Windows Azure
Web Sites
Building Web Apps at a Rapid Pace

Tejaswi Redkar

DYNAMIC DEPLOY

Windows Azure Web Sites

ISBN-13: 978-1491003541

ISBN-10: 1491003545

Printed by CreateSpace, an Amazon.com Company

http://www.CreateSpace.com/4363039

Publisher: Dynamic Deploy LLC
Technical Reviewers: Abhinav Dawra (ABHI); Harold Campos; Karsten Strøbæk; Krishnachytanya Ayyagari (KC); Rahul Rai; Saranya Sriram; Simon Gurevich; Stephen Kaufman
Artist: Tejaswi Redkar
Cover Designer: Tejaswi Redkar

Published by Dynamic Deploy LLC, e-mail orders@dynamicdeploy.com

For information on translations, publishing@dynamicdeploy.com

We offer great discounts on bulk purchases, Please contact bulksales@dynamicdeploy.com

The source code for this book is available to readers at https://github.com/dynamicdeploy/websitesbook.

DYNAMIC DEPLOY

I dedicate this book to all the children in this world. I wish each and every one of them a prosperous and bright future. They will make this world a better place.

I thank my wife Arohi and my sons Aaryan and Dhruv, for giving me the liberty to do what I love. I also thank my sister Aasawari for being with me when I needed her. I thank my parents for all the teachings. Finally, I thank God for gifting me the people I love.

CONTENTS AT A GLANCE

TABLE OF CONTENTS

FOREWORD

It is very rare in someone's career that one gets to work on their dream project. For me, this magic moment happened in late 2010 when a colleague of mine at Microsoft asked me to get involved in a new, high density Web hosting PaaS project in the Windows Azure organization. Being able to work on the intersection of running a cloud scale service and focusing on a great developer experience is a unique opportunity. With Windows Azure Websites (WAWS) we remain committed to doing both.

Traditional Web hosting has been around for a long time, but with the advent of cloud technologies, there is a need for a new breed of web application. Modern web applications need to be easy to develop, easy to integrate with other web services, serve all sorts of devices and support a large swath of open source technologies and languages. Above all, modern web applications need to be highly reliable, available and secure!

Building on the rock solid Windows Azure platform, WAWS is truly next generation web hosting. WAWS manages the lowest levels of stack on behalf of developers and site administrators and is available in most Windows Azure data centers. Scaling in WAWS is also quick and easy as web servers are kept "warm" by the platform so that sites can be scaled up or out on demand without any downtime.

The developer experience on WAWS is distinguished by supporting the diversity of many languages, developer tools and debugging options. WAWS gives first class support to .NET based applications but also supports PHP, Node.JS and Python. Support for Java and Ruby is on the way. Continuous integration, DevOps, diagnostics and troubleshooting are also deeply supported through integration with services like GitHub, TFS and NewRelic™.

To make sure WAWS carries the most impact for our customers, we have focused our development efforts on specific scenarios we call solutions. The solutions we focused on:

- Organizational Web Presence – WAWS is a powerful solution to build a websites for an organization, it allows for a scalable, secure and easy way to manage .com sites to be built either from scratch or from a large set of open source applications.
- Digital Marketing Campaigns – WAWS is a great fit for building micro-sites or social media applications for marketing needs. The diversity of tools and frameworks available allows for quick web app creation. The Auto Scale capabilities allow for confidence in cases where micro sites receive a lot of traffic.
- Business Applications – WAWS is a great solution for enterprise

developers who need to create applications for usage by their corporate colleagues. Using AAD allows for making sites available only for authenticated members of a corporation.

- PaaS \ SaaS Platform – one of the best features of WAWS is the ability to use the Windows Azure Pack (WAP) to install a private WAWS cloud, this allows organizations to realize the value of the cloud on their private networks and for hosting organization to build SaaS applications on top of a strong platform.

It is an honor to be able to write a forward for a book about WAWS, we have a lot of fun building the platform and interacting with our customers!

Nir Mashkowski
Principal Group Program Manager
Microsoft Corporation

ABOUT THE AUTHOR

 **Tejaswi Redkar** is a software architect with passion for writing. He works for Microsoft and has been working on the Windows Azure platform since its early days. He is also the author of "Windows Azure Platform" book published by APress. Currently, he works as the Director of Application Platform Technical Communities in Microsoft and covers a broad range of Microsoft technologies from User Experience to Business Analytics. His team has built more than 100 solutions on Windows Azure for Enterprises and ISVs. He is also the creator of http://www.dynamicdeploy.com and http://www.appsforazure.com .

Tejaswi has not only written about conceptual topics like Threading and Message Queuing, but also on broader topics, such as software ecosystems, business, and platforms. Tejaswi has a Master's degree in Computer Engineering from San Jose State University and an MBA from University of Wisconsin.

Tejaswi lives in the beautiful San Francisco Bay Area with his wife and two kids. When not working on what's next, he is either having pure fun with his family or bicycling on San Ramon trails.

You can find more details about him here:
LinkedIn: http://www.linkedin.com/in/tejaswiredkar
Follow him @tejaswiredkar, http://twitter.com/tejaswiredka
Amazon Author Site: http://www.amazon.com/author/tejaswiredkar
Blog: http://blog.dynamicdeploy.com
Creator of the following tools for Windows Azure:
http://www.dynamicdeploy.com
http://www.appsforazure.com

Tejaswi Redkar

ABOUT TECHNICAL REVIEWERS

Harold Campos

Harold is a Solution Architect in Microsoft Latin America. He is passionate about Cloud Technologies and believes he is working for the Best Company out there.

Stephen Kaufman

Stephen is a Solution Architect in the Americas Office of the CTO at Microsoft. He has served in many capacities throughout my career across a multitude of industries but it all boils down to that he is passionate about solving business challenges and building winning solutions.

Abhinav Dawra

Abhinav is working as a consultant with Microsoft Services in the App Dev space. He is a worldwide SME in Windows Azure for the Development and Integration community. He was also involved in writing some really useful IP in Windows Azure IaaS space.

Krishnachytanya Ayyagari (KC)

On professional front working as a Consultant at Microsoft with over 5.5 years of experience; completed my Masters from BITS, Pilani; worked on almost all Microsoft technologies from Winforms to Windows Azure and can speak and write C#, JAVA and C. On personal front son of Sai-Srinivas and husband of Shalini.

Saranya Sriram

Saranya is a veteran Technology Evangelist for Windows Azure and has been with Microsoft for almost a decade. She is a regular speaker at TechEd India for past 5 years and a variety of 3rd party conferences.

Simon Gurevich

Simon Gurevich is a Principal Consultant in Microsoft Services and has been building distributed applications throughout his professional career. Simon also leads a Worldwide Azure Community within Microsoft. Simon holds a Master degree in Computer Science and Mathematics.

Karsten Strobæk

Karsten works as architect/senior consultant for Microsoft Consulting Services out of Denmark. He has a Masters in Economics and Econometrics and more than 20 years of experience working with financial institutions on large and complex enterprise wide solutions.

Rahul Rai

Rahul specializes in .NET technologies and Windows Azure, on which he has worked on since its infancy. He has extensively worked on the many tenets of the Windows Azure platform in multiple customer engagements. Currently, he is working as a Consultant in Microsoft Services, India.

Tejaswi Redkar

"With the advent of Windows Azure, the role of developer has become paramount and DevOps gap has reduced. This book finely helps a developer step up to an operations role in a methodological fashion. Tejaswi has imparted his practical knowledge of working with Windows Azure Websites in a clear, crisp and concise manner."

-Rahul Rai, Consultant, Microsoft

"The best in this book that keep you to turn the page. Enjoyed reading it and will recommend to every developer or architect working on Windows Azure. A must read. Floored by the way dynamicdeploy.com was migrated to Windows Azure. Know it."

- Krishnachytanya Ayyagari, Consultant, Microsoft

"This book is a great effort by the author to teach people on Windows Azure Websites. This book not only focusses on WAWS but also talks about some of the key aspects which would be useful in creating performance rich and scalable web sites."

-Abhinav Dawra, Consultant, Microsoft

ACKNOWLEDGEMENTS

We never work alone. Everything you do today requires support of your friends, family, and colleagues to say the least. Even this book was not built in vacuum. I am fortunate enough to be surrounded by passionate and supportive people.

I would like to thank the following individuals for their contributions to my professional and personal life:

- Smt. Laxmi Natarajan, my school teacher who believed the author in me
- Prof. M.B. Unde from the National Chemical Laboratory, Pune for teaching me valuable engineering lessons
- Randy Bainbridge from Microsoft, who is one of the best managers I have worked with
- Penny Tong, for teaching me valuable work-life lessons
- Prof. Dan Harkey from San Jose State University for providing me with a teaching opportunity at the right time in my career
- Kui Jia, for selling me the Microsoft employment value proposition
- Rob Tiffany for helping me understand the self-publishing process
- My leadership team: Jeff Jurvis, Gianni Zorzino, and Norm Judah for fostering a knowledge management and readiness-driven environment
- The entire Microsoft for keeping the technology innovation in the world alive
- Finally, special Thanks to the technical reviewing team who honed this book to a publishable state -- Abhinav Dawra (ABHI); Harold Campos; Karsten Strøbæk; Krishnachytanya Ayyagari (KC); Rahul Rai; Saranya Sriram; Simon Gurevich; Stephen Kaufman

My professional life is incomplete without a personal network of amazing friends, co-workers, educators and students who have played an important role in shaping my life.

Tejaswi Redkar

Tejaswi Redkar

INTRODUCTION

This book provides you with detailed knowledge in developing web apps on Windows Azure Web Sites. Windows Azure Web Sites provides developers with a state-of-the-art cloud infrastructure for developing, testing, and deploying websites written not only in ASP.NET, but also in Node.js, PHP, and Python. It takes less than 5 minutes to deploy a website from your development machine to the cloud. This book will guide you through this process and after reading each chapter, you will be able to claim to be an expert in that topic.

This book not only educates you on the Windows Azure Web Sites features, but also to provides you with a deep understanding of using these features optimally in your own environment.

Who This Book Is For

The ideal reader of this book is a web apps or web services developer, a solution architect, a technology student, mobile apps developer, a developer entrepreneur, and a systems architect. This book is also for anyone interested in learning about Windows Azure Web Sites for developing personal or enterprise websites.

How This Book Is Structured

This book is primarily divided into two parts - the first part (Chapters 1-4) is dedicated to providing you knowledge of the features through hands-on examples and step-by-step guidance; and the second part (Chapters 5-10) is dedicated to applying these features in migrating and building real-world web solutions. The book structure provides you with a logical path of starting as an expert and finishing as an expert.

Chapter 1 discusses the basic concepts and the internals of the Windows Azure Web Sites **architecture**.

Chapter 2 gets you up to speed quickly in developing and deploying websites using popular tools like **WebMatrix** and **Visual Studio**.

Chapter 3 gets you setup with **Continuous Deployment** environments using **Visual Studio Online** (aka Team Foundation Service) and **GitHub**.

This chapter also educates you on different deployment options such as Visual Studio, Git, Dropbox, PowerShell, and FTP.

Chapter 4 is all about getting your website ready for **production** operations. It covers the **go-live** requirements for your website such as **scaling, security, diagnostics, and configurations**.

Chapter 5 starts with a case study in **migrating** dynamicdeploy.com from Windows Azure Cloud Services to Windows Azure Web Sites. This is also the chapter where I introduce the **Web Site Capability Model**.

Chapter 6 takes you through the journey of migrating the popular MVC Music Store to Windows Azure Web Sites. The chapter focuses on methodologies, tools and **best-practices** for completing the migration tasks.

Chapter 7 gets into the details of integrating **ElasticSearch** into the Music Store website. The chapter guides you through the ElasticSearch deployment process in Windows Azure Virtual Machines.

Chapter 8 gets into the details of integrating **custom analytics** into the Music Store website.

Chapter 9 is the lightening round with quick exposure to core capabilities required in building modern websites. This is the chapter where the popular **Storage Object Distribution pattern** is introduced.

Chapter 10 is all about developing and deploying **Node.js** websites and web services on Windows Azure Web Sites infrastructure.

Prerequisites

This is a cloud solution building book that helps you build web apps at a rapid pace. Without productive tools, building applications rapidly is rarely is breeze.

Listed below are the tools required for following the exercises from this book:

- Visual Studio 2012 or 2013
- Windows Azure Subscription (at least 3-month trial)
- SQL Server 2012 Express Database
- Git Tools for Windows
- Git Tools for Visual Studio 2012
- Visual Studio Online (aka Team Foundation Service) Account
- GitHub Account

All the discussions in this book assume that you are familiar with C# programming language, database development, and source control management (SCM) systems.

Downloading the Code

The readers of this book can download the source code from the book's GitHub repository at https://github.com/dynamicdeploy/websitesbook .
The website source code for Chapter 10 is available for download at https://github.com/dynamicdeploy/appsforazure .
The source code for this book is provided as-is with no support whatsoever.

Contacting the Author

You are very welcome to contact me via any one of the following options:
Email: tredkar@gmail.com
Twitter: @tejaswiredkar
LinkedIn: http://www.linkedin.com/in/tejaswiredkar/

Feel free to visit the Dynamic Deploy website http://www.dynamicdeploy.com

Chapter 1
ARCHITECTURE OVERVIEW

Windows Azure Web Sites (WAWS) is Platform as a Service (PaaS) done right. Microsoft calls WAWS *"PaaS for the Modern Web"*. PaaS is a type of cloud service where the infrastructure and the operating system is abstracted from the developer. You, as a developer, build an app and deploy it in PaaS without worrying about how the underlying infrastructure and operating system is setup. In the context of this book, PaaS is a public cloud service running in a provider's datacenter, such as Microsoft's Windows Azure Web Sites and Windows Azure Cloud Services.

My experience with WAWS spans over a couple of years in building real-world solutions, but excitement has been there for more than a few years. As a developer, I always thought Windows Azure Cloud Services had some overhead in building websites quickly. Sometimes, the migration cost outweighed the benefits in comparison to other PaaS and Infrastructure as a Service (IaaS) offerings. WAWS takes the real PaaS approach, the approach that the developers have been waiting for. Last year, I was helping a top consumer food products company to launch their largest web marketing campaign. The customer's marketing unit had a very clear vision of the channels they were going to target during this campaign. Their most significant requirement was faster time-to-market (TTM). Out of more than one hundred websites that needed to be launched over a period of 3 months, around 70% of them would be refreshed monthly, 10% would be refreshed daily, and the remaining ones would get recycled with new product launches. Their goal was to build a social marketing platform for their entire product portfolio. They tried working with several hosting companies, but no one could address their agility and global scale requirements. Such large initiatives require end-to-end platform automation which a lot of hosting companies don't provide. Their immediate next option was to look at cloud providers. This is where my team got involved and promptly recommended them to evaluate Windows Azure Web Sites. As I have mentioned earlier, their most significant requirement was achieving faster time-to-market. As expected, WAWS turned out to be a perfect fit for their campaign because they were able to launch their campaign around the world across multiple channels and languages at a pace they had never achieved before. WAWS is a core component in the Windows Azure portfolio of services, and is designed to meet a very specific need in building web applications (apps) in the cloud at a rapid pace. That is why I call it, *PaaS Done Right*.

In this chapter, I will provide a conceptual overview of WAWS, and its inner-workings. After reading this chapter, you will not only be able to decide if WAWS is the right fit for you, but also understand the value proposition of PaaS in general.

Why Windows Azure Web Sites?

I don't like to compare cloud offerings based on pricing right away. Pricing is important, but if you eliminate a cloud offering purely based on pricing, as with any other product, you are setting yourself up for a long-term disappointment. But you also need to make sure that the cloud offering you are choosing fits in your budget. You should always remember to start with a stable and large-scale cloud service provider. Cloud is about economies of scale, and hence the larger the provider, the better pricing you will get over the lifetime of your application. Amazon Web Services (AWS) and Microsoft's Windows Azure are constantly competing on price having reduced the pricing of their services several times over the past years. That said, your today's calculations may be invalid even a month from now if the pricing changes.

Below you will find some of the key benefits of WAWS from a developer's perspective.

Manageability

One of the key value propositions of WAWS is application manageability. If a cloud platform cannot manage your application, then in my opinion, it does not qualify as a PaaS. WAWS provides you with a management portal, an API, and PowerShell scripts for managing and monitoring your websites. After learning techniques in this book, you will no longer worry about infrastructure setups, and the time to market for your websites will be significantly shorter than before.

Development Tools

Your platform is only as good as your tools. Microsoft has always been a leader in development tools and WAWS is no exception. You will realize from the upcoming chapters that the learning curve for developers is minimal. Visual Studio and WebMatrix are the two Microsoft's development tools I would like to highlight here. The WAWS APIs have been integrated seamlessly into Visual Studio and WebMatrix, thus making it easy to extend your existing knowledge of running web applications on Microsoft's Windows platform into Windows Azure. Listed below is a brief description of these tools and the salient features of each.

Visual Studio

Unarguably, Visual Studio is the best development tool ever built. Its sweet spot is in building, debugging and testing any type of application you can build for the Windows operating system. It shines in developing ASP.NET websites for WAWS. You can develop, test and debug on your local machine, and then publish it in WAWS with a click of your mouse. Furthermore, you can now remotely debug your website running in WAWS, right on your local machine.

WebMatrix

WebMatrix is a simple yet powerful tool for building, editing and publishing websites quickly. It supports development and deployment of ASP.NET, Node.js and PHP websites for WAWS and on-premises. With its ability to run Node.js package manager (npm) and nuget package manager from within the integrated development environment (IDE), makes it a flexible tool for developing not only ASP.NET but also Node.js and PHP websites. In Chapter 10, you will learn to build a Node.js web service that stores and retrieves data from MongoDB, completely in WebMatrix. WebMatrix also integrates with WAWS API seamlessly and lets you publish websites from within the IDE to WAWS. Compared to Visual Studio, WebMatrix does lack in core debugging of complex websites in any programming language.

Rapid Deployment of Web Apps

Deployment of existing and new web applications is a breeze with WAWS. I will back my statement up by demonstrating a quick deployment in the next chapter. WAWS takes you from 0 to Multiple Web Apps in no time and zero start-up costs. I don't know of any other cloud service that offers this level of speed, and flexibility.

Well Defined Service Level Agreement (SLA)

SLA is the heart of any cloud service. It can make or break the platform. An incomplete or failed SLA may also drive the service provider out of business. Therefore, it is important to stick to a stable company that offers an SLA that is financially backed by credits and appropriate support. Microsoft takes great care in honoring its SLA and me being a Microsoft customer myself, have had received several credits when Windows Azure suffered outages. But, one important point to understand is that SLAs are not meant to address business continuity of your business app. They are designed to provide you with appropriate credit in case of infrastructure failures. Cloud providers are not liable for any loss in your business caused by violation of the SLA. Loss in business is still your responsibility and therefore you must take the necessary precautions, beyond SLAs, to protect your business from all failures. As of writing this chapter, the availability support for WAWS was 99.9%. The WAWS SLA document describes how this is calculated and your entitled credit if Microsoft does not meet the SLA.

You can download the latest Windows Azure Web Sites SLA from the following link:

http://www.microsoft.com/en-us/download/details.aspx?id=39303

Global Scale

For the sake of simplicity, I classify scale into two categories: Datacenter Scale and Application Scale.

Datacenter Scale

We live in a local world. Global sounds too grand considering how quickly people, systems, and applications can communicate in any part of the world. Sometimes, I can reach out to my relatives around the world faster than my family in the same town. But, there is a lot of groundwork involved in building such globally reachable application endpoints. You need datacenters that can provide worldwide access, plus applications that can scale globally. As of writing this chapter, there were in total 8 Windows Azure Datacenters around the globe capable of hosting WAWS. You have the choice of deploying your web application in one or more of these datacenters. These datacenters not only host WAWS, but also other Windows Azure services like Cloud Services, Virtual Machines, Windows Azure Storage, Windows Azure SQL Database, HDInsight, Reporting Services, etc.. So, you can replicate entire solution stacks around the globe and provide local endpoints at a global scale. Very few companies can offer you cloud at such a grand scale.

Application Scale

Application scale allows you to scale an application within the same datacenter. WAWS provides you with the infrastructure to scale your website horizontally (on multiple servers) as well as vertically (increase the size of your server). Scaling flexibility allows you to optimize your website's operational costs during peak and graveyard hours. WAWS provides you with the necessary datacenter and infrastructure constructs that empower you to rapidly build web applications at a global scale.

Multiple Platform Support

PaaS is about abstracting the infrastructure, not the application. So you shouldn't have to learn new programming languages for developing applications. In WAWS, you can build websites in ASP.NET, Node.js, PHP, and Python. Support for multiple web application platforms provides you with the flexibility to migrate existing web applications or design new ones leveraging your existing skillsets. WAWS protects the investment in you as a developer.

Flexibility with Free Tier

Let's be honest, developers don't like to pay for infrastructure. In WAWS, Microsoft made a brilliant move by offering a free tier with limited capabilities. In no time, you can deploy a web application and start unit or functional testing for free. This is a boon in disguise not only for developers but also for testers. How many times have you heard the statement, *"It works on my machine"*? WAWS brings an end to it. Deploy it quickly for free and reproduce the defect. Using the free-tier will improve your application lifecycle management (ALM) agility and thus will achieve a faster time to market. The service does not stop at the free tier, it provides you with the flexibility of scaling-out and scaling-up with Shared and Standard tiers. Shared-tier provides you with benefits such as scaling-out, but your website will always be running on a virtual machine instance that is shared with other Microsoft's customers. Standard-tier provides you with a reserved instance which allows you to scale-out, as well as scale-up by increasing the size of the reserved instance. You can also run multiple websites on the same Standard-tier instance.

You can find any new information on the pricing and features of each tier by navigating to the following URL
http://www.windowsazure.com/en-us/pricing/details/web-sites/

Fitting in Windows Azure Stack

Last year, I built the website Dynamic Deploy (http://www.dynamicdeploy.com) when the only PaaS option available on Windows Azure was Cloud Services. I would have gladly deployed it on WAWS, had it been available then. WAWS was launched much later than Windows Azure Cloud Services (Cloud

Services), and gained much less attention than Windows Azure Virtual Machines (VMs). But, developers who use WAWS love it and benefit from the flexibility it offers. I don't mean to say that WAWS replaces Cloud Services and VMs, but if an application is a right fit for WAWS, I recommend using it.

Table 1.1 below lists the core differences between WAWS, Cloud Services and VMs features that are most important to a developer.

Table 1.1: Feature Comparison between services

Features	WAWS	Cloud Services	WAVMS
Application Types	Web Sites and Web Applications	Web Sites, Web Applications, and background services	Any Application that can run on a VM
Data Security at rest	Not supported	Custom Encryption	Any
Data Security in transit	IP-based and Server Name Indication (SNI) based Secure Socket Layer (SSL)	SSL (HTTPS)	SSL, and any custom security that work on a VM
Identity Management	OAuth, Windows Identity Foundation (WIF) [1] ,Windows Azure Active Directory (WAAD), ASP.NET Membership Providers	OAuth, Windows Identity Foundation (WIF), Windows Azure Active Directory (WAAD), ASP.NET Membership Providers	OAuth, Windows Identity Foundation (WIF), Windows Azure Active Directory (WAAD), ASP.NET Membership Providers, Active Directory, Any custom identity management system supported

[1] http://www.cloudidentity.com/blog/2013/01/28/running-wif-based-apps-in-windows-azure-web-sites-4/

			on VMs
Relational Database Support	Windows Azure SQL Database and MYSQL [2](up to 20MB free)	Can access any database accessible over the TCP/IP protocol. Recommendation is to use Windows Azure SQL Database or SQL Server hosted in a virtual machine	Can access and host databases on VMs
ALM Support	FTP, GIT, VSOnline, Dropbox, BitBucket, etc.	VSOnline, GIT	Application dependent, not offered by VMs
Scalability	Quick Scale-Out and Scale-up	Scale-Out and Scale-up. Scale-Up requires re-deployment.	Scale-Out and Scale-Up. Scale-up requires reboot.
Multi-tier Applications	Can host only Web tiers	Can host Web and Worker roles	Can host Web, Worker and any custom tier.
Access to underlying OS and Virtual Machine	No	Yes (limited)	Yes
Free-tier	Yes	No	No
Third-party Apps Deployment	Yes (via App Gallery and Web Matrix)	No	Yes (via VMDepot, BitNami, Dynamic Deploy, and other VM stores)
Virtual Network Support	No	Windows Azure Virtual Network	Windows Azure Virtual Network
On-premises Integration (Line-of-Business Apps)	Yes (via Service Bus Relay)	Yes (via Service Bus Relay and Virtual Network)	Yes (via Service Bus Relay and Virtual Network)
Remote Desktop Access	No	Yes	Yes

---

[2] For more information on ClearDB's partnership with Microsoft, please visit https://www.cleardb.com/store/azure

Windows Azure In-Role Cache	No	Yes	No
Windows Azure Cache Service	Yes	Yes	Yes
Configuration Management	Web.config, Configuration in portal	Web.config ServiceConfiguration.cscfg ServiceDefinition.csdef	Web.config and any application specific configuration.
Supported Frameworks	.NET, Node.js, PHP, Python	Customizable to some extent where you can run most of the popular frameworks (e.g. .NET, Java, Node.js, etc.)	Completely customizable with choice of Windows and Linux
Operating Systems	Windows	Windows	Windows and Linux
Elevate Permissions	No	Yes	Yes
Startup Tasks	No	Yes	Yes (full control)
Deployment Mechanism	Git, FTP, Visual Studio Online/Server, Dropbox, API, PowerShell, more…	Visual Studio Online, Team Foundation Server, Git, API, PowerShell.	API, PowerShell

Table 1.1 provides you with a basis for comparing solution scenarios you can enable using the three compute services offered in Windows Azure.

Typical Scenarios

One size fits all does not exist in the cloud. The most versatile service of all is the Infrastructure as a Service (IaaS), but its management overhead makes it expensive compared to PaaS. In PaaS, the scenarios you can efficiently deploy are limited, but for the right fit, PaaS will provide you with an ideal hosting environment. The underlying infrastructure is completely abstracted so you can focus more on the business logic and quality attributes of your application.

WAWS was designed with specific application scenarios in mind. Listed below are some of the common scenarios for WAWS.

Internet Web Sites

This is the most-popular and an ideal fit for WAWS. Any public-facing website that requires a global presence and scale can be easily hosted in WAWS. One of my customers is the largest food products company in the world with 100+ different food brands. By hosting all these sites on WAWS, the customer is benefitting from the flexibility, scalability, security, reliability, and global scale of Windows Azure. The website owners make instant updates to the sites globally, instead of going through lengthy change control process that used to take days if not weeks. In my opinion, public facing websites will eventually be the dominant scenario in WAWS.

Time-bound Digital Campaigns

The digital marketing world has exploded with social media taking the central stage. All of today's marketing campaigns must include dedicated websites that have endpoints into social media giants like Facebook, Twitter, Pinterest, LinkedIn, etc., and the broader mobile ecosystem. Such websites have very specific characteristics as listed below:

- They are time bound (i.e. they have an expiration time aligned with the campaign)
- They have user interfaces supporting multiple device types (PCs, phones, tablets, kiosks, etc.)
- All the web interfaces are hosted on single website delivering same data but device-specific rendering capabilities
- If the campaign is successful, the site usage can explode exponentially demanding infrastructure scale and performance

With WAWS, you can bring up and take-down websites in minutes, and pay only for what you use. By designing your website with a Model View Controller (MVC) framework and multi-platform responsive design frameworks, you can quickly build a website that can render different device views and address the exploding demand. Once the campaign is complete, you can bring down the website in minutes, and then reuse the same pattern for any future websites.

Hosting Web-tier of a multi-tier application in the cloud

This scenario includes complex architectures involving more than one set of

Windows Azure services. WAWS can host the front-end web application of a complex n-tier architecture that may involve WAVMS or Cloud Service. In such architectures, where communication crosses boundaries, care should be taken in the areas of security, data transfer, performance and manageability because these can quickly increase your operating costs. In Windows Azure, each service has its own security boundary and unless they are connected to each other via virtual network, they need to expose external endpoints for communications. WAWS neither supports virtual network nor cloud services, so the only options are communicating over the public network, or a Service Bus Relay. Service Bus Relay adds communication overhead and therefore end-to-end performance and security testing is recommended. Before designing n-tier architectures with WAWS, I recommend designing a secure channel between multiple services in your architecture.

Data transfer across datacenters is charged and therefore in a multi-tiered architecture, you must define the data communication boundaries and estimate the costs upfront during the design phase. In WAWS, you don't have any storage available on the local machine, therefore, for any application –specific storage, you must use either Windows Azure Storage service or a relational database such as Windows Azure SQL database. When you design a multi-tiered website, you must co-locate the website, its storage mechanism, and any other integration service you need, in the same Windows Azure region (or datacenter), to avoid data transfer charges.

Windows Azure Regions

Windows Azure uses the concept of regions to manage the physical location of your applications and data. Currently, a region represents a Microsoft's datacenter location. When you deploy your website (or any Windows Azure service), you must select a region to host the service. At the time of writing this book, Windows Azure was available in the following regions East US, North Central US, West US, North Europe, West Europe, and East Asia.

Line of Business Application Integration

Line of Business (LOB) applications are either hosted on-premises, in the cloud (in VMs), or are offered as Software as a Service (SaaS). You can develop ancillary applications in WAWS that federate with these LOB enterprise applications. These ancillary applications can provide additional custom capabilities with seamless single sign-on experience. For example, you could build a reporting website that federates identity with Windows Azure Active Directory (WAAD) and Office 365 and displays custom business dashboards based on SharePoint data sources.

Architecture of WAWS

Although it is not required to understand the underlying WAWS architecture, architects and developers usually like to know the underpinnings of the system they develop applications on. This will somehow help you in designing your own systems.

WAWS is designed for the cloud from the ground-up. The architecture below illustrates all the core components of WAWS.

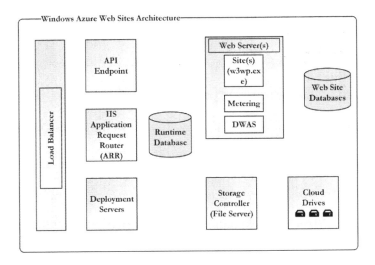

Figure 1.1: WAWS Architecture

The WAWS consists of a multi-tiered architecture with load-balancers, API Endpoints, and IIS Application Request Router (ARR) as the front-tier routing web requests to the appropriate back-end components. Listed below is the description of all the core components of WAWS from Figure 1.1.

Windows Azure Load balancer

The Windows Azure load balancer is part of the WAWS infrastructure and is abstracted from the developers. You don't have direct access to it, but all the website requests pass through it.

IIS Application Request Router (ARR)

ARR is probably the best kept IIS secret for developers. ARR is an IIS reverse proxy extension. It provides rules-based request routing as well as Content Delivery Network (CDN)-like caching capabilities. Although it is considered as an infrastructure component, it is an invaluable tool for developers building websites in the cloud and on-premises. You can download and read more information about ARR here.
http://www.iis.net/downloads/microsoft/application-request-routing

In WAWS, ARR is used:

- During provisioning, for deciding the back-end web server to host your website on, and forwarding the request accordingly
- For routing HTTP requests to the correct Web Server that is hosting your website

API Endpoint

API Endpoint is an independent entry point into the WAWS infrastructure. The API requests do not go through ARR, but through the load balancer to the API endpoint.

WAWS provides a REST API for several management tasks like provisioning a Web Server Farm, provisioning a Web Site, and capturing website logs. You can find the REST API reference here

http://msdn.microsoft.com/en-us/library/windowsazure/dn166981.aspx

In a large-scale environment, using the APIs, you can automate several tasks that typically require manual intervention. I highly recommend using APIs wherever possible. Most of the tools including WAWS PowerShell scripts, WebMatrix, and Visual Studio use the APIs.

Deployment Servers

The deployment servers also expose an independent entry point into the WAWS infrastructure. They are primarily used for FTP and WebDeploy based deployments.

Runtime Database (aka Hosting Database)

The runtime database runs on Windows Azure SQL Database and stores metadata about your subscription, hosting plan, website, and other system-level information. Based on this metadata WAWS makes provisioning and runtime decisions. The information that is usually contained in the app.config and web.config is also stored in the Runtime Database.

Storage Controller (File Server)

The Storage Controller provides Server Message Block (SMB) access to Windows Azure Drives that store your website contents. The Storage Controller makes sure that the drive consisting of your website contents is always available to the hosting web server. The architecture follows a centralized storage pattern where all the web servers hosting your website have a consistent view of the site contents. In some architectures, this is achieved by synchronizing contents between web servers, but it exposes the risk of data inconsistencies in case of synchronization failures. In centralized storage architecture, all the web servers point to the exact same shared drive, thus eliminating the need for synchronization.

Cloud Drives

The cloud drives are Windows Azure Drives that store the contents of your site. The drives are made available to web servers in the WAWS infrastructure by the Storage Controller via SMB protocol. Microsoft's primary reason for designing SMB access was to avoid using the Windows Azure Storage API directly thus providing direct on-premises compatibility.

Web Server Roles

The web servers are stateless web/worker roles customized for WAWS. Because the site contents are shared through the Storage Controller, they don't need synchronization. The web server consists of three primary services: Sites, Metering, and Dynamic Web Activation Service.

Sites

The sites represent your website that is provisioned on the web server. If the site is not active, it is either de-provisioned or moved to a high-density web server. In a scaled-out environment, multiple web servers will host the same website, and ARR will load balance the HTTP requests automatically.

Metering

Metering service runs in the web server and constantly monitors the resources used by your website. The metering service retrieves the hosting plan information from the runtime database and works with DWAS to apply constraints outlined in the plan. For example, the data collected by metering service is used for throttling bandwidth based on your hosting plan. In multi-tenant systems, metering service is an essential component for applying tenant-level constraints on system resources.

Dynamic Web Activation Service (DWAS)

The DWAS (based on Windows Activation Service) creates websites on the fly and applies appropriate constraints outlined in the hosting plan. When a new provisioning request comes in, the DWAS retrieves website metadata from the Runtime Database, website contents from the Storage Controller, and dynamically provisions the site on the web server it is running on. DWAS also participates in the quota enforcement, and site activation/de-activation decision process.

Web Site Databases

These are your website databases (aka application databases). They are provisioned only if your website needs them. For example, if your Drupal site needs a Windows Azure SQL database, WAWS can provision one for you. The databases are priced independently from WAWS. At the time of writing, 20MB usage of relational database storage was included in all the plans for free.

For more information on Windows Azure SQL Database Pricing, please visit the link

http://www.windowsazure.com/en-us/pricing/details/sql-database/

Publishing and Launching

WAWS makes clear distinction between publishing a website and launching it. When you publish a website, it is stored on the storage controller and is not created or launched on the web server until you start using it. When you start using the website, it is created/launched on the web server on-demand. The reason for dynamic launching is resource cost. The cost of unused resources in the cloud is high, and no matter what your perception is, from Microsoft's perspective, the resources are limited in the cloud. WAWS also offers a free-tier that takes up resources, and does not stop developers from creating dormant or unused websites. Microsoft wants to make sure that every resource is utilized optimally.

How It Works

In order to understand the runtime workings of WAWS, let's first define two terms:

Cold Site: A site that is published but not launched (is not provisioned on a web server). In a cold site, the site's metadata is stored in the runtime database and the site's contents are stored by the Storage Controller. This happens when you first publish your website.

Hot Site: A site that is provisioned on a web server and actively used. This happens when you access the site, and it is dynamically provisioned by WAWS on one of the web servers.

Figure 1.2 illustrates the request flow for provisioning and serving contents of a cold site.

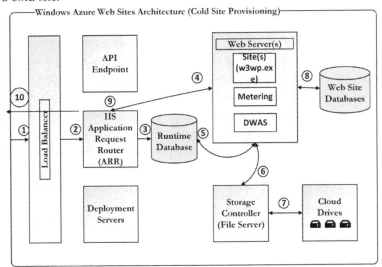

Figure 1.2: Cold Site Request

1. Let's assume that you are accessing the website http://www.dynamicdeploy.com which is published but not yet provisioned. From the header and domain information (based on configuration), the load balancer will redirect the request to WAWS (specifically to the ARR).
2. The ARR knows that this site has not been provisioned by checking its own cache
3. The ARR then retrieves the website metadata from the runtime database
4. Based on several parameters (e.g. resource usage) and constraints (e.g. hosting plans), it decides to route the request to the appropriate web server (aka web worker in the WAWS world)
5. Web Worker (DWAS) retrieves the website information from the runtime database for provisioning (or de-provisioning) purposes
6. The web server retrieves site's content from the Storage Controller.
7. The Storage Controller shares site's content with the web server via SMB connected Windows Azure Drive
8. If the website uses a backend database, the website starts loading data from the database if the request requires it to
9. The web server then serves the response back to ARR and in turn back to the requestor (10)

Microsoft's Impressive Claims

1) **Single WAWS instance has the ability to serve 13 million hits per day**

2) **You can have up to 10 reserved instances per region**

3) **These 10 instances have the ability to serve 1500 requests/second or 130 million hits/day**

4) **You can host up to 100 websites per geographic region per subscription**

Reference:

WAD B-329: Windows Azure Web Sites: An Architecture and Technical Deep Dive

Speakers: Karandeep Anand, Harsh Mittal

http://channel9.msdn.com/Events/TechEd/Eur ope/2013/WAD-B329#fbid=2iQ5K8OGhTf

Figure 1.3 illustrates the request flow for serving contents of a hot site.

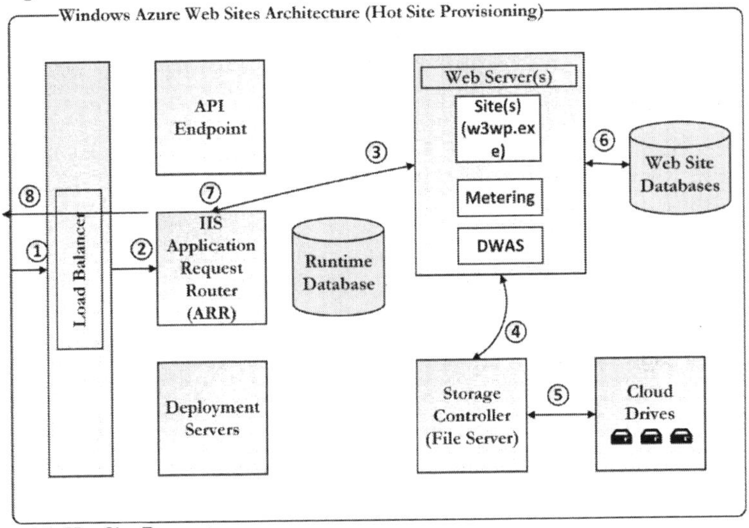

Figure 1.3: Hot Site Request

In case of a Hot Site requests, the website is already provisioned on the web server and ARR maintains the website's metadata in its cache. When the request comes in, ARR forwards this request to the appropriate web server without retrieving metadata from the runtime database. The website then serves the request normally. Because the site is already provisioned and the metadata is cached in ARR, most of the calls to the runtime database are eliminated.

How are Fault-Tolerance and Updates managed?

WAWS runs on Windows Azure Cloud Service

(WACS), which inherently supports update-domains and fault-domains. WAWS leverages the WACS fault domains to make sure two instances of the site are not deployed on the same hardware domain, and updates are applied on only one instance at a time. In case of a web server failure, the WAWS will follow the Cold Site request flow and re-provision the site. Any changes made to the site's structure are persisted by the Storage Controller on the shared drive.

Management Portal

Do judge a cloud service by its management portal. Management portal represents the developer's entry point into the cloud service and a serious cloud services provider will invest in building a sophisticated portal experience for managing applications. The Windows Azure team has continued to invest in providing a seamless cloud management experience across all its services. The current management portal is built on HTML 5 and provides you with the ability to manage all your Windows Azure services from one environment. WAWS is a newer service compared to Windows Azure Cloud Service or Storage Service, but the user interface seamlessly blends, and provides a consistent experience across all the services and regions.

In this section, I will go over some of the key WAWS usage scenarios for the management portal. During the course of the book, these scenarios will be covered in details.

TO USE ANY WINDOWS AZURE SERVICE, YOU NEED A WINDOWS AZURE SUBSCRIPTION. MICROSOFT OFFERS 3 MONTH FREE TRIALS THAT SHOULD BE SUFFICIENT FOR RUNNING MOST OF THE EXAMPLES FROM THIS BOOK. YOU CAN OPEN A NEW WINDOWS AZURE SUBSCRIPTION AT: HTTP://WWW.WINDOWSAZURE.COM

Creating a new Web Site

You can create a new website right from the portal. To do so, login to Windows Azure portal (http://manage.windowsazure.com) and then click on New > Compute > Web Site

Once you are there, you will have three options: - Quick Create, Custom

Create, and From Gallery. The first two options create a blank website, but the gallery option opens a gallery of readily available third-party web applications, as well as empty websites. It allows you to deploy ASP.NET, Node.js, Python, and PHP web applications. Figure 1.4 illustrates some of the Content Management System (CMS) applications available from the gallery.

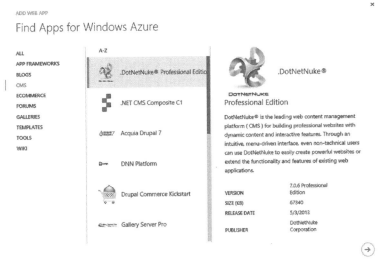

Figure 1.4: Web App Gallery

You can select any web application from the gallery and deploy it in WAWS. For a quick test, I deployed an empty PHP (PHP Empty Site) site with the domain name phpinfo.azurewebsites.net in the US West region. By default, WAWS provides you with the *.azurewebsites.net domain. You can configure custom domain names from the portal (only available for Shared and Standard plans).

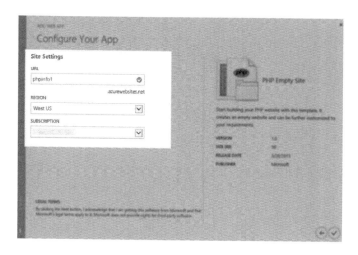

Figure 1.5: Configure your web application

After the site is ready, you will see it running in the websites list page as shown in Figure 1.6.

Figure 1.6: Web Sites list page

The websites page lists all the websites in your account. One account can be associated with administering multiple subscriptions. Each list item shows the status, subscription name, datacenter location (region), mode (or hosting plan), and URL of the website. If you have 1000 websites deployed, they all will be listed on this page. At the bottom of the page, each button represents an action.

Figure 1.7: Quick Commands for managing Web Sites

Browse: Will open a new web browser pointing to the site you have selected.
Stop, Delete and **Restart** are self-explanatory.
Manage Domains: Allows you to assign custom domains. It is grayed out for free hosting plans.
WebMatrix: Clicking this button will open the selected website in WebMatrix.

Install WebMatrix

From the portal, click on WebMatrix, which will ask you if you want to edit the live site. Click on "Edit live site directly"

Open phpinfo

Edit live site directly
Any saved changes will be made directly to the remote server

Edit local copy
Download a copy to the computer and make changes locally

☐ Do not ask me again for this site

Figure 1.8: Edit live site in WebMatrix

In index.php, add the following code, save the site and load the website.

```php
<?php
phpinfo()
?>
```

Listing 1.1: PHP Info

phpinfo() function outputs a large amount of system-level data including HTTP headers, PHP information, and operating system information. The web page will show details about the server your website is provisioned on. I have listed some interesting observations from the output (not shown) of phpinfo() you see in the browser:

1. Similar to Cloud Services, the operating system is on D:\Windows
2. The website is loaded from C:\DWASFiles\Sites\phpinfo
3. The server variables
   _COOKIE["ARRAffinity"],_SERVER["HTTP_COOKIE"]= ARRAffinity=zzz; WAWebSiteSID=aaa
4. Show that WAWS uses ARRAffinity cookie and a unique guid for each website
5. The HOME variable for your site points to a virtual directory C:\DWASFiles\Sites\phpinfo\VirtualDirectory0. This directory is mounted from the Storage Controller.
6. The computer name SERVER["COMPUTERNAME"] starts with RD, which proves WAWS is running on the Red Dog infrastructure (aka Windows Azure Cloud Services). Red Dog was Microsoft's internal code name for Windows Azure Cloud Services.
7. So, assuming you have enough knowledge about Windows Azure,

and if you connect the dots between the WAWS architecture and the server variables listed above, you will have enough evidence to prove that WAWS runs on Windows Azure Cloud Services.

Web Site Dashboard

On the websites list page, click on the website for navigating to the Quick Start page. From the quick start page you can download development tools, publish your app, integrate with your source control system, and navigate to specific menu like the Dashboard. The dashboard strives to be the aggregation page for administrative information and tasks.

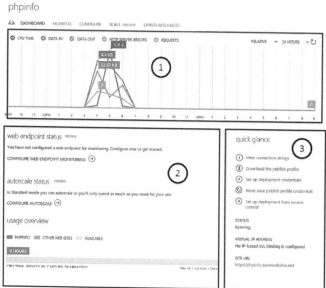

Figure 1.9: Dashboard page

The dashboard page has three distinct sections with the most common administrative tasks:

1) Monitoring Chart displays the CPU, data transfer, and HTTP errors and requests

2) Monitoring Configuration and Usage Overview section provides you with the ability to configure endpoint monitoring, setting up auto-scale, and shows the resource usage of your website

3) Quick Glance section provides links to connection strings, publishing profile, source control configuration, and general

information about the website endpoints

Throughout the book, while developing applications, you will learn each of these features in detail.

Monitoring your Web Site

The monitoring page displays monitoring chart and metrics in more detail. As the WAWS service matures, I am hoping to see more monitoring information about the website displayed here.

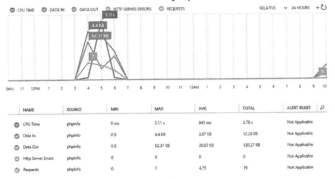

Figure 1.10: Monitoring Page

Configuring your Web Site

The configuration page allows you to configure most, if not all, of the website parameters, the runtime framework versions, certificates, Secure Socket Layer (SSL), custom domain names, application diagnostics, site diagnostics, application configuration settings (web.config), and more. I expect the configuration parameters on this page to grow over time as WAWS starts supporting more frameworks and provides more administrative flexibility.

What about web.config?

WAWS not only support ASP.NET but also Node.js, PHP, and Python. Web.config is an ASP.NET concept and understood only by the ASP.NET runtime. The configuration page allows you to create app settings that are common across

multiple runtime frameworks. You will observe in the later chapters that when you set app settings on the configuration page, the settings are added as environmental variables and available to all the language frameworks. A word of caution is that, in ASP.NET, these app settings take precedence over any web.config app settings. The configuration page app settings also reduces the risk of storing any sensitive information like passwords in the web.config file. This has been the concern of developers for years, and finally we see it addressed in the cloud. I still encounter mission critical web applications storing username and password in plain text in web.config files in spite of the understood risk.

Scaling your Web Site

Scalability is the ability of a system to grow and shrink proportionately based on the demand without encountering failures. WAWS is designed to handle internet-scale growth through manual as well as auto-scale. At the time of writing, the auto-scale features of WAWS were in preview. WAWS offers three plans and scaling features are directly tied to the plan you use.

Free: In the free tier, scaling feature is disabled. You can run up to 10 free independent websites, but you cannot scale a single website on multiple web servers.

Shared: In the shared tier, you can scale-out horizontally by adding more instances of your website. WAWS will automatically configure load balancing for it.

Figure 1.11 illustrates the scaling options available in the shared tier.

Figure 1.11: Scaling options in the shared tier

Standard: In the standard tier, you can not only scale-out by adding more reserved instances of your website, but also scale-up by increasing the size of your reserved instance. Standard tier also supports auto-scale. Auto-scale allows you to dynamically adjust the capacity of your website based on the load it is experiencing. In auto-scale, you can setup monitoring of the web server CPU and then setup a target action on the instance count variable of your website. The target action can increase or decrease the instance count of your web server based on the CPU usage range you have specified. Auto-scale feature is designed for optimizing your website cost by only paying for the capacity you need in a specific timespan.

Figure 1.12 illustrates the scaling options available in the standard tier.

Figure 1.12: Scaling options in the standard tier

In the future, I am hoping to see more auto-scale monitoring options like memory usage, and Windows Azure queue backlog, and custom triggers. You will learn about available scaling options in detail in Chapter 4.

Integrating with Development Tools

Developers say, "Your product is only as good as your development tools". In today's world, time-to-market and quality of a website is more important than the overall features available in your development framework. Over the years, you must have observed that frameworks that have better developer tools support succeed, while others fail. This is because, good development tools increase developer productivity and introduce less defects in the code. Microsoft's commitment to WAWS and its developer ecosystem is reflected in the investments made in development tools across multiple vendors. In the "Create a new website" section earlier, you learned how to easily deploy a new PHP website using Web Matrix. In addition to WebMatrix, WAWS also supports publishing your website from the following development and source control tools:

- File Transfer Protocol (FTP)
- Visual Studio
- Visual Studio Online
- Local Git Repository
- GitHub
- Dropbox
- BitBucket
- Codeplex
- Any external Git and Mercurial repository

From the Dashboard page, clicking the "Setup Deployment from Source Control" link opens up a popup window where you can start the source control integration process. I have covered details of continuous integration in Chapter 3.

Creating Linked Resources

From the Linked Resources section, you can link your website to other Windows Azure resources like SQL databases and Windows Azure Storage accounts from the portal thus allowing you the ability to scale and monitor all the linked resources together. In large-scale applications, most of the times, databases are the biggest bottleneck and therefore administrators spend a lot of time not only configuring but also continuously maintaining databases. Even if you scale-up a website, if you cannot scale the backend database along with it, it can still bring your website down. Linked resources allow you to scale a database along with your website.

Figure 1.13 shows a SQL database named "cfdb-2013-2-1-18-9" linked to the website named "mynodeapps".

Figure 1.13: Linked Database

After you create a linked resource, it is automatically displayed in the Scale section of the website (shown in Figure 1.14), from where you can scale it along with the website.

linked resources
_____

CFDB-2013-2-1-18-9
SQL DATABASE   Manage scale for this database

Figure 1.14: Manage scale for a linked database

Pricing

Although pricing is not the top deciding factor in selecting a cloud platform, it does play a significant role in committing to a platform. If all things are equal, pricing makes the difference. I believe that the competition will ultimately eliminate pricing as a significant deciding factor. The pricing of cloud services across multiple vendors have been on a sliding path due to competitive pressures. WAWS offers three plans Free, Shared, and Standard tier. Pricing is usually based on the compute hours, virtual machine (server) size, storage, memory, network bandwidth, and sometimes premium services like SSL and custom domains. In most of the cases, compute time will be your most significant expense. The next one would be database if your website requires it. In WAWS, you can always start in a free tier and then gradually move to shared and standard tiers if the demand increases. This will help you succeed (and fail) fast without investing your life savings.

Because pricing is a volatile component of cloud services, I will just include a link to the WAWS pricing page.

http://www.windowsazure.com/en-us/pricing/details/web-sites/

Management API

WAWS exposes a REST-based Management API for writing custom deployment automations. The Windows Azure PowerShell Cmdlets also call these REST APIs behind the scenes. You can find the complete list of cmdlets here

http://msdn.microsoft.com/en-us/library/windowsazure/jj152841.aspx

and the REST API reference here

http://msdn.microsoft.com/en-us/library/windowsazure/dn166981.aspx

The API references and cmdlets constantly change based on addition of new features, and therefore I have included links to them.

Top 3 Things to Consider

Before making the final decision on moving to WAWS, consider these three recommendations:

1) Compatibility

Is your website compatible with the features offered by WAWS? Key discovery points include:

Identity Management:

Usually identity management needs significant change when moving from one environment to another because it highly depends on how tightly a website is integrated with the identity provider. OAuth and Claims-based websites are easier to move, whereas Active Directory/LDAP-based sites will require significant attention in migration.

Storage:

WAWS is restrictive on local storage and therefore if your website requires local disk storage, it will need to be refactored to use Windows Azure storage or a SQL database.

Session State:

In WAWS, sessions are managed using ARR Affinity cookie. The web servers themselves are stateless and therefore if your application is not designed for sharing session state across multiple-instances, you will not be able to take advantage of WAWS scaling features. I recommend designing stateless websites either in the cloud or on-premises.

2) Development Tools

Invest in Development Tools, they will improve the website quality and reduce time required for fixing bugs. The return on investment (ROI) of development tools such as Visual Studio and (the free WebMatrix) is high and Microsoft also offers promotions to Most Valuable Professionals (MVPs), Partners, and BizSpark (http://www.bizspark.com) members.

3) Pricing

All else equals, pricing matters. Study pricing carefully and create your own spreadsheet for calculating pricing for your website. I recommend the practice of revising the pricing on every design change. For static and simple websites, it might be cost effective to host your application with a traditional hosting company. But, if you want flexibility in deploying multiple websites on a single server and scaling out dynamically, WAWS can prove to be financially viable.

What is Windows Azure Pack?

Windows Azure Pack is guidance accompanied by tools and utilities for building Windows Azure-like functionality in your own datacenter. It is

specifically designed for hosting companies. It runs on **Windows Server 2012 R2** and **System Center 2012 R2**. As a public cloud evangelist at heart, I have kept **Windows Azure Pack** out of scope for this book. It deserves a book of its own. For more information on **Windows Azure Pack**, please visit the following website.

http://technet.microsoft.com/en-us/library/dn296435.aspx

Summary

WAWS is the fastest way to develop websites in the cloud, and at the cheapest possible price (free). In this chapter, we explored the fundamental concepts that make up WAWS. You also learned some popular website scenarios for running on WAWS. The high-scale architecture and management capabilities of WAWS allows you to rapidly build global websites at internet scale. The inner working knowledge of WAWS will help you design multi-tenant systems of your own. Finally, you learned the top three things I recommend before deciding your cloud platform. These recommendations are based on my experience in building hundreds of websites and cloud services on Windows Azure.

Microsoft has designed WAWS with cloud first in mind and therefore has become the fastest growing service in Windows Azure. I expect to see significant growth in features and adoption of WAWS in the next couple of years.

If you are designing a new website, WAWS will empower you to deploy this site in minutes, and then scale on-demand. I have built several websites on WAWS and will share my experiences and recommendations with you throughout this book. In the next chapter, you will learn multiple ways of quickly deploying a website to WAWS.

Chapter 2
WEB SITES QUICK START

WAWS supports a variety of deployment options. The concepts we covered in Chapter 1 will help us dive deeper into deployment exercises from a variety of tools. The goal of this chapter is to make you comfortable working with these tools for deploying your own websites.

Developers are passionate about the tools they use and therefore I will try to provide an unbiased approach demonstrating website deployments. You can then decide for yourself on the right deployment tool for your solution.

It's all about the App

Infrastructures are designed to support applications. In PaaS, you are responsible only for your applications, and you instruct the infrastructure to deploy and manage them through configuration. WAWS manages your applications for you in Windows Azure. As a developer, you can now only focus on quickly building high-quality web apps of your choice, and let WAWS manage them for you.

In the following sections, I will provide you with simple walkthroughs on different ways of deploying websites into Windows Azure.

Deploying a Web Site using the Web App Gallery

Web App Gallery is a collection of third-party web applications you can deploy to WAWS from Windows Azure portal. It is similar to WebMatrix but is completely web-based. Listed below are the steps required to deploy a WordPress website using Web App gallery.

Step 1: Login to Windows Azure portal

Navigate to http://windows.azure.com and login to your Windows Azure account.

Step 2: Click the New command button at the bottom of the portal page

Figure 2.1: New Button

Step 3: Click on Compute > Web Site > From Gallery

Figure 2.2: Select From Gallery

Step 4: Select Blogs > WordPress

Figure 2.3: Select WordPress

Click the → button to navigate to Configure Your App page

Step 5: Configuring Your App

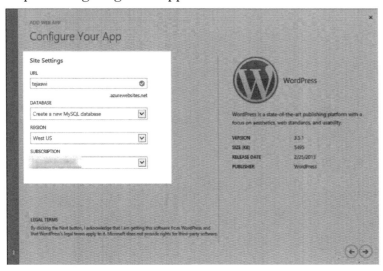

Figure 2.4: Configure Your App

On the *Configure Your App* page, enter a unique domain name, select "Create a new MySQL database", and select any region you wish to deploy your application to. If you have multiple subscriptions, you may select the appropriate subscription you want to deploy it under. Depending on the configuration parameters required by the web application, the *Configure Your App* page will display different options.

Step 6: Providing MySQL information

On the next screen, provide the name for your MySQL database, select the same region as the website, and check "I agree" to ClearDB's legal terms.

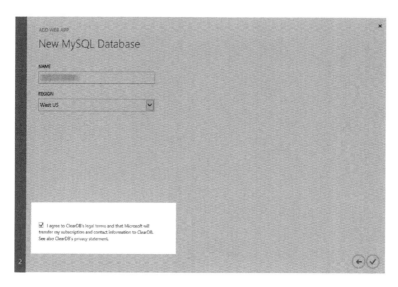

Figure 2.5: MySQL Database Information

If you don't select the same region for the database as your website, you will incur data transfer charges.

Finally, click the complete button to create the WordPress website.

Step 7: Accessing the blog website

After the website is created, it will show up in the websites list and the status will change to Running as shown in Figure 2.6.

Figure 2.6: Web Sites List

Click on the URL to navigate to the WordPress configuration page, and then click on the website name to go to the website's dashboard.

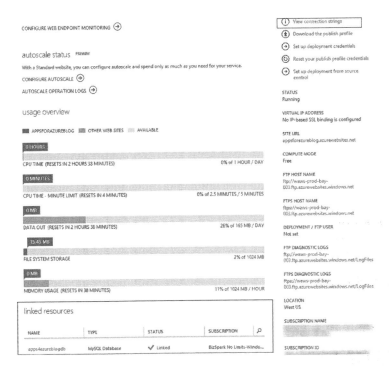

Figure 2.7: Web Site Dashboard

Note that on the Dashboard page, WAWS automatically links the MySQL database. You can retrieve the database connection string by clicking on the "View connection strings" link under the "quick glance" section of the website's dashboard page.

Figure 2.8: Linked Database

If you click on the database name, you will navigate to ClearDB's MySQL database management page.

Figure 2.9: Database Management Page

"Where does this database exist?" you may ask. ClearDB runs part of their infrastructure in Windows Azure datacenters offering MySQL as a service within each region. On ClearDB's website, click on the Endpoint Information tab to observe more details about the MySQL database created for you.

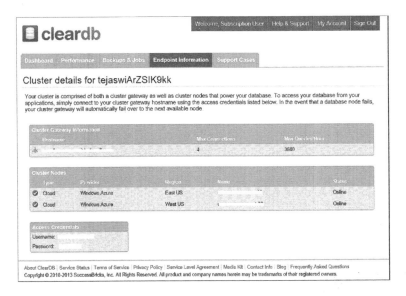

Figure 2.10: MySQL Endpoint Information

Note that a MySQL clustered database is automatically created for your WordPress site. The cluster is comprised of a cluster gateway that your application connects to and two database instances – West US (primary), and East US (secondary). WAWS selected East US as the secondary node because I selected West US as my primary region. In Windows Azure datacenters are automatically paired based on regions – West US | East US, North US | South US, etc. In an event of a primary node failure, ClearDB's cluster gateway will automatically fail over to the secondary node. Your web application maintains connection only with the cluster gateway.

Step 8: Configuring WordPress

Click on the website URL to go to the WordPress configuration page.

Figure 2.11: Configure WordPress

Enter all the required details and click Install WordPress. Once successful, click on the Login button to navigate to the administrator dashboard.

Figure 2.12: WordPress Installed

Step 9: Login using admin

After the website is created, you can log into the site using the admin credentials you just created.

Figure 2.13: WordPress Login

Click on the Login button to go to the Dashboard page.

Figure 2.14: WordPress Admin Dashboard

Step 10: Customizing WordPress

On the Dashboard page, you can customize your theme and plugins for your WordPress blog. I used the Sublime theme that was listed in the featured themes section. Navigate to the website URL (e.g. http://tejaswi.azurewebsites.net) to open your blog home page.

Hello world!

Figure 2.15: Dynamic Deploy Blog

Step 11: Downloading Publish Profile

You can also open the live WordPress site in WebMatrix. From the website dashboard page on Windows Azure portal, download publish profile and save it to a known secure location on your computer.

Figure 2.16: Download publish profile

The publish settings file consists of sensitive information like passwords and connection strings for your website. WebMatrix and other tools use this file to communicate with WAWS API.

Step 12: Opening Web Site in WebMatrix

Now, I would like to add advertisement banners to the template pages of my blog for monetizing my blog articles. WAWS integrates with WebMatrix allowing you to edit web pages on the live site. To edit your blog template, open WebMatrix, and select Open > Remote.

Figure 2.17: Open WebMatrix

Figure 2.18: Open Remote

Next, select Import publish profile and select the publish settings file that you saved in the previous step.

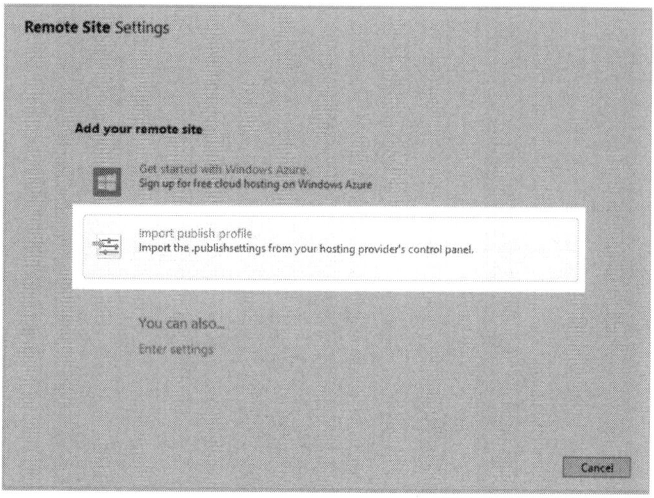

Figure 2.19: Import publish profile

WebMatrix will load the connection profile as shown in Figure 2.20. Click on Validate Connection to validate the connection with your website running on WAWS. The Validate Connection action calls the WAWS API and checks if you can communicate with the WAWS infrastructure.

Pop Quiz: At this stage, is the website Hot or Cold?

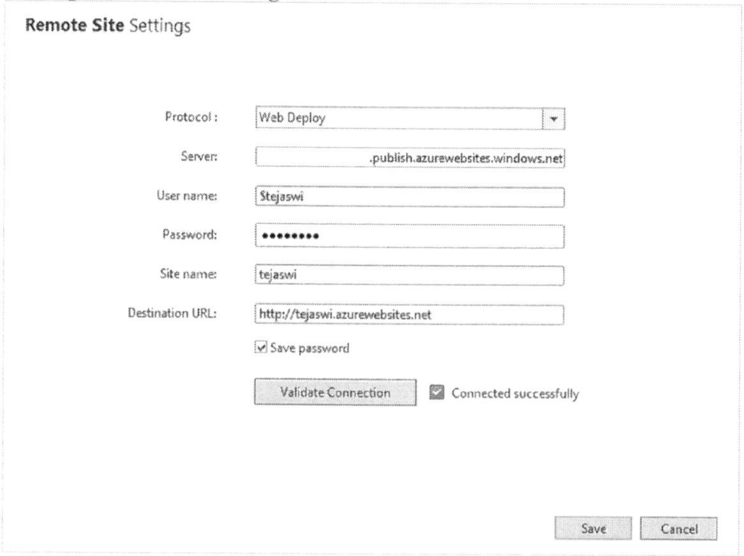

Figure 2.20: Validate Connection

The website is Hot because it is already running on a virtual server. Once you click the Save button, WebMatrix will open the WordPress website as shown in Figure 2.21.

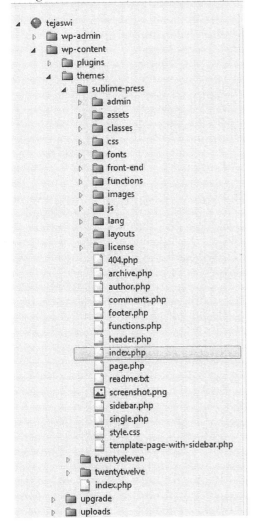

Figure 2.21: Web Site Open in WebMatrix

Step 13: Editing in WebMatrix

WordPress has a template model that is out of scope for this book. To change the main page template, I must edit the index.php file in the themes/sublime-press directory. Every theme has its own directory and you need to edit only the active theme. As shown in Figure 2.22, I have added my Google AdSense code snippet into my main page template.

```
<?php endif; ?>
<!-- Post Header Starts -->
    <header>
<!-- Title Starts -->
        <h1 class="single-title-home"><a href="<?php the_permalink(); ?>" title="<?php the_title(); ?>"><?php echo the_title(); ?></a></h1>
<!-- Title Ends -->

<!-- Meta Starts -->
        <div class="post-meta" >
            <span class="awesome-icon-calendar"></span><?php echo 'On' ?> <?php the_time('j'); ?> <?php the_time('M'); ?>, <?php the_time('Y'); ?> ?>
            <span class="awesome-icon-user"></span><?php echo 'By' ?> <?php the_author_posts_link(); ?>
        </div>
<!-- Meta Ends -->

    </header>
<!-- Post Header Ends -->
        <script type="text/javascript"><!--
google_ad_client = "------------------";
/* search468x60 */
google_ad_slot = "----------";
google_ad_width = 468;
google_ad_height = 60;
//-->
</script>
<script type="text/javascript"
src="http://pagead2.googlesyndication.com/pagead/show_ads.js">
</script>
```

Figure 2.22: Advertisement Banner Code Snippet

You don't have to add advertisement, you can add any text you feel like for testing purposes, but I wanted to show you a real-life scenario of what most bloggers would do.

Step 14: Saving and Running the Web Application

Save the page and click the Run button to open the website in a browser window. You should see your edits appear immediately on the web page.

Figure 2.23: Run website with banner

You can further enhance your blog site by editing the theme templates further and adding content. Note that because you are editing the website live, the changes you save are saved back to the server in the cloud.

Exercise Summary

In this exercise, you learned how to quickly create a WordPress website backed by a MySQL database using the Web App gallery, and editing the website using WebMatrix. In the next exercise, you will learn to deploy web apps using WebMatrix.

Deploying a Web Site using WebMatrix

In this section, you will learn to deploy websites using WebMatrix gallery.

Step 1: Creating a Windows Azure SQL Database (Azure SQL) Server

If your website requires a Windows Azure SQL Database, I recommend creating an Azure SQL DB server before deploying any websites in WAWS. Creating a server is free, you will be charged only when you create a new database.

Login to Windows Azure portal, navigate to New > Data Services > SQL Databases > Quick Create and create a new database server and a database named tejnop120.

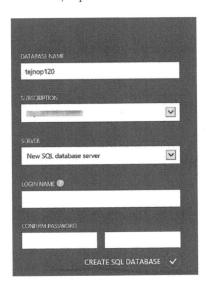

Figure 2.24: Create a new Azure SQL Database

Although WebMatrix lets you create the database from the tool, I strongly recommend creating the database from the portal first for keeping it independent of the website installation. This way, their installations are loosely coupled. Note down the server name, administrator login name and password for your database, you will need them when you install the website. The database page will list all the details required for connecting to the database, and menu for monitoring, scaling and configuring the database.

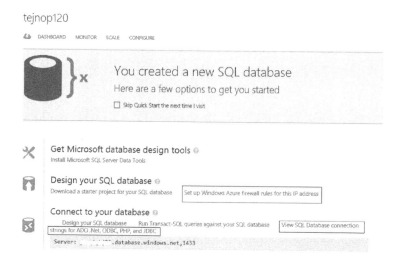

Figure 2.25: Database Connection Strings

Azure SQL DB has firewall enabled by default, therefore access to the database server from your local machine is restricted. If you want to connect to the database from tools on your local machine (e.g. from SQL Server Management Studio), click the "Set up Windows Azure firewall rules for this IP address" link to add a firewall exception for your router's IP address.

Step 2: Signing In to Windows Azure Account

Open WebMatrix and sign into your Windows Azure account as shown in Figure 2.26.

Figure 2.26: Sign In

Enter your Windows Azure credentials and sign in.

Step 3: Opening WebMatrix Application Gallery

Click on New > App Gallery to open the application gallery.

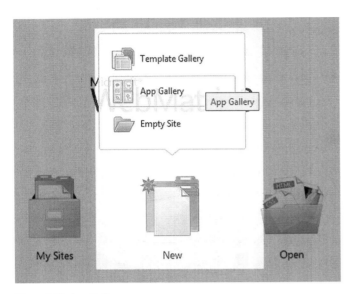

Figure 2.27: App Gallery

Similar to the web app gallery from the portal, the WebMatrix App Gallery has pre-built third-party applications available for deploying to WAWS. The number of websites are more than those offered by the web portal gallery because it also includes the ones you can deploy locally. Only the websites that have the Windows Azure icon can be deployed to WAWS. So, that reduces your selection significantly. One more difference between the web portal web app gallery and WebMatrix is that the latter downloads and installs applications on your local machine first and then you have to synchronize it with WAWS. I personally dislike this approach as it violates the "No Downloads" cloud principle I believe in.

Step 4: Selecting Orchard Content Management System (CMS)

From the applications list, select Orchard CMS. Orchard is a popular CMS built in .NET. In previous exercise, we deployed WordPress, a PHP-MySQL CMS, in this exercise we will deploy Orchard, an ASP.NET-SQL Server CMS. Notice the consistency in deployment procedure between ASP.NET and PHP websites.

Figure 2.28: Select Orchard CMS

The next screen provides you with more information about Orchard. Click Next again to proceed to the configuration screen.

Step 5: Configuring and Installing

On the Prerequisites screen, enter your website name, subscription, and datacenter location.

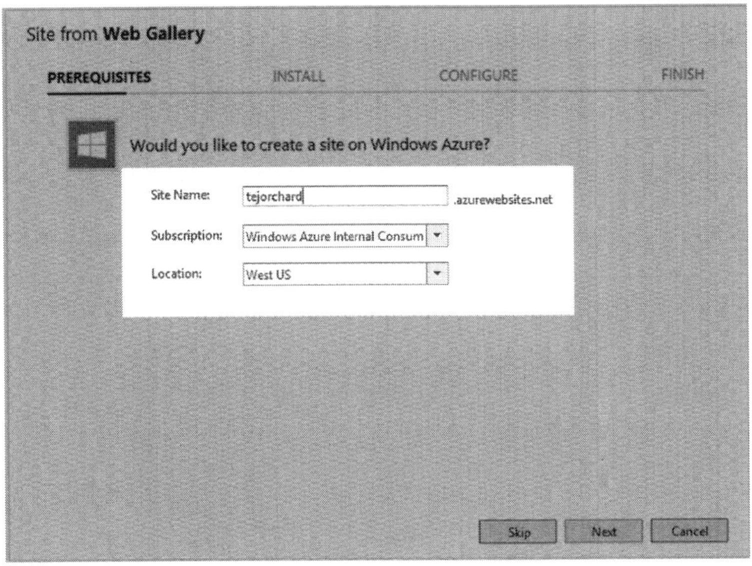

Figure 2.29: Prerequisites

Note that Orchard does not ask you for the database connection during the installation steps. This is because, Orchard captures this information during configuration and then creates database tables. Click Next to install Orchard.

Site from **Web Gallery**

PREREQUISITES	INSTALL	CONFIGURE	**FINISH**

Install Completed Successfully

View installer log

Here is what was installed:

✔ Orchard CMS

Figure 2.30: Installation Complete

As I have mentioned earlier, WebMatrix installs the application locally and then opens up a browser pointing to the local installation. "Install complete" specifies that Orchard CMS has been installed on your local machine, not in WAWS. Ignore the browser page and look for the dialog shown in Figure 2.31.

tejorchard.azurewebsites.net is ready! Click Publish whenever you want to upload your changes.

Figure 2.31: Publish

Step 6: Publishing the Web Site

Click on the Publish link to publish the Orchard installation to WAWS. Click Continue on the Publish Preview dialog.

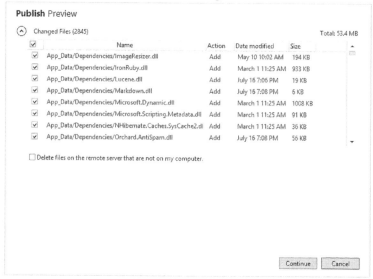

Figure 2.32: Publish Preview

After the application is published, you will see a publish message as shown in Figure 2.33

Figure 2.33: Publish Complete

Pop Quiz: When the publishing is complete, is the site HOT or COLD?

Step 7: Setting Up Orchard

Click on the website URL to navigate to the Orchard Setup page. On this page you will specify administrator password and the Azure SQL database information. Select the "Use an existing SQL Server, SQL Express database" option. You can get the ADO.NET connection string for the database portal page.

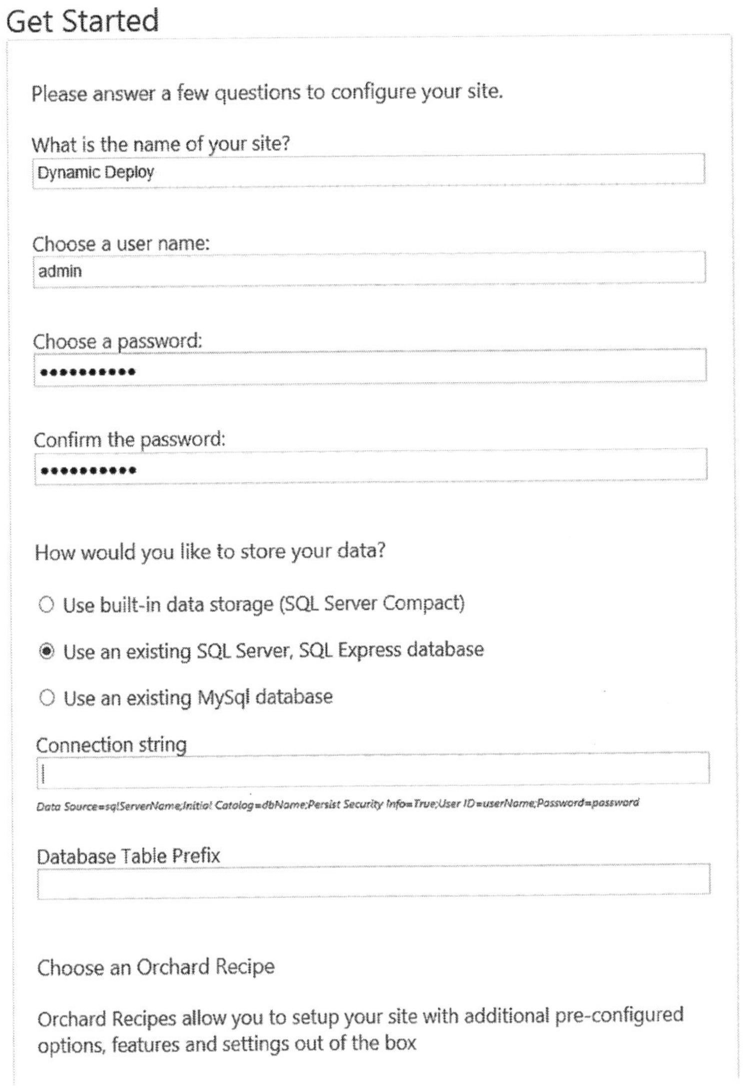

Get Started

Please answer a few questions to configure your site.

What is the name of your site?

Dynamic Deploy

Choose a user name:

admin

Choose a password:

●●●●●●●●●●

Confirm the password:

●●●●●●●●●●

How would you like to store your data?

○ Use built-in data storage (SQL Server Compact)

◉ Use an existing SQL Server, SQL Express database

○ Use an existing MySql database

Connection string

Data Source=sqlServerName;Initial Catalog=dbName;Persist Security Info=True;User ID=userName;Password=password

Database Table Prefix

Choose an Orchard Recipe

Orchard Recipes allow you to setup your site with additional pre-configured options, features and settings out of the box

Figure 2.34: Setup Orchard

Step 8: Customizing Orchard

After the website is created, you can customize it by navigating to the admin page http://[website name].azurewebsites.net/Admin

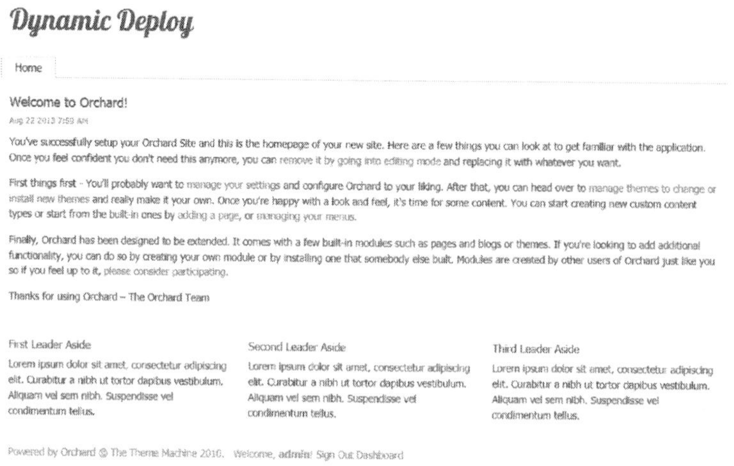

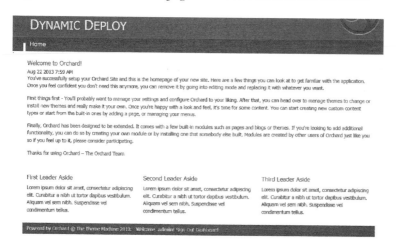

Figure 2.35: Default Orchard Theme

Figure 2.36 shows the main page with a different theme installed.

Figure 2.36: New Orchard Theme

You can further customize Orchard by editing it in WebMatrix and then publishing back to WAWS.

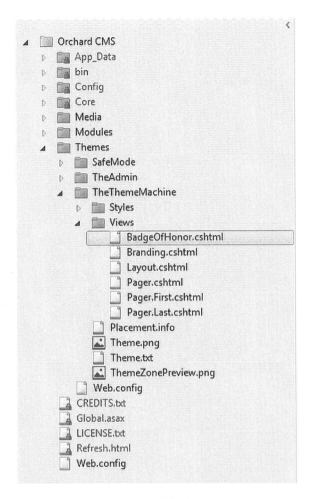

Figure 2.37: Edit Orchard in WebMatrix

Exercise Summary

In this exercise, you learned how to provision a website from WebMatrix. You also learned to create an Azure SQL database and then configure Orchard CMS to point to that database. My personal preference is to use the web portal to create a website and then load it in WebMatrix just to avoid the local installation of the website. In the next exercise, you will learn to provision a custom ASP.NET website using Visual Studio.

Deploying a Web Site using Visual

Studio

Windows Azure developers love Visual Studio because it abstracts all the underlying configuration intricacies and allows you to rapidly deploy applications and services to the cloud. It also has built-in support for deploying websites to WAWS. In this section, you will learn to deploy a custom ASP.NET website to WAWS.

Step 1: Creating an empty website from Windows Azure portal

Login to Windows Azure portal and create a new website (e.g. named storagesearch) by clicking on New > Compute > Web Site > Quick Create

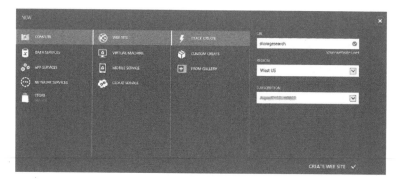

Figure 2.38: New website

We will deploy an ASP.NET website from Visual Studio to the website in WAWS.

Step 2: Creating a new website in Visual Studio

Open Visual Studio and create a new ASP.NET application.

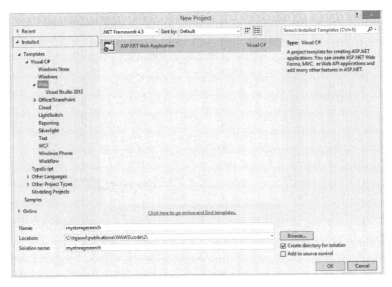

Figure 2.39: New ASP.NET web application

Step 3: Selecting web application template

Next, select a Web Forms template and click on the Change Authentication button.

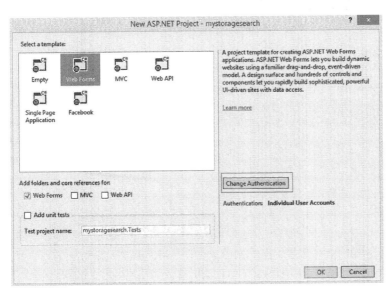

Figure 2.40: Select Web Forms

Step 4: Selecting Authentication

On the Change Authentication window, select the No Authentication option.

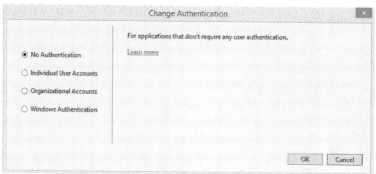

Figure 2.41: Select No Authentication

Because we selected the No Authentication option, Visual Studio will not generate any authentication (or membership) classes in the code. I am recommending this option in order to keep the exercise flow concise and simple. In a real-world web application, you will typically configure the authentication type right when you create the web application.

For more information on the listed authentication types, please refer to the following URL

http://www.asp.net/visual-studio/overview/2013/creating-web-projects-in-visual-studio#auth

Step 5: Running the website locally

Run the website locally by pressing F5.

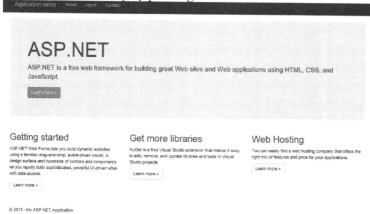

Figure 2.42: Running website locally.

Step 6: Deploying the website to WAWS

In this step, you will learn how to deploy your website from Visual Studio directly to WAWS. Because Visual Studio uses management API and web deploy to communicate with WAWS, you need to download your website's publish profile file from its dashboard page as shown in Figure 2.43.

Figure 2.43: Download publish profile

Next, right-click on the website project (e.g. StorageSearch) in Visual Studio and select Publish to open the Publish Web dialog box. On the Publish Web window, click on the Import button to select the downloaded publish-profile file.

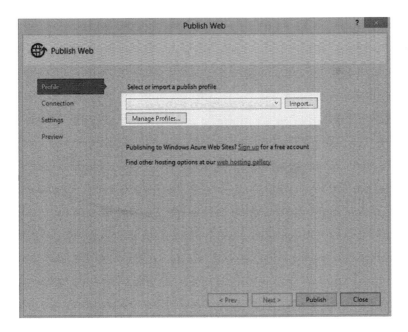

Figure 2.44: Click import

Browse and select the publish-profile file you downloaded from the WAWS portal.

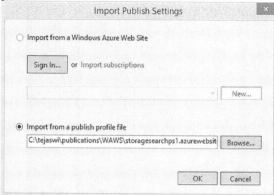

Figure 2.45: Import profile file

After you import the publish-profile, you can validate the connection with WAWS by clicking the Validate Connection button as shown in Figure 2.46.

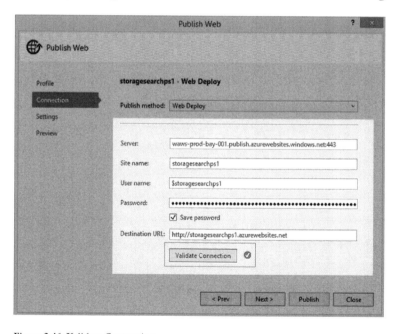

Figure 2.46: Validate Connection

Click Next to open the Settings screen to specify the configuration and database connection if any exists.

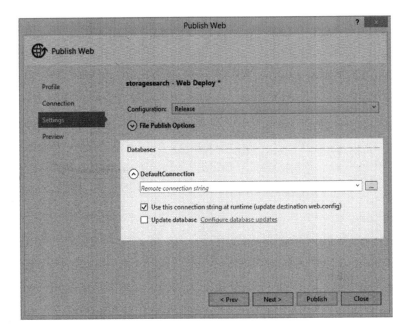

Figure 2.47: Settings

Finally, on the Preview screen, click Publish to deploy the website.

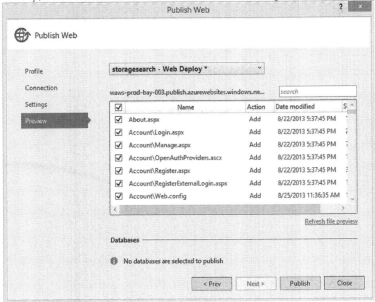

Figure 2.48: Publish

After you click the Publish button, Visual Studio will upload all the files to WAWS, publish the website and start a browser window pointing to the website's URL.

Step 7: Testing Your Web Site

After the website deployment is complete, the browser will display the Default.aspx page shown in Figure 2.49.

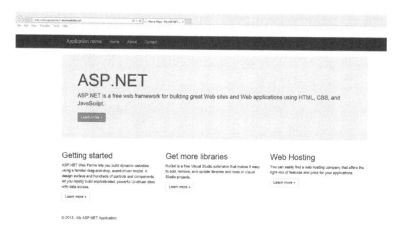

Figure 2.49: Web site running in WAWS

Step 8: Remote Debugging a website in Visual Studio[3]

Remote debugging is one of the most advanced features in Visual Studio. It allows you to debug a live running website on your local machine. To remotely debug the live website you deployed to WAWS:

1) Add website to Server Explorer.
   Open Visual Studio Server Explorer and expand the Windows Azure node as shown in Figure 2.50.

---

[3] http://weblogs.asp.net/scottgu/archive/2013/11/04/windows-azure-import-export-hard-drives-vm-acls-web-sockets-remote-debugging-continuous-delivery-new-relic-billing-alerts-and-more.aspx

Figure 2.50: Expand Windows Azure node in Server Explorer

2) Right-click on the Web Sites node and select Add New Site....

Figure 2.51: Add New Site

3) Sign-in to with your Windows Azure account and click Cancel.

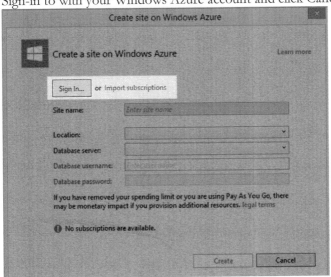

Figure 2.52: Sign In with your Windows Azure account

4) Refresh the Web Sites node to list all the deployed websites.
5) Next, open the website project in Visual Studio and add the following lines of code to Default.aspx.cs

```
protected void Page_Load
(object sender, EventArgs e)
```

```
{
  if(User.Identity.IsAuthenticated)
  {

     Trace.Write("Authenticated");
  }
}
```

Listing 2.1: Code for debug

Add a breakpoint next to the "if" statement.

6) Publish the website to WAWS, but this time select the "Debug" configuration profile as shown in Figure 2.53.

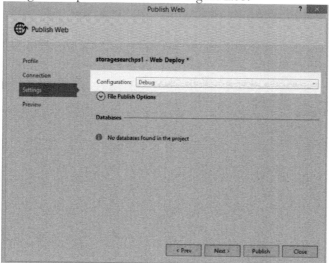

Figure 2.53: Select Debug Configuration during publishing

7) After the website is published, right-click on the website name in Server Explorer and select Attach Debugger.

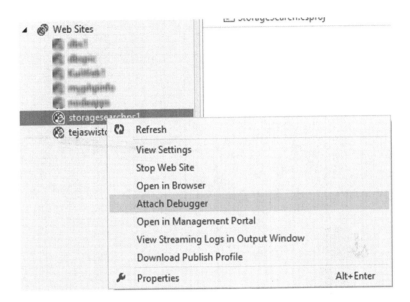

Figure 2.54: Attach Debugger

Visual Studio will remotely attach the debugger to the selected website running in WAWS. As shown in Figure 2.55, the debugger will then stop the website's execution when it hits the breakpoint you set in Listing 2.1 (i.e. at if(User.Identity.IsAuthenticated)).

```
1 reference
public partial class _Default : Page
{
    0 references
    protected void Page_Load(object sender, EventArgs e)
    {
        if(User.Identity.IsAuthenticated)
        {
            Trace.Write("Authenticated");
        }
    }
}
```

Figure 2.55: Remote Debugger stopped at the breakpoint

Note that you can track all the website's variables (shown in Figure 2.56) and change them dynamically as if you were debugging a website locally.

Figure 2.56: Track variables locally

If you encounter an error while attaching the debugger, stop and start the website from the Server Explorer and then attach the debugger again.

Exercise Summary

In this section, you learned how to deploy and remotely debug a custom ASP.NET website in WAWS from Visual Studio. Remote debugging is an invaluable tool for complex websites when you want to track the change in variables as the HTTP request transitions from one page to another. In Chapters 5 and 6, you will learn to migrate complex ASP.NET websites to WAWS.

Summary

In this chapter you learned three different tools for deploying websites into WAWS – Web App Gallery, WebMatrix, and Visual Studio. There are even more options like FTP, PowerShell, Git, etc. that you will learn in the next chapter. The goal of this chapter was to familiarize you with WAWS and its integration with Visual Studio. With this knowledge, you can already start deploying your websites to WAWS. WAWS allows you to focus on rapid development and continuous improvement because in today's world of mobile applications, there is no time to think through and implement an entire idea in a single release. In the next chapter, you will learn to setup continuous deployment of websites from source control management tools, which will help you rapidly integrate tested code into production environments.

Bibliography

Microsoft Corporation. (2012). *Windows Azure Web Site Documentation.*

Retrieved from Windows Azure :
http://www.windowsazure.com/en-
us/documentation/services/web-sites/?fb=en-us

Tejaswi Redkar

Chapter 3

CONTINUOUS DEPLOYMENT

Continuous deployment is the process of automating releases of your solution on every successful build. The deployment destination can be a development, testing, staging, or production environment. Software development has transformed significantly in the past few years. Product is divided into features that are designed, implemented and tested instantly without spending upfront time in writing entire product design specification. Features are prioritized and released at a faster pace. Today's development tools have also adapted to these changes and thus provide you with built-in ability to continuously integrate and deploy your applications.

WAWS is designed with continuous deployment support from the ground up. WAWS not only integrates with Microsoft's Visual Studio Online, but also third-party source control management (SCM) systems or file share. In this chapter, you will learn to continuously deploy websites from popular SCMs to WAWS.

What is Continuous Deployment?

In continuous deployment, the variance between the tested code residing in SCM and the live production environment is kept minimal. This means when a developer tests and checks-in the code, the build and release processes are triggered automatically. The deployments can be made into development, testing, stating, or production environments depending on your software development processes. Figure 3.1 illustrates the continuous deployment process graphically.

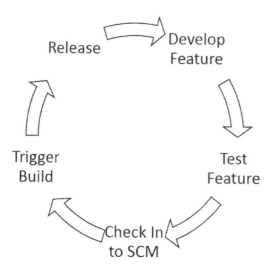

Figure 3.1: Continuous Deployment

In its simplest form, following is the sequence of steps that happen in a typical continuous deployment process:

1) Developer develops a feature
2) Developer/Tester tests the feature based on the quality attributes associated with that feature (e.g. unit, functional, scale, performance, etc.)
3) Once the tests are passed, the source code associated with the feature is checked into the SCM system
4) Checking-in triggers an automated build within the SCM. The build also runs a series of automated tests called quality gates to make sure the feature does not break any core application functionality.
5) If the build and automated tests succeed, the binaries are released to the production system and production-related tests are run on it

These five steps are a simplistic description of what actually happens in a large-scale environment consisting of hundreds of developers. For products with large product code base and thousands of developers building hundreds of features, continuous deployment is employed in a risk-averse manner by applying automated as well as manual quality gates. The product is then released in preview for testing, and then continuously improving the code quality through continuous deployment.

Why Continuous Deployment?

Continuous deployment provides you with the following benefits:
Business Agility

With continuous deployment, you build a process for continuously improving the quality of your product and also adaptability to business changes.

Technical Agility

Technical agility is the ability to quickly respond to technical requirements like adding new features, fixing defects, and retracting features. Technical agility in turn improves business agility.

Operational Agility

Operational agility is the ability to quickly respond to infrastructure events like security breaches, system lockups, scale-up/down, and operational cost management. With continuous deployment, the operational team can quickly modify infrastructure based on operational requirements of the business. This modification may require shutting down some virtual machines due to security breach or releasing a particular branch of an application in the staging environment.

Continuous Deployment with Visual Studio Online (VSOnline)

Note: Team Foundation Service is now called Visual Studio Online. So, there might be some references to Team Foundation Service (TFS) in this book.

VSOnline is Microsoft's foray into the SCM SaaS market. As of writing this book, VSOnline features were focused in three primary areas: Source Code Management, Team Collaboration, and Build-Test-Deploy. VSOnline itself runs on Windows Azure and therefore it was designed from the ground up with Windows Azure integration in mind. WAWS integrates with VSOnline out-of-the-box. In the following exercise, you will learn to manage and deploy a website from VSOnline. Only development of code will be done on the local machine. Build, Test, and Deploy will be executed in the cloud by VSOnline. We will follow a step-by-step process to understand continuous deployment from VSOnline to WAWS.

Step 1: Creating a VSOnline Account

Navigate to http://tfs.visualstudio.com and create an account. Signing up is free and you can have up to 5 free users. To create an account, you need to create a namespace that establishes your unique VSOnline endpoint.

Account Creation
Identity Provider
Windows Live™ ID
Account URL
https://
.visualstudio.com/
Create Account
By clicking Create Account, you are agreeing to the Terms of Service and the Privacy Statement.

Figure 3.2: Create VSOnline account

You can then create any number of projects under this namespace. Once you create an account, you should see a dashboard as shown in Figure 3.3.

Recent projects & teams
New
Browse
Dynamic Deploy Portal
8 hours ago
Dynamic Deploy Windows Stor...
Storage Search

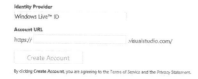

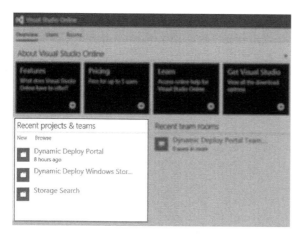

Figure 3.3: VSOnline Portal Page

The portal lists existing projects and provides an interface for creating new ones.

Step 2: Creating a new team project

Click on the New team project button to create a new team project.

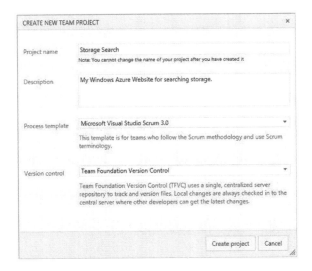

Figure 3.4: New Team Project

Specify a project name, description, process template and the version control system as "Team Foundation Version Control". After you click on the Create project button, VSOnline creates a new project with artifacts specific to the selected process template. Click on "Navigate to project site" button to go to the project dashboard website.

Figure 3.5: VSOnline Project Dashboard

The VSOnline dashboard provides you with access to the four pillars of your application lifecycle:

Code: Provides you with access to the project source code

Work: Provides you with ability to create sprint backlogs, task management, and defect management

Build: Provides access to source code build plans and scripts

Test: Provides you with ability to create test plans and test cases

The dashboard also provides an administration interface for managing team members, sprint schedules, and work areas. Since VSOnline is an ever-improving cloud service, I envision more services being added as it matures.

Step 3: Setting up WAWS and VSOnline integration

1) Login to your Windows Azure portal and navigate to the dashboard page of the storagesearch website you created in the previous chapter. If you did not create one, you can still create a new one in the portal.

2) From the website's dashboard page, click on the "Set up deployment from source control" link to open the "Setup Deployment" popup window.

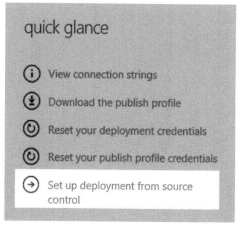

Figure 3.6: Set up deployment from source link

3) Select Visual Studio Online from the list as shown in Figure 3.7.

SET UP DEPLOYMENT
Where is your source code?
Visual Studio Online
Local Git repository
GitHub
Dropbox
Visual Studio Online provides a complete solution for software management, source control, issue tracking, build and test automation, and more.

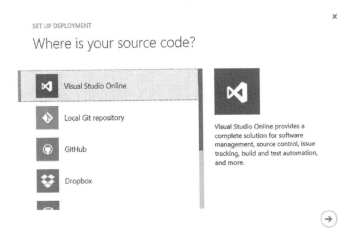

Figure 3.7: Select VSOnline

4) On the "Authorize VSOnline Connection" screen, specify the namespace you created while creating your VSOnline account and click Authorize Now button. You may also create a new VSOnline account from this screen by clicking on the "Create a VSOnline account now" link.

SET UP DEPLOYMENT
Authorize connection
Existing user
https:// dynamicdeploy .visualstudio.com
Authorize Now
New user
Don't have an account yet? Create an account now.

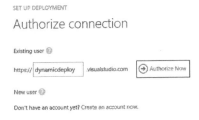

Figure 3.8: Authorize connection

5) VSOnline uses OAuth protocol to federate authentication and provide single sign-on between WAWS and VSOnline. The OAuth orchestration requires you to accept the connection request between WAWS and VSOnline. Click on the Accept button to proceed.

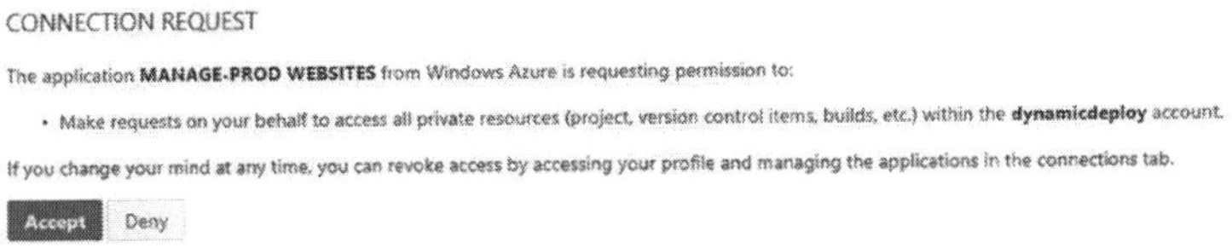

CONNECTION REQUEST
The application MANAGE-PROD WEBSITES from Windows Azure is requesting permission to:
Make requests on your behalf to access all private resources (project, version control items, builds, etc.) within the dynamicdeploy account.
If you change your mind at any time, you can revoke access by accessing your profile and managing the applications in the connections tab.
Accept
Deny

Figure 3.9: Connection Request

If the authentication is successful, Windows Azure portal will ask you to select a source control repository (project) from your VSOnline account.

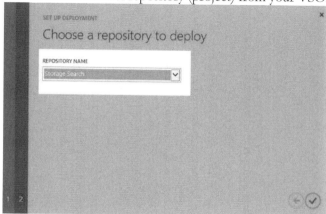

Figure 3.10: Source Control Repository

Once the connection is established, the Deployments section will list the connection information and also replace the "WebMatrix" button from the bottom menu to Visual Studio. VSOnline linking assumes that you will check-in you code from Visual Studio.

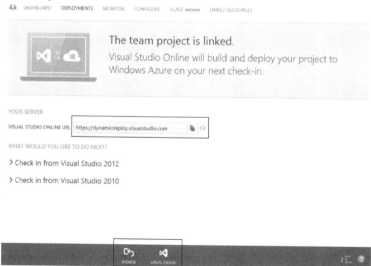

Figure 3.11: VSOnline Linked Page

The deployments page also lists instructions for checking in code from multiple versions of Visual Studio into VSOnline. Although Figure 3.11 lists Visual Studio 2012 and 2010, the deployment process is supported from

Visual Studio 2013 as well.

Step 4: Checking In Source Code and Building

1) Understanding the VSOnline Build Architecture

Before checking in your code, it is important to understand how the VSOnline build engine works. VSOnline is a distributed system in which Build Service can run on an independent group of machines. VSOnline already hosts a Build Service called Hosted Build Controller that runs in the cloud. In most simple projects, I recommend using Hosted Build Controller. But, for larger projects with complex build processes, you can configure VSOnline to work with your own Build Service. Your own Build Service can be hosted in Windows Azure Virtual Machines or in your datacenter. Creating your own Build Service is out of scope for this book. Figure 3.12 illustrates the high-level build process in VSOnline.

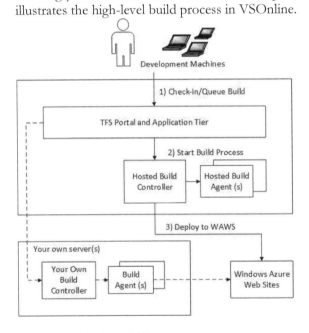

Figure 3.12: VSOnline Build Process

From Visual Studio, when you check-in the code or queue a build, VSOnline queues a build with the Build Controller, which then instructs the Build Agents to build the project. After the build is successful, Build Controller initiates a process to deploy your website.

Note: Hosted Controller Limitations

At the time of writing, the VSOnline Build Service
was in preview and therefore the Hosted Controller
had limitations on software installed. When you
check-in your code in VSOnline, any external
binary references are not automatically checked-in
and therefore builds may fail when using the
Hosted Controller. As a workaround, I recommend
creating a folder named lib in your Visual Studio
project and copy all the external binary references
there. Check-in these assemblies along with the
project. Edit the build definition source settings in
Visual Studio to add the lib folder path as an
Active working folder. Hosted Build Controller will
then have access to these assemblies during the
build process. If you are using your own Build
Service, then you can pre-install these libraries on
your Build Agent machines, or continue following
the binary check-in process. You can find more
information on which binaries are pre-installed on
the VSOnline Hosted Controller here
http://listofsoftwareontfshostedbuildserver.azure
websites.net/

You can also find more information on Hosted
Build Controller here

http://tfs.visualstudio.com/learn/hosted-build-
controller-in-vs

Figure 3.13 illustrates the "lib" folder that I created in my Visual Studio
project and added dependent assemblies to this folder.

Figure 3.13: Visual Studio Folder with Binaries

2) Adding VSOnline to your project

After adding the lib directory in your project, add the solution to your VSOnline by right-clicking on the solution, selecting "Add Solution to Source Control". Enter the required VSOnline information of your account.

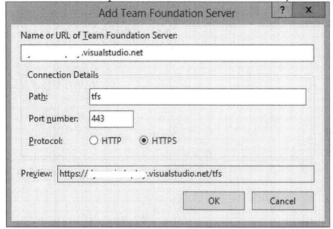

Figure 3.14: Add Team Foundation Server

You will be asked to enter your VSOnline credentials and select the project from your VSOnline account.

3) Checking in your code

Now the VSOnline and your code are linked. You need to still check-in the code to trigger a build followed by deployment. The build may fail if all the files, including the lib directory, are not checked-in correctly. One precautionary step I usually take is adding the lib folder to Source Settings property of the build as shown in Figure 3.15.

Figure 3.15: Source Settings

You can modify the Source Settings of your build by navigating to Team Explorer and editing the build definition as shown in Figure 3.16.

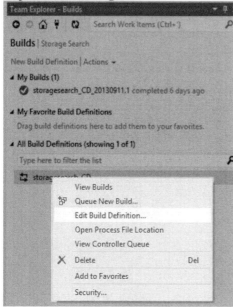

Figure 3.16: Edit Build Definition

4)   Verifying Continuous Deployment

If the build is successful, the website will be automatically deployed to WAWS as shown in Figure 3.17.

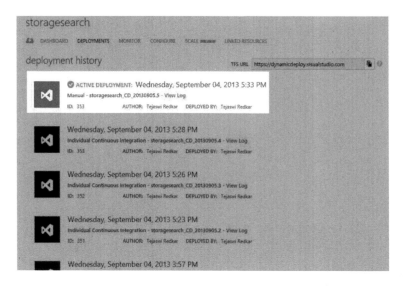

Figure 3.17: Active Deployment

Every time you (or any developer on your team) checks-in code, VSOnline will build and trigger a deployment. You can view In Progress, Active and Historical deployments under the Deployments section in WAWS portal. Typically, in large scale projects, you will have a dedicated Build Controller with the capability to automatically deploy to WAWS. In that case, you can change the default Hosted Build Controller to your Builder Controller from the Edit Build Definition dialog in Visual Studio.

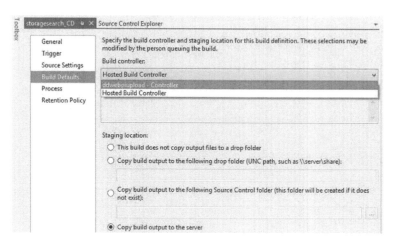

Figure 3.18: Changing Build Controller

In Figure 3.18, ddwebpiupload is the name of a dedicated build controller I have associated with my VSOnline account. I built it by installing a VSOnline Build Service on a Windows Azure Virtual Machines and pointed it to VSOnline as its source control system.

5)   Building Manually

You can also queue a build manually by right-clicking on the build definition and selecting "Queue New Build…" as shown in Figure 3.19.

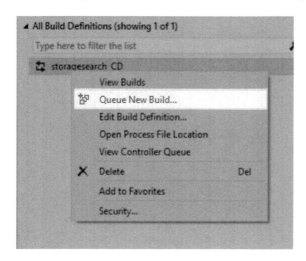

Figure 3.19: Queue New Build

After you queue a build, build controller triggers the build and deployment process. You can view the queued builds on VSOnline portal or directly from Visual Studio's builds section of the Team Explorer. On other hand, you can also queue the build directly from the VSOnline portal. Figures 3.20, 3.21, 3.22, and 3.23 illustrate the status of Queued, Completed, and Deployed builds in the VSOnline portal respectively, and WAWS deployment status in Windows Azure portal.

Figure 3.20: Queued Build in VSOnline portal

Figure 3.21: Completed Build in VSOnline portal

Figure 3.22: Deployed Build in VSOnline portal

Figure 3.23: Deployment Status in Windows Azure portal

Exercise Summary

In this exercise, you learned how to configure continuous deployment between WAWS and Microsoft's Visual Studio Online. You also learned the limitations of the default Hosted Build Controller and workaround to include your own assemblies into the build process. With continuous deployment, you can integrate any new features and changes rapidly into your website. Typically, in large-scale environments, deployments have quality-gates that run automated tests before pushing the code into to production environments. With continuous deployment, you can even back-out and replace bad deployments very quickly. Since VSOnline is an ever improving service, I recommend you to keep a track of the latest released features of VSOnline.

Continuous Deployment with GitHub

In recent years, GitHub and Microsoft have added support for each other's tools thus providing continuous deployment options for developers maintaining their projects in GitHub. Microsoft has created a Git add-in for Visual Studio to check-in code from Visual Studio directly to GitHub. In return, GitHub has also built a GitHub for Windows application that you can download from the URL http://windows.github.com/. GitHub for Windows provides a simple graphical user interface for executing Git commands.

In this section, you will learn to link WAWS with GitHub for continuous deployment. For this exercise, you will need to download:

Note: Visual Studio Tools for Git is integrated into Visual Studio 2013, for Visual Studio 2012, you can download the tools from the link below.
http://visualstudiogallery.msdn.microsoft.com/abafc7d6-dcaa-40f4-8a5e-d6724bdb980c

---

WAWS' Best Kept Secret "Project Kudu"

Project Kudu is the software service behind Git deployments in Windows Azure Web Sites. The service itself does not depend on Windows Azure and therefore you can deploy it in your own datacenter and enjoy WAWS-like deployment functionality. For information on how Kudu works, please refer to the URLs below.

References:

https://github.com/projectkudu/kudu

https://github.com/projectkudu/kudu/wiki/Kudu-architecture

https://github.com/projectkudu/kudu/wiki

Step 1: Understanding Continuous Deployment process from GitHub

In this integration, software developers commit and synchronize their code with their GitHub repository, that triggers an event (or fires a hook) notifying WAWS to initiate a Git pull on the source code branch from GitHub. Figure 3.24 illustrates the interactions between WAWS and GitHub that occur during continuous deployment.

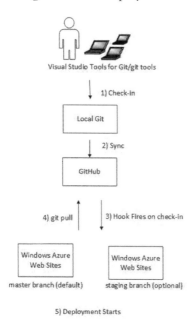

Figure 3.24: GitHub Continuous Deployment

WAWS supports deployment from specific source code branches (e.g. master), thus allowing you to have clear separation between staging and production deployments if required.

Step 2: Creating a GitHub Account

Using a browser, navigate to http://www.github.com and create a new account. You can create and follow multiple repositories from this account.

Figure 3.25: Creating new GitHub account

Figure 3.25 illustrates your GitHub home page after you open an account.

Step 3: Creating a new GitHub repository

A new repository will store your website source code. From the top right corner of your GitHub account page, click on "Create a new repo".

Figure 3.26: Create a new repo

On the create repository page, provide your repository details.

> Note: Please make sure that the repository is public and "Initialize this repository" checkbox is not checked. While checking in code from Visual Studio add-in for Git, I received an error message

due to naming conflicts caused by initialization.

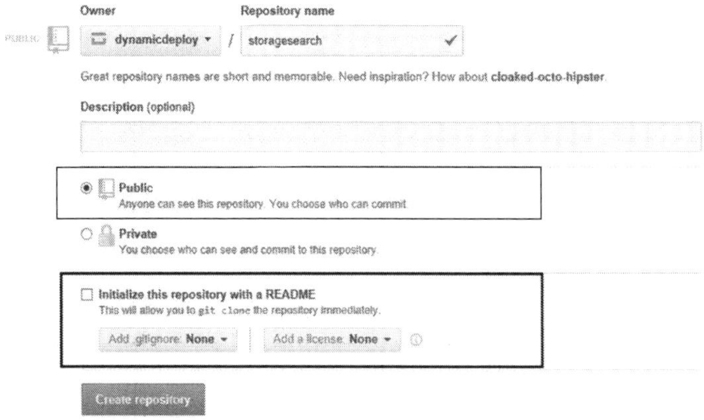

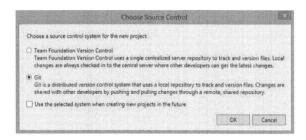

Figure 3.27: Repository details

Click Create repository button to create your source code repository in GitHub.

Step 4: Checking in source code

Open your website solution in Visual Studio and add it to source control using the "Add Solution to Source Control" option. Because you have installed the Git add-in, you will be provided with two options – Team Foundation Version Control and Git. Select Git and click OK.

Figure 3.28: Choose Source Control

Visual Studio creates a new local Git repository for you in the same directory as the project source code, as shown in Figure 3.29.

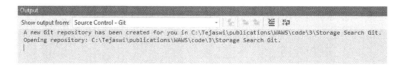

Figure 3.29: Initialize Local Git Repository

Git gives you the flexibility to work locally on your source code and then synchronize contents with GitHub when you are ready. This allows you to have a two-phase check-in process. First commit locally, and then synchronize it with GitHub.

Next, right-click on the Visual Studio solution and click Commit to check-in your source code to the local Git repository. Note that the source code is still on the local machine and not synchronized with GitHub.

Figure 3.30: Commit Source Code

You will be asked to configure user name and email address before committing the changes.

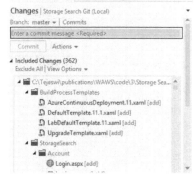

Figure 3.31: Configure Git Credentials

On the credentials dialog, specify your GitHub account credentials.

Figure 3.32: Git Settings

Click on Update to go back to the Commit changes page.

Figure 3.33: Commit Changes

Enter a comment for the change set and click on Commit. You don't have to specify credentials every time you commit changes.

Figure 3.34: Committed Changes

We still haven't synchronized the source code with GitHub. To do so, click on the Commits link to navigate to the Commits window as shown in Figure 3.35.

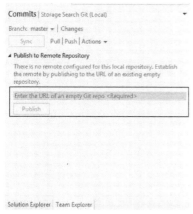

Figure 3.35: Commits Windows to Publish

From this window you can synchronize your locally committed source code to GitHub. The "Sync" button is grayed out because you haven't linked the local Git repository to GitHub yet. You will need to get the URL of the GitHub repository and then publish it. In order to get the URL of GitHub repository, navigate to the GitHub repository page. If you have created the repository as per the instructions, you should see the repository as shown in Figure 3.36.

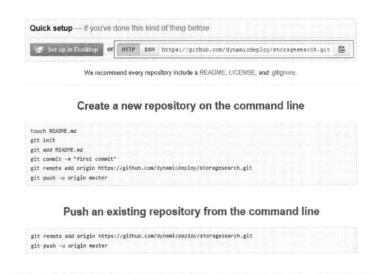

Figure 3.36: GitHub Repository Page

Copy the Git URL from the Quick setup section and paste it in Visual Studio Remote Repository textbox as shown in Figure 3.37.

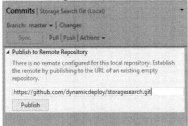

Figure 3.37: Publish to Git

Clicking on the Publish button opens up a screen to enter your username and password to connect to GitHub, which if you proceed enables the Sync button.

Figure 3.38: Sync to GitHub

Click the Sync button to synchronize the source code with GitHub. After all the code gets uploaded to GitHub, your repository should look similar to Figure 3.39.

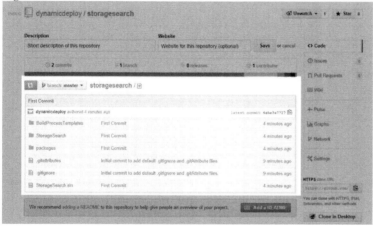

Figure 3.39: GitHub Repository with uploaded source code

You have now configured GitHub as the source code repository for your website. Next, you have to create a website and link it to this GitHub repository for continuous deployment to WAWS.

Step 5: Creating a new website

The next logical step is to create a new website from the Windows Azure portal as shown in Figure 3.40.

Figure 3.40: Create a new website

Step 6: Linking GitHub with the website

On the website landing page, click on the "Integrate source control" link. From the list of source control systems, select GitHub.

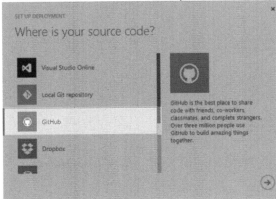

Figure 3.41: Select GitHub Source Control

On the next page, GitHub will request authorization for accessing your account.

Figure 3.42: Allow GitHub Access

Once you allow access to the GitHub account, WAWS will ask you to select the repository and the branch (master by default) to deploy.

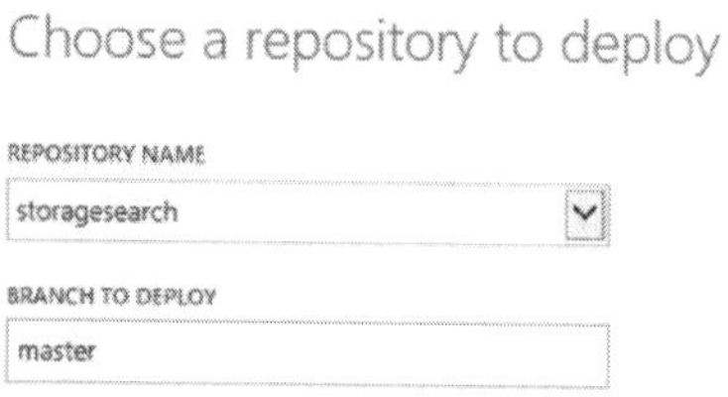

Choose a repository to deploy

REPOSITORY NAME

storagesearch

BRANCH TO DEPLOY

master

Figure 3.43: Select repository and branch to deploy

The website is now linked to the GitHub source repository. If you check-in source code changes into GitHub, it will trigger a deployment. Remember that from Visual Studio, you have to first commit the source code to the local Git repository and then synchronize to GitHub for the deployment to trigger. To test it, make minor changes to the source code and synchronize the code to GitHub. You should immediately see a deployment being triggered on your website's Deployments section. You can also trigger simultaneous deployments to staging and production websites, depending on how the source code is checked-in. WAWS gives you the flexibility to configure the deployment process as per your requirements. Figure 3.44 illustrates an active deployment that is linked to a GitHub repository.

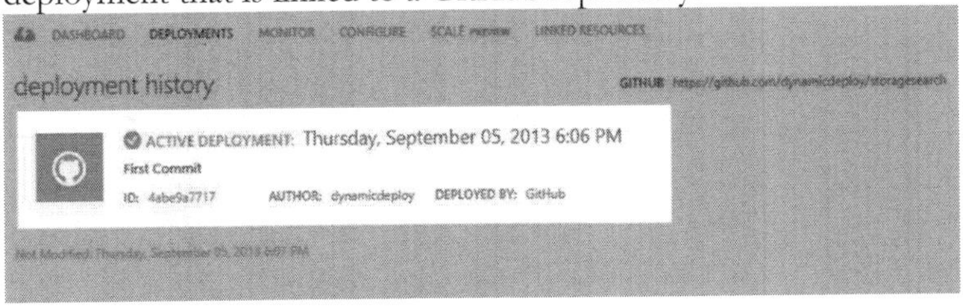

Figure 3.44: Active Deployment Linked to GitHub

You can also link WAWS to local or CodePlex Git repositories. The procedure is similar to the one described above, and therefore I will not be covering the remaining Git repositories in this book. For publishing from a local Git, the Windows Azure Training Kit (https://github.com/WindowsAzure-TrainingKit) provides several examples and is continuously updated by Microsoft.

Deploying from Dropbox

Dropbox is known for its consumer-friendly file storage, syncing, and sharing service. It is not an enterprise-grade source control system. But, Microsoft decided to make Dropbox a hook into deploying WAWS. For consumers who already have Dropbox accounts and host websites from there, this feature reduces barriers to entry for adopting WAWS. In this section I will provide instructions for deploying a website to WAWS from your Dropbox folder. You will need a Dropbox account to understand the steps in this exercise. I also recommend downloading and installing the Dropbox desktop client.

Step 1: Linking WAWS to Dropbox

As seen in previous exercises, create a new website from Windows Azure portal and click on "Integrate with source control". From the source control list, select Dropbox as shown in Figure 3.45.

Figure 3.45: Select Dropbox Source Control

In the next dialog, you will be asked to authorize the creation of folders in your Dropbox account. This is because, WAWS creates a named folder in your Dropbox account for storing websites.

Figure 3.46: Authorize Access to Dropbox Folder

Click Allow to authorize the transaction. Next, in the "Set up publishing" dialog, specify a folder name that will be created in /Apps/Azure folder.

Figure 3.47: New Folder in Dropbox

WAWS will be now linked to your Dropbox folder /Apps/Azure/[folder name you specified].

Figure 3.48: Linked Dropbox Folder

Note that you can sync the Dropbox folder from portal by clicking the sync button. Verify with the Dropbox desktop tool the path of the newly created folder.

Figure 3.49: Dropbox Folder Path on local machine

The Dropbox folder is empty when it is created. You need to upload your website files to this folder.

Step 2: Copying Source Code to Dropbox

For your website to be deployed to WAWS, you need to copy all the website files in the newly created Dropbox folder, and click Sync button on the Windows Azure portal. As shown in Figure 3.50, I have copied all the files from the StorageSearch website into the storagesearchdropbox folder that was created above.

> **Note: If your source code consists of sensitive information, do not copy into the Dropbox folder. Only copy binaries and files required for running the website.**

↑ ▸ Tejaswi Redkar ▸ Dropbox ▸ Apps ▸ Azure ▸ storagesearchdropbox

Name

- Account
- App_Data
- App_Start
- bin
- Content
- Images
- lib
- obj
- Properties
- Scripts
- About.aspx
- About.aspx.cs
- About.aspx.designer.cs
- Bundle.config
- Contact.aspx
- Contact.aspx.cs
- Contact.aspx.designer.cs
- Default.aspx
- Default.aspx.cs
- Default.aspx.designer.cs
- favicon.ico
- Global.asax
- Global.asax.cs
- Site.Master
- Site.Master.cs
- Site.Master.designer.cs
- Site.Mobile.Master
- Site.Mobile.Master.cs
- Site.Mobile.Master.designer.cs
- StorageSearch.csproj
- StorageSearch.csproj.user
- StorageSearch.csproj.vspscc
- ViewSwitcher.ascx
- ViewSwitcher.ascx.cs
- ViewSwitcher.ascx.designer.cs
- Web.config
- Web.Debug.config
- Web.Release.config

Figure 3.50: Web Site Copied to Dropbox

Step 3: Synchronizing Deployment

The last step in deploying your website is to click the Sync button on the website's Deployments page.

Figure 3.51: Sync Dropbox

The website will be automatically deployed to Windows Azure as shown in

Figure 3.52.

Figure 3.52: Web Site deployed from Dropbox

Although I don't see Dropbox as a popular source control repository for WAWS, it is definitely worth exploring scenarios that may arise from this integration. For example, you could create image and other media driven websites based on randomly uploaded content into Dropbox. There are a lot of public events where photographs are taken and lost in mobile devices and Facebook accounts. If you can automatically upload event-specific content to a Dropbox folder shared by attendees, you can dynamically create website for that event.

Deploying with FTP

This is the simplest form of deploying websites to WAWS. WAWS exposes FTP endpoints for every website created. Below is a step-by-step procedure for deploying websites to WAWS using FTP.

Step 1: Create a new website

As illustrated in earlier exercises, create a new website from Windows Azure portal. Next, create FTP deployment credentials by clicking "Reset your deployment credentials" on the website dashboard page.

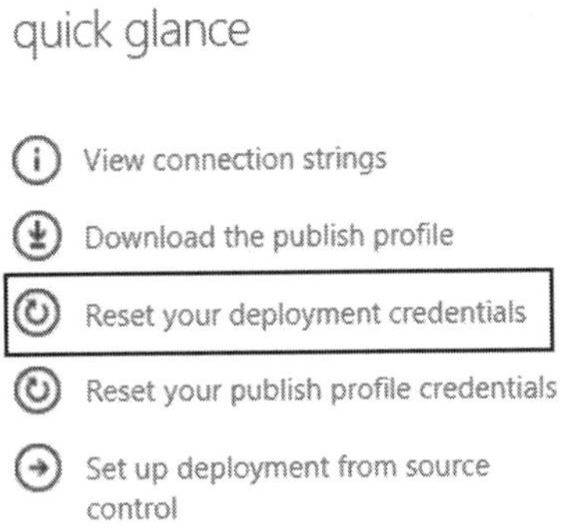

quick glance

(i) View connection strings

(↓) Download the publish profile

(↻) Reset your deployment credentials

(↻) Reset your publish profile credentials

(→) Set up deployment from source
control

Figure 3.53: Reset Deployment Credentials

Specify a new user name and password you will use for connecting the FTP client.

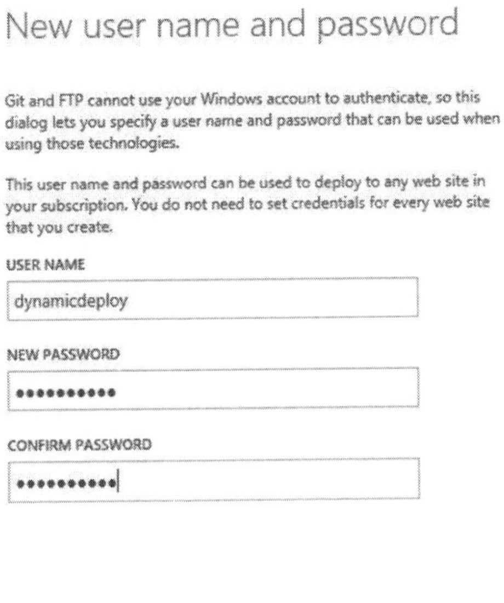

New user name and password

Git and FTP cannot use your Windows account to authenticate, so this dialog lets you specify a user name and password that can be used when using those technologies.

This user name and password can be used to deploy to any web site in your subscription. You do not need to set credentials for every web site that you create.

USER NAME

dynamicdeploy

NEW PASSWORD

●●●●●●●●●●

CONFIRM PASSWORD

●●●●●●●●●●

Figure 3.54: FTP User

Step 2: Open an FTP client to WAWS and upload files

Note down the FTP connection information for the website from the dashboard page as shown in Figure 3.55.

FTP HOST NAME
ftp://waws-prod-bay-
003.ftp.azurewebsites.windows.net

FTPS HOST NAME
ftps://waws-prod-bay-
003.ftp.azurewebsites.windows.net

DEPLOYMENT / FTP USER
storageearchftp\dynamicdeploy

FTP DIAGNOSTIC LOGS
ftp://waws-prod-bay-
003.ftp.azurewebsites.windows.net/LogFiles

FTPS DIAGNOSTIC LOGS
ftps://waws-prod-bay-
003.ftp.azurewebsites.windows.net/LogFiles

Figure 3.55: FTP Connection Information

Using your favorite FTP client, connect to the websites' FTP endpoint. I have used FileZilla, but you can use any FTP client for this purpose.

Filename	Filesize	Filetype	Last modified	Permissions	Owner/Gro...
..					
LogFiles		File folder	9/10/2013 5:04:...		
site		File folder	9/10/2013 5:04:...		

Figure 3.56: FTP Connection and folder list

The /site/wwwroot folder is where you should upload the website's files. After uploading, the folder structure looks like Figure 3.57.

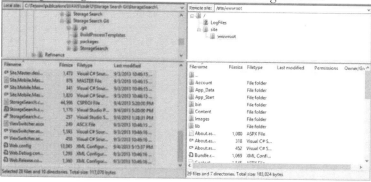

Figure 3.57: Folder Structure in WAWS

After all the files are uploaded, you can test the website by navigating to website's home page. In all the exercises, I am using the same storagesearch website we built earlier in this chapter.

Deploying with PowerShell Cmdlets

Microsoft has released a set of PowerShell cmdlets for running administrative tasks on Windows Azure services. The set also includes cmdlets for managing WAWS. You can download the latest version of the cmdlets source code from https://github.com/WindowsAzure/azure-sdk-tools. You can also install the Windows Azure PowerShell tools from Web Platform Installer (http://www.microsoft.com/web/downloads/platform.aspx), which is the recommended installation method.

In this section, you will learn to use PowerShell cmdlets for creating websites and pushing contents of the website from local Git repository to WAWS. Below is a step-by-step procedure for deploying websites using PowerShell Cmdlets.

Step 1: Setting up a local Git environment

From GitHub, download your favorite local Git client. In this exercise, I am using GitHub for Windows from http://windows.github.com. Connect the Git client to GitHub by specifying the user name and password.

Figure 3.58: Connect GitHub for Windows

From the GitHub repository page you created in Figure 3.39 earlier, click on "Clone in Desktop" button to clone your GitHub repository on your local machine.

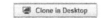

Figure 3.59: Clone in Desktop

Note that this clone is different to the one you created using Visual Studio for Git earlier in the chapter. I wanted to try this specifically to simulate multiple development and deployment environments from the same machine. At the end of this exercise, you will realize what I am trying to test here.

Step 2: Installing PowerShell cmdlets

Next, download and install Windows Azure PowerShell cmdlets using the

Windows Platform Installer

http://www.microsoft.com/web/downloads/platform.aspx

Figure 3.60: Install Windows Azure PowerShell

After installing the cmdlets, open PowerShell prompt and type the following to list all the cmdlets associated with the word website.

```
>help website
```

For interacting with the WAWS API, we need to download the Windows Azure publish settings file. You can either download it from the WAWS dashboard or using the cmdlet

```
>Get-AzurePublishSettingsFile
```

This will open a browser and download the publish settings file for your subscriptions. Save the file locally to a known location.

Note: The .publishsettings file is a highly sensitive file containing certificate thumbprints to access your subscriptions from anywhere. Please save the file in a secure environment.

To execute remaining cmdlets, we need import the publish settings file as an input to all the cmdlets you will run during the PowerShell session.

```
>Import-AzurePublishSettingsFile "Path to the
.publishsettings file"
```

This sets the session context and now you can run all the Windows Azure cmdlets. To list all the Windows Azure Web Sites in your subscription, call the cmdlet

```
>Get-AzureWebsite
```

Step 3: Creating a new website

Windows Azure cmdlets lets you create a new website and simultaneously initialize if with a Git or GitHub repository. Open GitShell.exe and navigate to the local Git repository you created in the previous step. Now, create a new website called "storagesearchps" and initialize it with the –GitHub option as shown below.

```
>New-AzureWebsite   -Name   storagesearchps   -
Location "West US" -GitHub
```

This command will create a new website in the West US region and initialize it with the GitHub repository from the local directory. You can verify the deployment in the deployments section of the website portal as shown in Figure 3.61, and also test the website by navigating to its home page.

Figure 3.61: Web site deployment status

Step 4: Pushing changes to WAWS

Now, if you have followed the earlier exercise "Continuous Deployment with GitHub", you must have realized that there are two website Git environments on the local machine– one from the GitHub exercise and another from the current PowerShell exercise pointing to the same GitHub repository. So, if you change the source code, and commit the changes from one of these local environments, do you think both the website deployments will be triggered in WAWS? Let's verify.

1) Open the storagesearch project in Visual Studio and make a simple change to the Default.aspx as shown in Figure 3.62

```
<hgroup class="title">
    <h1><%: Title %>.</h1>
        <h2>Windows Azure Web Sites Book Rocks!!!</h2>
</hgroup>
<p>
```

Figure 3.62: Simple Code Change

Also comment the Response.Redirect function call from Default.aspx.cs. Please make sure you are working on the same project that was used in the GitHub and PowerShell exercises.

2) Committing the source code

From Visual Studio, commit the source code to your local Git.

Figure 3.63: Commit Source Code

Next, synchronize the source code with GitHub by clicking the Sync button in Visual Studio.

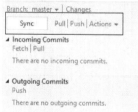

Figure 3.64: Synchronize with GitHub

These changes are synchronized to the GitHub repository which is linked to two different websites – One from the GitHub exercise and another from the PowerShell exercise from the previous sections of this chapter. Because of this double linking, GitHub will fire events/hooks to both the websites, and each of these websites will run a Git pull on the repository. The result is that the same code will be auto-deployed to two different websites. This feature is extremely useful in geo-distributing your application across multiple

Windows Azure data centers. One website can be served from Western United States, whereas the second one can be served from Northern Europe or Asia depending on the website's user base. Figure 3.65 and 3.66 illustrate the status of auto-deployments in two different websites triggered by the same GitHub repository.

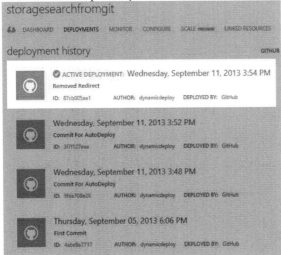

Figure 3.65: Auto Deployment on website 1

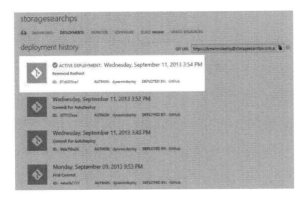

Figure 3.66: Auto-deployment on website 2

In both the figures, note that the check-in comments are shown to match the Git commits. You can create a naming convention for the commit comments that will help you visually identify the purpose of each deployment.

Summary

Continuous Deployment reduces your time-to-market for every release drastically, but to configure it, you need to do some upfront work. In real world, you can implement automated tests that will run after every check-in and automatically create a quality gate for the deployment. Team culture is an important aspect in building an efficient continuous deployment system. In this chapter, you learned to configure continuous deployment with Visual Studio Online, GitHub, Dropbox, FTP, and PowerShell. I chose these five because of their unique setup requirements. There are more source control systems that WAWS supports, but the overall configuration process is similar to the ones covered in this chapter. Based on my experience, the most popular ones are VSOnline and GitHub. In the next chapter, you will learn the operational capabilities of WAWS.

Bibliography

Microsoft Corporation. (2012). *Windows Azure Web Site Documentation.*
Retrieved from Windows Azure :
http://www.windowsazure.com/en-us/documentation/services/web-sites/?fb=en-us

Chapter 4
OPERATIONS

"Programming is only the tip of an iceberg in building products", a point my professor always stressed on. Maintenance of software is an expensive task with support and operations staff constantly servicing customer requests. A successful software product needs an end-to-end strategy from its inception to sustainability. In today's world, cloud platforms are designed to relieve you of some of the mundane operations tasks like patching, scaling, and re-deploying applications. The cloud operating system provides the fabric required for today's computing tasks. Therefore, the cloud platforms strive to reduce your operating costs by offering built-in management infrastructure and tools. In WAWS, the operating system is completely abstracted from the developer. As a developer, you can develop, test, and deploy your product in production in WAWS without worrying about maintenance of the underlying operating system.

In this chapter, you will learn the skills required to efficiently operate your WAWS on your own. The Windows Azure portal provides you with monitoring, configuration management, scaling, and linking capabilities that you can leverage for complete management of your website. Some of these features are also available via the service management API. Operations is the next logical topic to learn after learning continuous deployment in the previous chapter. The objective of this chapter is to educate you on the tasks required for deploying websites in production and operating them in WAWS.

What is Operations?

In the cloud era, operations is concerned with the sustainability of your service in providing expected results to the website users. The expected results are usually derived from an agreement a customer signs during the subscription process. This type of agreement is also called a Service Level Agreement (SLA). The SLA of a service clearly defines the constraints and limitations of the service that every customer must understand. For example, if Windows Azure SQL Database offers 99.9% availability SLA, then it should adhere to this agreement. But, you shouldn't be surprised if it does not meet a 99.99% availability SLA.

WAWS has a well-defined SLA you can download from this link http://www.microsoft.com/en-us/download/details.aspx?id=39303

Note from the SLA, that Microsoft offers 99.9% availability SLA on WAWS and offers a 10% credit if it goes below 99.9%, and a 25% credit if the availability drops below 99%. In order to meet these SLAs, the WAWS infrastructure must be designed to exceed its SLA. Microsoft also provides you with additional features like auto-scaling for adding redundancy to your websites to exceed the SLA offered by WAWS. But, the redundancy comes at a price and is not offered for free.

This chapter covers features offered by the Windows Azure portal for managing websites. In a multi-tiered large-scale applications, you need specialized operations management software like System Center Operations Manager that will provide you with capabilities in monitoring all the tiers of your application from one central console.

The Hosting Plans

In order to effectively operate your website, you need to first understand the features and capabilities of WAWS. Microsoft offers three hosting plans and the features as well as pricing differs across them. Table 4.1 lists the capabilities offered by each plan.

Table 4.1: WAWS Hosting Plans Comparison

	Free	Shared	Standard
Price[4]	Free	33% discount in Preview $0.013/hour (~$10/month)	At GA: $0.10/hour per CPU Small: 1 CPU Medium: 2 CPUs Large: 4 CPUs
Number of	Up to 10 per Region (60)	Up to 100	Up to 500

---

[4] WAWS Pricing Site: http://www.windowsazure.com/en-us/pricing/details/web-sites/

sites			
Maximum scale	1 instance	6 instances	10 instances
Scale-out	Not supported	Scale-out up to 6 instances	Scale-out up to 10 instances
Scale-up	Not supported	Not supported	Small, Medium, and Large instance types
Auto-scale	Not supported	Not supported	Supported
Storage	1GB (shared by all sites)	1GB (shared by all sites)	10GB (shared by all sites)
Storage transactions	1 hour/day 2.5 minutes for every 5 minutes enforcement period. Shared by all sites in a region	4 hours / day. 2.5 minutes for every 5 minutes enforcement period per site	Full resources on box
SQL database	1 GB for all sites in a region. Enforced once an hour	512MB per site. Enforced once an hour	Full resources on box
MySQL (via ClearDB)	Standard SQL Database	Standard SQL Database	Standard SQL Database
Database Storage	Includes one 20MB database	Includes one 20MB database. Can purchase additional in Windows Azure Store.	Includes one 20MB database. Can purchase additional in Windows Azure Store.
Data Transfer	Ingress - Unlimited Egress - 165MB/day (5GB/month)	Ingress – Unlimited Egress – Windows Azure bandwidth rates (above 5GB/month)	Ingress – Unlimited Egress – Windows Azure bandwidth rates (above 5GB/month)
Custom domains	Not Available	CNAME and A-Record	CNAME and A-Record

SSL	Not Available	Available	Available
SLA[5]	Not Available	Not Available in Preview	99.9% Monthly
Support	None	None in Preview	Available

For latest information on WAWS pricing, please visit the following link.
https://www.windowsazure.com/en-us/pricing/details/web-sites/

Scaling

Cloud thrives on scaling. On-demand scale-out and scale-up features optimizes scaling operations and costs associated with it. WAWS support both scale-up and scale-out features. At the time of writing, scale-up features were available only in the Standard plan, whereas, the scale-out features were available in Shared and Standard plans. The Free plan did not support scaling. In this section you will learn to scale-up and scale-out your website on WAWS.

Scale-Out versus Scale-Up

Before deciding on whether to scale-out or scale-up a website, you need to understand the differences between the two.

Scaling Out in WAWS

Scaling-out means increasing the request processing capabilities of your application by adding identical redundant infrastructure to run your application. Typically, a load-balancer distributes the incoming requests on these multiple redundant instances of your application. The processing power of each infrastructure unit is kept the same. Care must be taken to scale-out all the infrastructure components accordingly to avoid bottlenecks in your architecture. For example, if your application uses a database, then when you scale-out your application, you need to make sure that your database is capable of processing the surge in requests. Figures 4.1 and 4.2 illustrate the scale-out concept with block diagrams.

---

[5] http://www.microsoft.com/en-us/download/details.aspx?id=39303

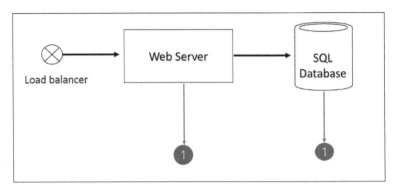

Figure 4.1: Single Instance Deployment

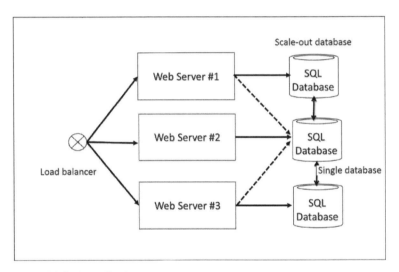

Figure 4.2: Scale-out Deployment

The deployment in Figure 4.1 includes one website and one SQL database, similar to the WordPress blog we deployed in Chapter 2. If the website becomes popular and you start getting requests that exceed the capacity of a single instance, in WAWS, you have the option to scale-out by adding not only multiple instances of the identical web servers but also multiple instances of the database.

Note: The biggest roadblock I have observed in scaling-out websites in real-world is the ability of the website to handle distributed sessions. Most of the developers still develop websites with in-memory sessions, which does not scale in the scale-out model. In-Memory Session objects are bound to each machine instance and are available only on that instance. My recommendation is to use distributed sessions either using Azure SQL database or Windows Azure Caching.

Scaling Up in WAWS

Scaling up is the process of increasing the HTTP (or any) request processing ability of your application by adding more power to the same unit of deployment. Scale-up does not add redundancy, but instead, improves the capacity of the existing infrastructure. This may include increasing the CPU, memory, and disk capacity of the server, or even adding a high-capacity load balancer to your network. In Figure 4.3, a small virtual machine instance is upgraded to a large machine instance to increase the HTTP request processing ability of your application.

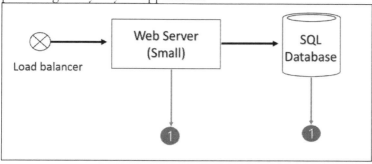

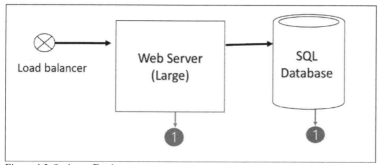

Figure 4.3: Scale-up Deployment

Although commonly practiced, I usually recommend against scaling up your infrastructure unless you have ruled-out scaling-out with proper architecture validation. The reason is that scaling-up does not provide you with automatic redundancy like scaling-out does. Therefore, the availability of you website would always be at risk in a scale-up model because the instance itself becomes a single point of failure in the architecture. But, in scenarios where your website requires large amount of memory for caching and processing power for running intense algorithm, you will need to scale-up your infrastructure. A single instance in WAWS (Shared and Standard plans) provides availability of 99.9%, but if you want to exceed that availability percentage, then you can scale-out your website for additional redundancy and fault tolerance.

Scaling Your Web Site in WAWS

To scale your website, open the Windows Azure portal and navigate to your website's landing page. The portal menu will show a Scale menu option as shown in Figure 4.4.

Figure 4.4: Scale Menu

Click on the Scale menu to open the scaling page. If the website is running in Free mode, change it to Shared mode because scaling is not supported in Free mode. After you change to the Shared mode, you can increase your website instances manually to scale it out.

Figure 4.5. Scale-out Shared Web Site

The Shared plan supports manual scaling from the portal. For auto-scaling, the website must be running in a Standard mode. After you change the website's mode to Standard, the auto-scale configurations are displayed on the page as shown in Figure 4.6.

Figure 4.6: Auto-scale configuration

Observe that the standard mode supports auto-scale based on instance size (scale-up), schedule, and CPU.

Following are some of the scaling patterns you can setup by navigating to the Scale page.

Scale-Up

You have the ability to scale-up (or scale-down) your website's instance size from Small (1 core, 1.75 GB Memory) to Medium (2 cores, 3.5GB Memory), or Large (4 cores 7GB Memory).

Scale-Out

Listed below are some of the scale-out patterns you can use for your website:

1) **CPU-Only Metric Scaling Pattern**

Requirement: Scale-out my website to 3 instances when the CPU threshold crosses 80%, and scale-down my website to 1 instance when the CPU threshold goes below that. Figure 4.7 illustrates the configuration for this scaling pattern on the portal page.

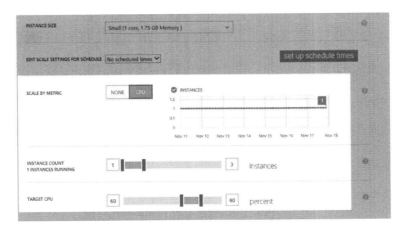

Figure 4.7: Scale by CPU metric only

In CPU-only metric pattern, you configure scaling based on CPU usage of the virtual machine instance on which the website is running on.

> Note: WAWS monitoring system checks the CPU of your website once every five minutes and based on the configuration you have set, adds instances as needed at that point in time. In the above configuration, WAWS will add 2 more instances if the CPU usage is more than 80%. If CPU usage is low, WAWS will remove any excess instances once every two hours. To optimize on scale-out patterns, you need to understand the load patterns of your website.

2) Schedule-based Scaling

Requirement: For my website:
i. Run 3 instances during week days
ii. Run 1 instance during week nights, but increase it to 2 if CPU threshold crosses 80%
iii. Run 1 instance during weekends

To configure schedule-based scaling, you need to first setup schedule times by clicking on the "set up schedule times button" on the Scale page. In the "Set up Schedule Times" window, specify your settings for week days, week nights, weekends, and time zone.

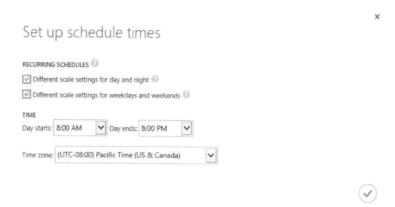

Figure 4.8: Set up Schedule Times

Figure 4.9, 4.10, and 4.11 illustrate the week day, week nights, and weekend configuration (a) on the portal respectively.

Figure 4.9: Weekday Scale Schedule

In Figure 4.9, note that the CPU metric is turned off, which means that irrespective of the CPU usage, WAWS will run at least 3 instances of the website during week days.

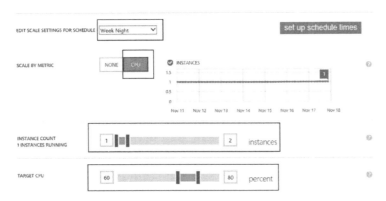

Figure 4.10: Week night schedule

In Figure 4.10, note that in the week nights, we are also enabling the CPU metric as an added constraint before deciding to scale-out.

Figure 4.11: Weekend schedule

In Figure 4.11, note that the CPU metric is turned off, and we are instructing WAWS to run only one instance of the website during weekends.

Note: Running Quick Tests

I recommend the following tools to quickly load test the websites and generate scale as needed.

Web Capacity Analysis Tool (WCAT):
http://www.iis.net/downloads/community/2007/
05/wcat-63-(x64)

Load Impact: http://www.loadimpact.com

Pingdom: http://tools.pingdom.com

Web Page Test: http://www.webpagetest.org/

Neustar:
http://www.neustar.biz/enterprise/resources/we
b-performance/free-website-performance-test

WAWS makes scaling a simple operational task by providing you with an intuitive graphical user interface on the portal. Although today's sophisticated virtualized on-premises platforms can offer similar capabilities, the upfront investment required for building such infrastructure is prohibitively expensive for developers. WAWS lowers barriers to entry in scaling your website. This capability allows any small development team to compete with larger players without investing heavily in infrastructure.

Monitoring

You can monitor your websites from the WAWS Monitor page. A Microsoft partner named New Relic also offers Windows Azure specific monitoring capabilities. In this section, you will learn how to monitor your websites using the portal as well as New Relic's Application Performance Management for WAWS.

Performance Monitoring using the portal

On the Monitor page of your website, there are certain default metrics listed on the page as shown in Figure 4.12.

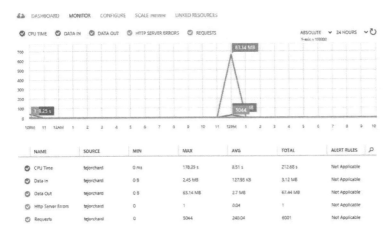

Figure 4.12:Monitor page metrics

There are some additional metrics available that you can add by clicking on the "Add Metrics" button from the bottom menu.

From "Select Metrics to Monitor" screen, you can select or remove the metrics that are available for monitoring.

CHOOSE METRICS

Select Metrics to Monitor

NAME	UNIT
☑ CPU Time	Milliseconds
☑ Data In	Bytes
☑ Data Out	Bytes
☑ Http 401 errors	Count
☑ Http 403 errors	Count
☑ Http 404 errors	Count
☑ Http 406 errors	Count
☑ Http Client Errors	Count
☑ Http Redirects	Count
☑ Http Server Errors	Count
☑ Http Successes	Count
☑ Requests	Count

Figure 4.13: Metrics available to monitor

Table 4.2 lists the metrics you can add for monitoring your website from the portal.

Table 4.2: Web Site Metrics

Metric	Description
CPUTime	The website's CPU usage
Data In	Data received by the website from clients
Data Out	Data sent by the website to the clients
Requests	The total number of requests handled by the website
HTTP Server Errors	Number of HTTP internal server errors
HTTP Successes	Number of HTTP success messages sent
HTTP Redirects	Number of HTTP redirect messages sent
HTTP Client Errors	Number of HTTP client error messages

HTTP 401 errors	Number of HTTP 401 Unauthorized messages
HTTP 403 errors	Number of HTTP 403 Forbidden messages
HTTP 404 errors	Number of HTTP 404 Not Found messages
HTTP 406 errors	Number of HTTP 406 Not Acceptable messages.

In Standard mode, you can configure rules for receiving alerts by monitoring web endpoints. But, before setting up alerts, you must configure web endpoint monitoring in Windows Azure portal.

Web Endpoint Monitoring

In Standard mode only, WAWS lets you monitor up to 2 endpoints from up to 3 geographic locations. WAWS then tests response time and uptime of web URLs you have configured for each website. Each geographic location will run the test every five minutes. Uptime is monitored using HTTP response codes, and response time is measured in milliseconds. WAWS considers a site not functioning if the response time is greater than 30 seconds or the HTTP response code received is greater than 400.

To configure endpoint monitoring for your website:

1) Set your website to run in Standard mode from the Scale section of the website in Windows Azure portal
2) Navigate to the Configure section of the website
3) Go to the Monitoring section to enter your endpoint settings
4) Enter a name for the endpoint
5) Enter the URL for the service that you want to monitor. For example, http://www.dynamicdeploy.com
6) Select one or more geographic locations from the list. If you have a global user base, then configure one endpoint in each continent.
7) Repeat the previous steps for creating a second endpoint.
8) Click Save.
9) Once saved, the data will be available on the Dashboard and Monitor tabs

Figure 4.14: Web Endpoint Monitoring

In Figure 14, I have configured two endpoints from 3 different test locations. If your entire user base is in one continent, then you can choose two geographic locations from the same continent. There are 8 geographical locations (corresponding to Windows Azure datacenters) to choose from:

1) Chicago, Illinois (US)
2) San Antonio, Texas (US)
3) San Jose, California (US)
4) Ashburn, Virginia (US)
5) Dublin, Ireland
6) Amsterdam, Netherlands
7) Hong Kong
8) Singapore

As an optional step, you can setup alerts after configuring web endpoints.

Receiving Alerts

You can configure alerts based on the endpoint monitoring you configured. When the value of a configured metric crosses the threshold assigned to an alert rule, the rule becomes active and registers an alert. Optionally, on configured alerts, you can setup email notifications for administrators. When the rule becomes active, a notification email is sent.

To create a new alert,

1) Navigate to the Windows Azure Management Portal.
2) In the navigation pane, click Management Services.
3) On the Management Services page, click Alerts, and then click Add Rule button at the bottom. The Create Alert Rule wizard appears.
4) In the Define Alert section, provide the information, and then go to the next page.

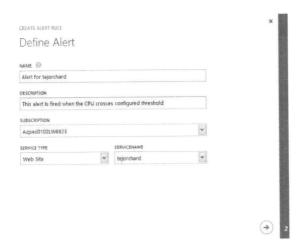

Figure 4.15: Configure Alert

5) On the Define a condition for notifications page, select the metric, condition, threshold value, email action, and enable the rule.

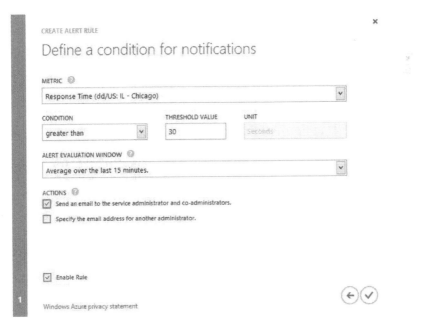

Figure 4.16: Define alert condition

6) Click the check icon to complete the configuration. The alert will then appear in the alerts list as shown in Figure 4.17.

Figure 4.17: Alert list

After the alert is set up, the administrators will receive an email notification when the alert is fired.

Monitoring Resource Usage

Each Windows Azure subscription supports running up to 100 websites per region in Shared website mode. Each website shares pool of resources with other websites in the same geo-region configured to run in Shared mode. Usage quotas of each website are listed under its Dashboard management page. Figure 4.18 illustrates the usage overview of a Shared website.

Figure 4.18: Shared website usage overview

In Standard mode, a website is allocated dedicated resources on the virtual machine it is running on. The maximum number of Standard mode websites you can run per region is 500. Figure 4.19 illustrates the usage overview of a Standard website.

Figure 4.19: Standard website usage overview

When a subscription's usage quotas are exceeded, Windows Azure stops all the shared websites running in that subscription for that quota interval. The websites are restarted in the next quota interval.

Performance Monitoring using New Relic

In this section you will learn to monitor your website using New Relic's performance monitoring service. New Relic provides deep insight into your application's performance and reliability. New Relic Standard is free to Windows Azure users. Listed below is a step by step procedure for enabling New Relic's performance monitoring for your website.

Step 1: Installing New Relic through the Windows Azure Store

1) Login to the Windows Azure Management Portal.
2) In the lower pane of the management portal, click New.
3) Click Store.
4) In the Choose an Add-on dialog, select New Relic and click Next.

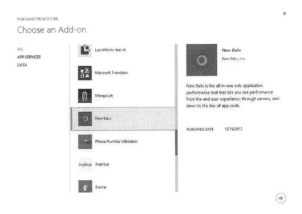

Figure 4.20: New Relic Add-on

5) In the Personalize Add-on dialog, select the New Relic plan that you want

Tejaswi Redkar

Figure 4.21: Personalize New Relic

6) Enter a name for the New Relic service.
7) Select the region to deploy the service to; for example, West US.
8) Click Next.
9) In the Review Purchase dialog, review the plan, pricing, and legal terms. If you agree to the terms, click Purchase.

Figure 4.22: Review New Relic Purchase

10) After you click Purchase, a New Relic account will be created for you and it will be listed in the add-ons list.

Figure 4.23: New Relic in the add-ons list

11) Click on the Connection Info button at the bottom to retrieve your New relic license key.
12) Note down the license key because you will need it when you install the New Relic nuget package.

Step 2: Installing New Relic Nuget package

The New Relic Web Sites Agent is available as a NuGet package, and can be added to your Web Site using either Visual Studio or WebMatrix.

Installing Visual Studio Nuget Package

Listed below is a step by step procedure for enabling New Relic monitoring in a Visual Studio website.

1) Open your Windows Azure Web Site in Visual Studio
2) Open the Package Manager console by selecting Tools > Library Package Manager > Package Manager Console
3) Set your project to be the Default Project at the top of the Package Manager Console window.

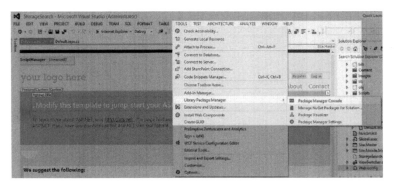

Figure 4.24: Package Manager Console

4) On the Package Manager command prompt, run the following command to install the package:

```
Install-Package NewRelic.Azure.WebSites
```

5) In the license key prompt, enter the New Relic license key you noted from the Windows Azure Store in earlier step.

Figure 4.25: License Key Prompt

The package installation creates a new folder named newrelic in the solution.

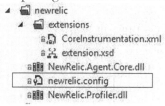

Figure 4.26: NewRelic folder

Installing WebMatrix Nuget Package

Listed below is a step by step procedure for enabling New Relic monitoring in a WebMatrix website.

1) Open your Web Site in WebMatrix by clicking on the WebMatrix button from the website's dashboard
2) On the Home tab of the ribbon, select NuGet.
3) In the NuGet Gallery, set the source to nuget.org and then search for newrelic.azure.websites.

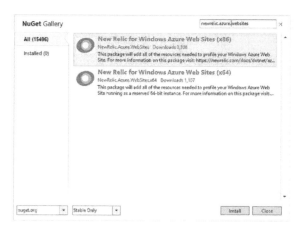

Figure 4.27: New Relic for Windows Azure Web Sites

4) Select the New Relic for Windows Azure Web Sites entry, and then

click Install.

5) The package installation will create a folder named newrelic in the solution, as shown in Figure 4.28.

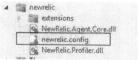

Figure 4.28: NewRelic Folder in WebMatrix

6) Expand this folder and open the newrelic.config file. In this file, replace the value REPLACE_WITH_LICENSE_KEY with the New Relic license key you noted from the Windows Azure Store in earlier step.

Step 3: Configuring and Publishing the Web Site.

1) For the New Relic package to start sending monitoring information to the New Relic service, you need to manually add some configuration in App Settings of your website's configuration from Windows Azure portal.

2) Sign in to the Windows Azure management portal and navigate to your Web Site's "Configure" section.

3) In the Developer Analytics section, select either Add-on or Custom. You can configure New Relic with any one of the option.

4) The Custom option requires you to manually specify New Relic's license key, whereas, the Add-on option allows you to select your existing New Relic licenses. Figure 4.29 illustrates the user interface for both the options.

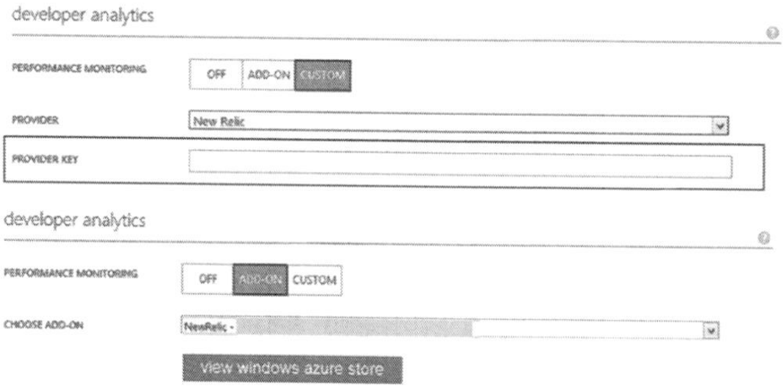

developer analytics

PERFORMANCE MONITORING	OFF	ADD-ON	CUSTOM
PROVIDER	New Relic
PROVIDER KEY	

developer analytics

| PERFORMANCE MONITORING | OFF | ADD-ON | CUSTOM |
| CHOOSE ADD-ON | NewRelic - |

view windows azure store

Figure 4.29: Developer Analytics Options for New Relic

5) After selecting one of the options in Developer Analytics, click Save. While saving, the values listed in Table 4.3 are automatically

added to the App Settings of your website.

Table 4.3: New Relic Configuration Settings

Key	Value
COR_ENABLE_PROFILING	1
COR_PROFILER	{71DA0A04-7777-4EC6-9643-7D28B46A8A41}
COR_PROFILER_PATH	C:\Home\site\wwwroot\newrelic\NewRelic.Profiler.dll
NEWRELIC_HOME	C:\Home\site\wwwroot\newrelic

Step 4: Monitoring your website's performance in New Relic

To monitor your web application from the New Relic dashboard:
1) Navigate to the Add-Ons section in the Windows Azure portal
2) Click on the New Relic add-on to navigate to the add-on's dashboard page
3) Click the Manage button to go to the New Relic's application page.
4) From the New Relic's menu bar, select Applications > (application's name). Figure 4.30 and 4.31 illustrate the App Server and Browser requests monitoring dashboards.

Figure 4.30: App Server Dashboard for the website

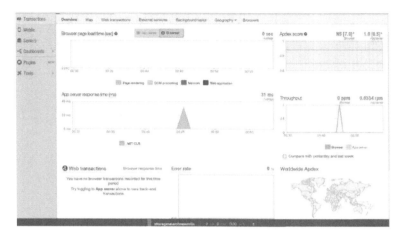

Figure 4.31: Browser Dashboard for the website

Note: For more information on New Relic's user interface, please visit the following website.

https://docs.newrelic.com/docs/site/the-new-relic-ui

Top 10 Performance Gain Recommendations

In this section I will list the most popular generic tips for building high-performance websites. The recommendations are browser-centric and applies to any websites whether it is running on WAWS or not.

Tip 1: Understand the problem with Load/Stress Test

Don't follow any performance recommendations blindly. First try to understand if the performance of a website can be improved, and at what cost. I recommend running quick online tests with http://www.webpagetest.org (or similar tools) to get a performance map of your website. The test results will show you the response times and if there is any quick room for improvement. These tests will provide you with details on how a browser views your website. I have found these recommendations invaluable in optimizing website's performance.

For example, after running as a quick test using webpagetest.org on

http://www.dynamicdeploy.com , I was able to pinpoint which static objects were
not being cached. In IIS, you can enable caching of static content by adding
the following XML fragment in your web.config.

```xml
<?xml version="1.0" encoding="UTF-8"?>
<configuration>
  <system.webServer>
    <staticContent>
      <clientCache
cacheControlMode="UseMaxAge"
cacheControlMaxAge="20.00:00:00" />
    </staticContent>
  </system.webServer>
</configuration>
```
Listing 4.1: Enable client-side caching in IIS

The above fragment caches the static content in the browser for 20 days.
Figures 4.32 and 4.33 depict the before and after results of enabling static
caching on the website.

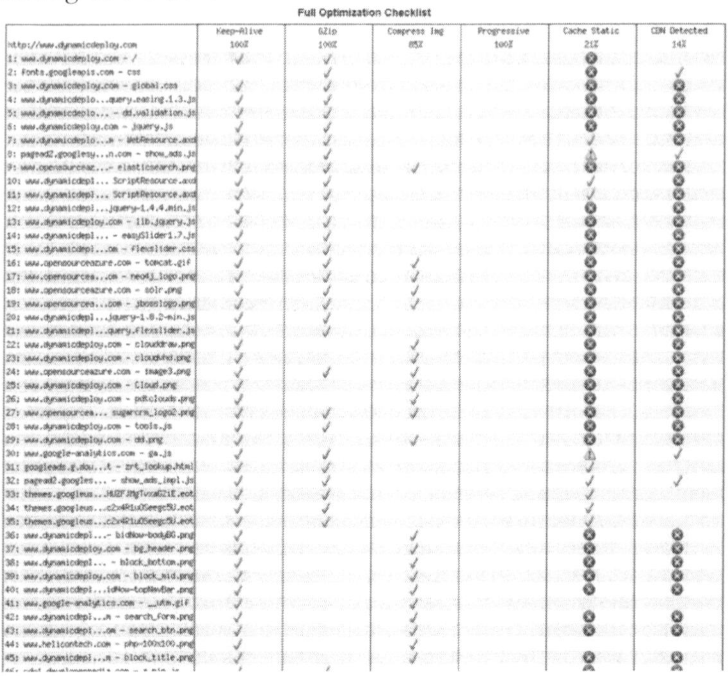

Figure 4.32: Before Enabling Static Cache

http://dynamicdeploytest.cloudapp.net/	Keep-Alive 100%	GZip 100%	Compress Img 84%	Progressive 95%	Cache Static 78%	CDN Detected 14%
1: dynamicdeploytest.cloudapp.net – /	✓	✓				
2: fonts.googleapis.com – css		✓			✗	
3: dynamicdeploytes...pp.net – global.css	✓	✓			✓	✗
4: dynamicdeploytes...query.easing.1.3.js	✓	✓			✓	✗
5: dynamicdeploytes... – dd.validation.js	✓	✓			✓	✗
6: dynamicdeploytes...app.net – jQuery.js	✓	✓			✓	✗
7: dynamicdeploytes...jquery-1.4.4.min.js	✓	✓			✓	✗
8: pagead2.googlesy...n.com – show_ads.js	✓	✓				✓
9: www.opensourcear...– elasticsearch.png	✓	✓			✗	✗
10: www.opensourceazure.com – tomcat.gif	✓	✓	✓		✗	✗
11: www.opensourcea...om – neo4j_logo.png	✓	✓	✓		✗	✗
12: www.opensourceazure.com – solr.png	✓	✓	✓		✗	✗
13: www.opensourceazure.com – image3.png	✓	✓	✓		✗	✗
14: dynamicdeployte...dapp.net – tools.js	✓	✓			✓	✗
15: dynamicdeployte... sugarorm_logo2.png	✓	✓	✓		✗	✗
16: dynamicdeployte...net – lib.jquery.js	✓	✓			✓	✗
17: dynamicdeployte... – easyGlider1.7.js	✓	✓			✓	✗
18: dynamicdeployte...t – WebResource.axd	✓	✓			✓	✗
19: dynamicdeployte... ScriptResource.axd	✓	✓			✓	✗
20: dynamicdeployte... ScriptResource.axd	✓	✓			✓	✗
21: dynamicdeployte...et – Flexslider.css	✓	✓			✓	✗
22: dynamicdeployte...jquery-1.8.2-min.js	✓	✓			✓	✗
23: dynamicdeployte...query.flexslider.js	✓	✓			✓	✗
24: dynamicdeployte...net – clouddraw.png	✓	✓	✓		✓	✗
25: dynamicdeployte...net – cloudwhd.png	✓	✓	✓		✓	✗
26: dynamicdeployte...app.net – Cloud.png	✓	✓	✓		✓	✗
27: www.google-analytics.com – ga.js	✓	✓	✓			✓
28: dynamicdeployte...net – pdhclouds.png	✓	✓	✓		✓	✗
29: dynamicdeployte...sxdapp.net – dd.png	✓	✓	✓		✓	✗
30: googleads.g.dou...t – zrt_lookup.html	✓	✓	✓		✓	
31: pagead2.googlet... – show_ads_impl.js	✓	✓			✓	✓
32: themes.googleus...HUZFJMgTwxaG21E.eot	✓	✓			✓	
33: themes.googleus...c2x4R1sOSeegc5U.eot	✓	✓			✓	
34: themes.googleus...c2x4R1sOSeegc5U.eot	✓	✓			✓	
35: dynamicdeployte...– bidNow-bodyBG.png	✓		✓		✓	✗
36: dynamicdeployte...net – bg_header.png	✓		✓		✓	✗
37: dynamicdeployte... – block_bottom.png	✓		✓		✓	✗

Figure 4.33: After Enabling Static Cache

As seen in Figures 4.32 and 4.33, I was able to improve the caching of static objects from 21% to 78% by just enabling it in IIS. It did not require any change to my website source code. As a website developer, you must take these recommendations seriously because they will improve the performance of your website drastically.

Tip 2: Enable Content Delivery Network (CDN)

Note in Figure 4.33, the test also recommended enabling CDN because only 14% of the static objects are in the CDN, and most of them are Google Analytics objects. None of the objects from dynamicdeploy.com are cached in the CDN. CDN is a network of storage servers distributed across the globe to cache the website content closer to your users. At the time of writing, Windows Azure CDN was not available to new users because the Windows Azure team is redesigning their CDN network. For more information on the previous CDN's functionality, please refer to the following URL

http://www.windowsazure.com/en-us/develop/net/common-tasks/cdn/ .

CDN has usually data-transfer and storage costs associated with it and is based on the total storage you are using across the entire CDN network. That means if you have 1 GB or images cached in 20 CDN locations, you will be paying for 20GB of storage. You will also be charged for the data transfer cost associated with copying the images from their source datacenter to the CDN nodes. In a scenario where a couple of your traveling users access the website from 20 different CDN locations in the world, you will still be charged for the storage and data transfer. Therefore, I recommend including

CDN in calculating your storage costs before deciding whether to use it or not. For a worldwide high-volume website, CDN improves performance several times because the static content is loaded from the server closest to the user.

Tip 3: Use the right image format

Nowadays websites are studded with images and other media formats. Images increase the download size of web pages thus reducing the response time. It is essential to understand the optimal format and use for each image. The three common web image formats are: JPEG, GIF, and PNG. I recommend using JPEG format for photographs, and PNG (or GIF) formats for images with text and solid colors such as background, reports, etc.. GIF file size is usually larger than PNG, therefore weigh them carefully in terms of download time versus quality.

Tip 4: Optimize JavaScript and CSS

Remove unneeded characters (such as tabs, spaces, comments) from JavaScript and CSS files to reduce its file size. All the text you have included in JavaScript and CSS is downloaded because the code is run in the browser instead of the server.

For example,
This CSS:

```
.dynamicdeploy-head {
  color: #bbffff;
  font-size: 12px;
  font-weight:bold
}
```

can be re-written as:

```
.dynamicdeploy-head{color:#bbffff;font-size:12px;font-weight:bold}
```

You can find the list of tools for optimizing CSS at this link:
http://sixrevisions.com/css/css_code_optimization_formatting_validation

Listed below are some of the popular tools for minifying JavaScript:

1) JavaScript Code Improver
   (http://jcay.com/id-190119110113039.html)
2) JSMIN (http://www.crockford.com/javascript/jsmin.html)
3) YUI Compressor (http://developer.yahoo.com/yui/compressor/)
4) Firebug (http://getfirebug.com/)

Each file required for loading a web page is downloaded individually using a separate HTTP connection from browser to the file. Therefore, if you combine the CSS and/or JavaScript files into a smaller number of files, the number of downloads will be reduced thus reducing the HTTP connection overhead.

Tip 5: Use CSS sprites

To reduce the number of HTTP requests, CSS Sprites combine multiple background images into a single image and use the CSS background-image and background-position properties to display the appropriate image segment. Web-based CSS Sprite Generators (e.g. http://spritegen.website-performance.org/ and http://csssprites.com/) let you upload images to be combined into one CSS sprite, and then outputs the CSS code for rendering the images.

Tip 6: Use Web Server Compression

Web server compression is one of the key methods for reducing response times. Although it can be an effective technique in most of the scenarios, it can also adversely affect the performance when not used properly. If the object being compressed are already in compressed format, then using compression may adversely affect the performance. Compression reduces the response time of an HTTP request by compressing the size of the HTTP response. The most popular compression format for HTTP responses is GZip developed by the GNU project and standardized by RFC 1952. Most of the times, GZip can reduce the response size by about 70%.

You can find more details on enabling IIS compression here
http://technet.microsoft.com/en-us/library/cc771003(v=ws.10).aspx

Tip 7: Reduce DNS Lookups

When you type www.dynamicdeploy.com into your browser, the browser contacts a DNS resolver to return the web server's IP address. This orchestration typically takes 20-120 milliseconds. The browser needs the IP address before downloading anything from the web server. DNS lookups are usually cached for improving the lookup performance.

When the browser does not detect a DNS lookup in its cache, it tries to contact the DNS resolver for every unique hostname embedded in the web page. On the other hand, multiple unique hostnames enable parallel downloads that takes place in a page. For example, your images may be residing on a mysupercdn.com server whereas your web pages may be served by the host dynamicdeploy.com. In this case, the browser can download the page and images in parallel and the load is distributed between the mysupercdn.com and dynamicdeploy.com. As a rule-of-thumb, I recommend between two and four unique hostnames for an image and media driven websites for optimizing DNS lookups. With this configuration, you can safely distribute your static content from the CDNs and let the web server deliver dynamic content, thus optimizing the degree of parallelism.

Tip 8: Remove all 404s

For large websites, it is common to keep residual links even after the content it points to has been removed. Sometimes, the URL links are entered incorrectly and the errors are not visible visually on a web page. Most of the times, these broken links are forgotten after a new feature is released or an old one is disabled. The web server responds to the absence of content with HTTP 404 status code to the browser. HTTP requests are expensive so a 404 code will unnecessarily slow down the response time of your web page. Most of the online web page tests (like http://www.webpagetest.org) provide you with warnings related to missing content. Figure 4.34 shows a red alert on an image URL that was not loading correctly in my website because the URL was entered incorrectly in the CSS file.

Figure 4.34: 404 Alert in webpagetest.org

Tip 9: Follow the Web Development Checklist

While developing my own website, I was searching online for a checklist that would help me validate a website against most commonly required validation tasks such as search engine optimization (SEO), mobile device testing tools, security tools, usability, monitoring, etc. These tasks are common across most of the public facing websites, but are difficult to keep a track of. Finally, I found "Web Dev Checklist" (http://webdevchecklist.com/) by browsing through several pages of search results. Web Dev Checklist provides you with a simple checklist to follow before you release your website into production environment. I recommend following this checklist diligently before every release of your website.

Tip 10: Practice Continuous Performance Monitoring

Continuous performance monitoring is the process of continuously monitoring the key performance metrics of your website even after it goes live. At a regular interval (preferably several times during the day), run automated performance tools that will warn you on any degradation in user experience. Establish a benchmark each day and strive towards improving it during every release.

Constantly monitor the web server's performance metrics (request queue, CPU usage, Memory, Requests/sec, etc.) and error logs in an attempt to pinpoint any bottlenecks. These results will help you decide whether to scale-out, scale-up, or scale-down the web server infrastructure. In WAWS, you can automate the performance monitoring followed by a scaling action either by using the Windows Azure PowerShell cmdlets or building your own tools that call Windows Azure Service Management API.

Tip 11 (Bonus): Run Windows Azure Web Sites in .NET 4.5 and on a 64bit platform
In the general section of your website's Configure tab, you have the option of running the website in .NET 4.5 Framework and 64bit platform. I am including this as a bonus tip because the platform option is available only in Standard mode. Based on my testing and analysis of large-scale websites, most of them run at least 20-30% faster on 64bit platform.

Configuring Diagnostics

Diagnostics is the runtime information to determine the overall health of your website. In WAWS, you can enable diagnostics in your website and then retrieve the logs for debugging your website. In this section you will learn how to enable and acquire diagnostic logging for your website running in WAWS.

Enabling Logging

To enable logging for your website, login to the Windows Azure portal and navigate to the Configure page of the website. On the Configure page, use the application diagnostics and site diagnostics sections to enable logging. You can also select the logging level and the logs storage destination to either file system or Windows Azure storage.

> **Note: If you choose Windows Azure storage, then make sure you select a storage account within the same region as the website to avoid any data-transfer costs.**

Figure 4.35: Diagnostics Logging Options

As shown in figure 4.35, the diagnostics is split into two sections – application diagnostics and site diagnostics. Application diagnostics consist of logs created by the application. In ASP.NET, you can use the System.Diagnostics.Trace class to log information to the application diagnostics.

Site diagnostics allows you to enable system-level logging as listed below:

Web Server Logging

Setting this option logs HTTP requests and responses for the website using the W3C extended log file format. You can even specify quota and retention policy for the generated logs.

Detailed Error Logging

Setting this option logs detailed error messages for 400 or greater HTTP status codes that indicate a failure.

Failed Request Tracing

Setting this option logs traces of failed requests, including time taken to process the request in each component.

Log Storage

You can set the logs storage to be File System or Windows Azure storage. Setting the option to File System stores the diagnostics information on the web server's file system, and can be accessed using FTP, or downloaded as a zip file using Windows Azure PowerShell cmdlets. Setting the option to storage saves application diagnostics logs to the specified Windows Azure storage account in a table named WAWSAppLogTable. The site diagnostics allows you to store the log files as blobs in your own Windows Azure Blob storage container as shown in Figure 4.36.

Figure 4.36: Container name to storage site diagnostics

To test diagnostics, I modified the following code from Default.aspx.cs in the storagesearch website.

```
if (User.Identity.IsAuthenticated)
{

System.Diagnostics.Trace.TraceInformation(string.
Format("User logged in {0}", User.Identity.Name));
}
```
Listing 4.2: Logging Code

This code will write a trace output every time an authenticated user navigates to default.aspx.

Downloading Logs

Diagnostic information stored on the web server's file system can be downloaded using FTP, Windows Azure PowerShell, or the Windows Azure Command-Line Tools.

Using FTP

Before downloading the log files from the web server's file system, you need to set the login password by clicking the "Reset your deployment credentials" link from the quick glance section on the website's dashboard page. The FTP HOSTNAME and DEPLOYMENT/FTP USER list the hostname and user name for the FTP account respectively. Next, you can connect to the web server using your favorite FTP client. Figure 4.37 shows the file structure you will see after you FTP to the web server.

Figure 4.37: Web server file structure

WAWS creates the following structure for storing log files:

Application logs are stored in /LogFiles/Application/ in text format. These text files will contain the log messages from Listing 4.2.

Failed Request Traces are stored in /LogFiles/W3SVC#########/ in xml format. There is one XSL file that specifies formatting instructions to the browsers.

Detailed Error logs are stored in /LogFiles/DetailedErrors/ in html format listing HTTP errors

Web Server logs are stored in /LogFiles/http/RawLogs in text format. You may use a utility such as Log Parser (http://www.microsoft.com/en-us/download/details.aspx?id=24659) for parsing these log files.

Deployment logs are stored in /LogFiles/[deployment method]. In Figure 4.37, I have deployed the website using GitHub and therefore the logs are stored in /LogFiles/Git folder.

Using PowerShell

To download log file using PowerShell:
1) Start PowerShell command prompt
2) Import .publishsettings file
   ```
   >Import-AzurePublishSettingsFile   "Path   to
   the .publishsettings file"
   ```
3) Download the logs by calling the cmdlet
   ```
   Save-AzureWebSiteLog -Name [websitename]
   ```

The save command will download the logs files and save in the current directory as logs.zip.

Downloading from Windows Azure Blob storage

For downloading table data and blob files from Windows Azure storage, you can use a tool like ClumsyLeaf's CloudXplorer or TableXplorer

http://clumsyleaf.com/products/cloudxplorer

or Azure Storage Explorer

http://azurestorageexplorer.codeplex.com/

Figure 4.38 shows the application logs in the Windows Azure Table storage (WAWSAppLogTable)

Figure 4.38: Application Logs in Windows Azure Table Storage

Figure 4.39 shows the Windows Azure Blob storage structure that is created for storing site diagnostics.

Name	Size	Date modified	Type
RD00155D50E51F.log	215 KB	10/15/2013 3:31:53 P...	Text Docume

- dOI
  - ddvhds554
  - sitediagnostics
    - STORAGESEARCH
      - 2013
        - 10
          - 15
            - 22

Figure 4.39: Site diagnostics in Windows Azure Blob Storage

Streaming Logs

WAWS supports streaming of logs as they are generated by the application and the web server. You can use the Windows Azure PowerShell cmdlets or Windows Azure Command-Line tools for streaming logs from WAWS directly to your desktop.

To stream logs using PowerShell:

1) Start PowerShell command prompt
2) Import .publishsettings file
   ```
   >Import-AzurePublishSettingsFile "Path to
   the .publishsettings file"
   ```
3) Download the logs by calling the cmdlet

```
Get-AzureWebSiteLog -Name [websitename] -Tail
```

This command downloads logs as they are generated, into the PowerShell window as shown in Figure 4.40.

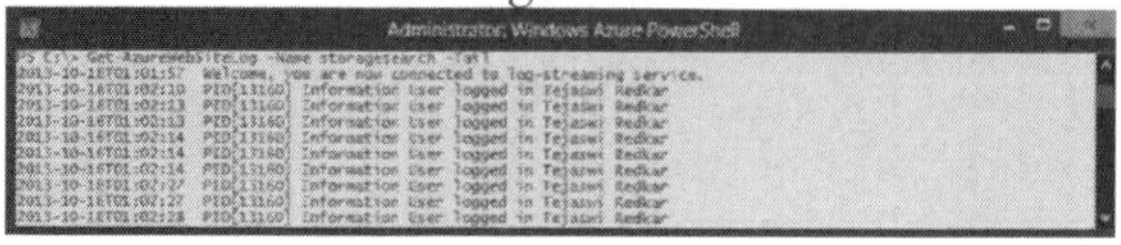

Figure 4.40: WAWS Log Streaming

The command runs like a server and prints logs to the console. This tool may be good when the website logs occasionally. If the logs are larger in volume, then the output from this tool may render unreadable.

Configuring Custom Domains

Domain names are a brand asset. Today's internet giants and advertising media lives by the domain name brand, therefore, it is important to have your website associated with your business domain name. By default, all the websites created in WAWS run under the *.azurewebsites.net domain. This domain is owned by Microsoft and you won't be allowed to purchase any certificate tied to this domain. Most of the websites need their own domain name because that is their fundamental identity on the web. WAWS supports running your websites under your own domain name, but only in Shared and Standard modes. In Free mode you must use the azurewebsites.net domain. In this section, you will learn to run your website under your own domain name.

Note: To proceed further, you will need to change the hosting plan of your website to either Shared or Standard. You can change the plan by navigating to the Scale section of the website in Windows Azure portal, and changing the WEB SITE MODE to Shared or Standard. Save the setting to take effect.

When you purchase a domain name from a domain name registrar, you can either use CNAME (Alias record) or A record to point the domain name to your website running in WAWS. That means your users don't need to type the *.azurewebsites.net domain name for your website.

CNAME (Alias record)

A CNAME is used to map a domain such as www.dynamicdeploy.com or blog.dynamicdeploy.com, to the <yourwebsite>.azurewebsites.net domain name. Typically, you cannot map bare domains such as dynamicdeploy.com or wildcard domains such as *.dynamicdeploy.com. You must use A record mapping for bare and wildcard domains. CNAME is the recommended method for mapping domain names because it insulates the website from the underlying IPAddress changes, whereas A record depends on the static IPAddress of the underlying website.

I have registered a domain called cloudapicentral.com on Namecheap.com (http://www.namecheap.com). For this domain name, I want to create a CNAME record at the domain registrar's website such that when a user types www.cloudapicentral.com in the browser, the domain registrar points the request to my Windows Azure website http://storagesearch.azurewebsites.net. Next, I want to create a blog site in WAWS (tejaswi.azurewebsites.net) and point the CNAME record blog.cloudapicentral.com to this website. This is a two-step process and the user interface for configuring a CNAME record may be different for your domain name registrar. The procedure to create a CNAME record with Namecheap is as follows:

1) Login to Namecheap (or your domain name registrar)
2) Navigate to Manage Domains and click on the domain (cloudapicentral.com)
3) From the left hand menu, click on the "All Host Records" link
4) Add a CNAME record that points the www record to storagesearch.azurewebsites.net as shown in Figure 4.41.

HOST NAME	IP ADDRESS/ URL	RECORD TYPE	MX PREF	TTL
@	http://www.cloudapicent	URL Redirect	n/a	1800
www	storagesearch.azurewel	CNAME (Alias)	n/a	1800

Figure 4.41: CNAME Record

In Figure 4.41, @ - equals http://cloudapicentral.com without www. So, @ points to www.cloudapicentral.com which in turn points to www, which has a CNAME alias pointing to storagesearch.azurewebsites.net.

5) Save the changes

Note: DNS is a network of servers distributed around the world and therefore it may take some time for the change to propagate through the DNS

network. Till the CNAME is propagated, you cannot set the CNAME for your website.

6)   You can track the propagation of the CNAME using this web tool http://www.digwebinterface.com/ (or http://www.dnsstuff.com)

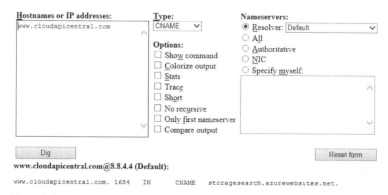

www.cloudapicentral.com@8.8.4.4 (Default):

www.cloudapicentral.com. 1684   IN   CNAME   storagesearch.azurewebsites.net.

Figure 4.42: Track CNAME propagation

7)   Next, in the subdomains section, add blog as a subdomain CNAME as shown in Figure 4.43.

Figure 4.43: Sub-domain CNAME

8)   Track the CNAME in http://www.digwebinterface.com/

9)   After the changes propagate through the Domain Name System (DNS) network, you need to navigate to the Configure section of your website on the Windows Azure portal, and add the new domain name (www.cloudapicentral.com) by clicking on the Manage Domains button as shown in Figure 4.44

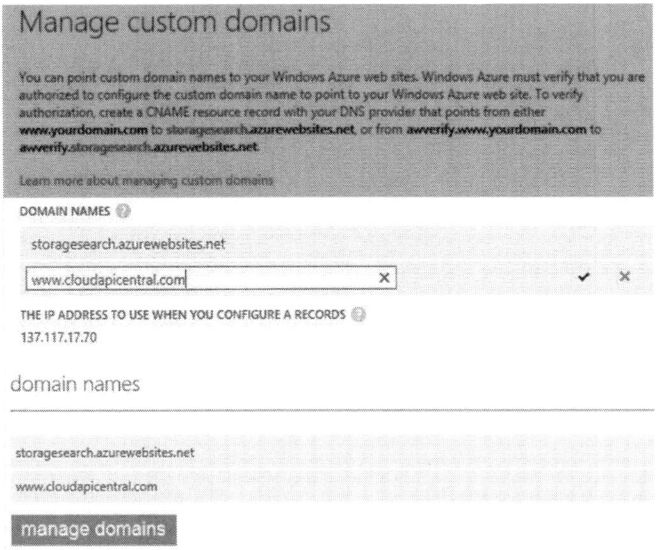

Figure 4.44: Manage Custom Domains

10) Similarly, add blog.cloudapicentral.com domain to the tejaswi.azurewebsites.com website configuration

11) Next, you can test both the links by navigating to http://www.cloudapicentral.com and http://blog.cloudapicentral.com

A record

An A record lets you map bare domains (e.g. dynamicdeploy.com) as well as wildcard domains (e.g. *.dynamicdeploy.com) to the IP address of website running in WAWS.

In order to configure an A record, you must first configure a CNAME record for Windows Azure to verify the user of the domain name. The CNAME that you configure is used for verification purpose only. For example, if the domain name is cloudapicentral.com, the hostname or CNAME record will be awverify.cloudapicentral.com and its value will be awverify.[yourwebsitename].azurewebsites.net

(e.g. awverify.storagesearch.azurewebsites.net), as shown in Figure 4.45.

HOST NAME	IP ADDRESS/ URL	RECORD TYPE	MX PREF	TTL
@	http://www.cloudapicent	URL Redirect ⌄	n/a	60000
www	storagesearch.azurewe	CNAME (Alias) ⌄	n/a	60000

SUB-DOMAIN SETTINGS ▼

awverify.www.cloudapic	awverify.storagesearch.	CNAME (Alias) ⌄	n/a	60000
		⌄	n/a	
		⌄	n/a	
		⌄	n/a	
		⌄	n/a	
		⌄	n/a	

Figure 4.45: Verification CNAME

1) Login to your domain name registrar's website and add the CNAME setting for awverify.[yourwebsitename].azurewebsites.net.
2) After this change is propagated through the DNS network, you can configure the A record in the portal.
3) Navigate to your website Dashboard in the Windows Azure portal
4) Click on the Manage Domains link on the Configure tab to open the Manage Custom Domains dialog box
5) Note the IP address of the website that is listed in the dialog box as shown in Figure 4.46.

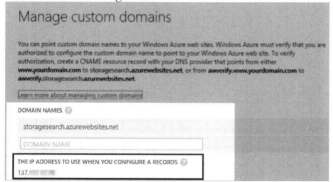

Figure 4.46: A record IP address

6) Login to the domain registrar's website and add an A record with cloudapicentral.com pointing to storagesearch.azurewebsites.net as shown in Table 4.4.

Table 4.4: A record values

Alias	TTL	Type	Value
awverify.cloudapicentral.com	60000	CNAME	awverify.storagesearch.azurewebsites.net

cloudapicentral.com	7200	A	137.117.17.70

After the changes propagate through the Domain Name System (DNS) network, you need to navigate to the Configure section of your website on the Windows Azure portal, and add the new domain name (www.cloudapicentral.com) by clicking on the Manage Domains button as shown in Figure 4.44 earlier in the chapter.

Figure 4.47 and 4.48 illustrate the A records propagated through the DNS network.

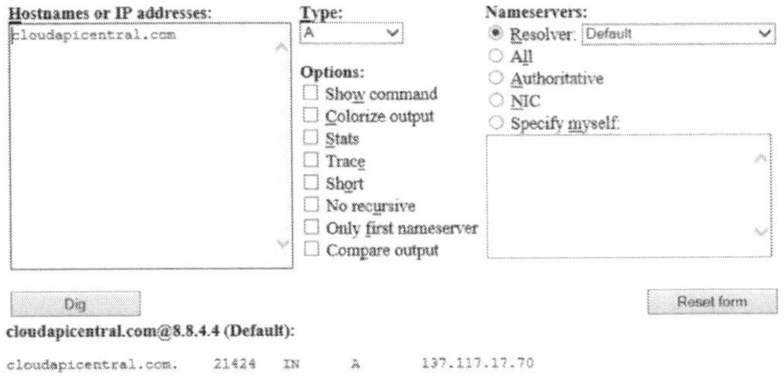

Figure 4.47: A-record for cloudapicentral.com

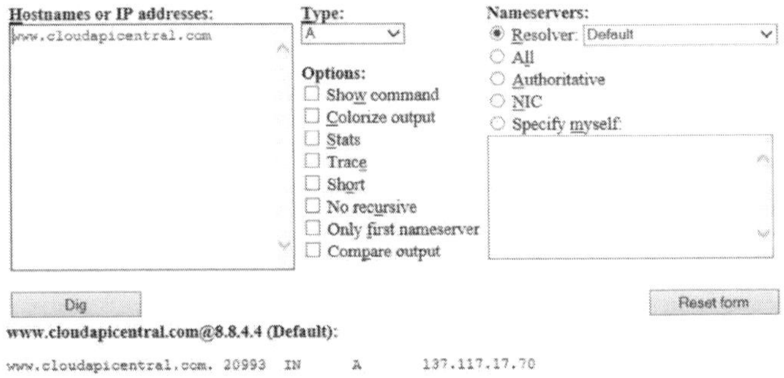

Figure 4.48: A record for www.cloudapicentral.com

DNS knowledge is crucial for understanding how cloud infrastructures work. Windows Azure is based on a sophisticated DNS infrastructure hosted in Microsoft's datacenters. Windows Azure then adds another layer of DNS capabilities that are specific to each Windows Azure service.

In this section, you learned to configure CNAME and A records to point your custom domains to your websites running in WAWS. To some extent, this knowledge also applies to other services in Windows Azure such as Cloud Services, Virtual Machines, Storage Accounts, and Mobile Services.

The next logical step after configuring custom domains is adding your custom Secure Socket Layer (SSL) certificates so that the users can access your website using a secure HTTP channel (https). In the next section, you will learn to configure your own custom SSL certificate.

Configuring SSL Certificate

SSL does not equate security. SSL creates an encrypted channel between a browser and the website thus allowing transfer of sensitive information without tampering. SSL is just one component of your secure development lifecycle. SSL also provides a method of authentication between the website user and the website owner because an SSL certificate is issued by a publicly trusted authority called Certificate Authority (CA). Browsers are pre-configured to trust certificates created by trusted authorities and therefore typically browsers do not display any warning messages. If you create your own certificate, browsers will warn users of an untrusted certificate. In this section, you will learn how to create your own (self-signed) certificate, acquire a certificate from a trusted authority and configure your website to support SSL encryption.

> Note: In WAWS, SSL certificates are supported only for websites running in Standard mode.

Acquiring an SSL certificate

The first step to getting SSL setup for your website is to acquire an SSL certificate signed by a Certificate Authority (CA). You can buy SSL certificates from most of the domain registrars and hosters such as GoDaddy.com and Namecheap.com. The certificate you receive must meet the following requirements to be used in WAWS:
1) The certificate must contain a private key.
2) The certificate must use a minimum of 2048-bit encryption.
3) The certificate must be created for key exchange, exportable to a Personal Information Exchange (.pfx) file. This will be needed because the certificate that you upload must be in the .pfx format
4) The certificate's subject name must match your custom domain used to access the website. For example, if you website's custom domain is www.dynamicdeploy.com then your certificate's subject name must also be www.dynamicdeploy.com
The domain *.azurewebsites.net is owned by Microsoft and therefore you

will not be allowed to acquire SSL certificate mapping to it.

> **Note: Sometimes you receive certificates with extensions other than .pfx such as .crt. In that case, you can either use a tool like OpenSSL or an online service like https://www.sslshopper.com/ssl-converter.html to convert certificates from one format to another.**

The Certificate Authority will request you to generate a Certificate Signing Request (CSR) , send it and the CA will reply with a certificate as a completion of the CSR. You can either you IIS Manager or OpenSSL to generate a CSR.

Because Certificate Authorities take time to create a certificate, for the purpose of this book, I recommend creating a self-signed certificate. Creating self-signed certificates are recommended only in development environments. In production, you must use a certificate from a Certificate Authority.

> **Note: To create a wildcard certificate for multiple domains (dynamicdeploy.com, www.dynamicdeploy.com, blog.dynamicdeploy.com,) you should use *.[yourdomainname].com (e.g.: *.dynamicdeploy.com). For a single domain name (e.g. www.dynamicdeploy.com), you must use the exact name of this domain that users will type in the browser (e.g. www.dynamicdeploy.com) to navigate to your website.**

Listed below is a step-by-step procedure for generating a self-signed certificate.

1) Open the makesslcert.cmd file in notepad located in the source code for Chapter 4.
2) In the makecert.exe command, note that the makecert.exe command takes an argument (CN=%1) for the domain name of your website.

```
makecert.exe -n "CN=%1" -in "Center Root CA" -
ss my -e "07/01/2022" -eku 1.3.6.1.5.5.7.3.1 -pe
-sky   exchange   "%~dp0certs\mysslcert.cer"   -sv
"%~dp0certs\mysslcert.pvk" -len 2048
   pvk2pfx  -pvk  "%~dp0certs\mysslcert.pvk"  -spc
"%~dp0certs\mysslcert.cer"                   -pfx
"%~dp0certs\mysslcert.pfx" -pi Pass@word1
```

3) Save the file.
4) Open Visual Studio Developer Command Prompt to run the makecert.exe utility
5) Browse to Chapter 4 source code directory and execute the makesslcert.cmd with the argument of your exact domain name.

For example
```
makesslcert.cmd www.clouapicentral.com
```

6) Enter the Private Key password (Pass@word1) in the Create Private Key Password dialog and click OK.

Figure 4.49: Create Private Key Password

7) In the Enter Private Key Password dialog, enter the same password (Pass@word1) and click OK

Figure 4.50: Enter Private Key Password

8) Then Enter Private Key Password will exit with a Succeed message in the command prompt, and a cert folder will be created with your certificates in it.

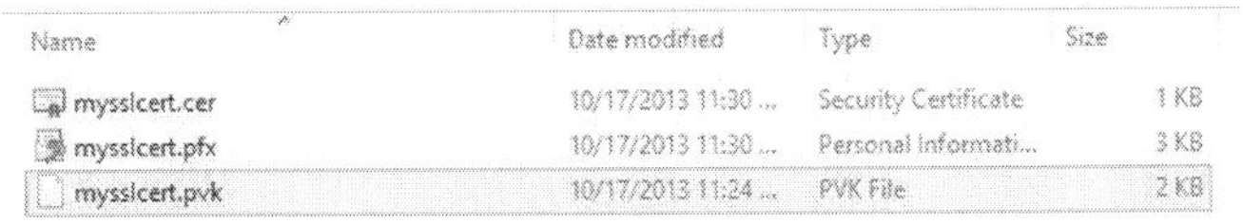

Name	Date modified	Type	Size
mysslcert.cer	10/17/2013 11:30 ...	Security Certificate	1 KB
mysslcert.pfx	10/17/2013 11:30 ...	Personal Informati...	3 KB
mysslcert.pvk	10/17/2013 11:24 ...	PVK File	2 KB

Figure 4.51: cert folder with certificates

Uploading the certificate to the website

Acquisition of certificate is the only time consuming step in configuring SSL for your website. Listed below is a step-by-step procedure for uploading the generated SSL certificate to your website.

1) Navigate to your website's Scale section on the Windows Azure portal
2) Change the website's plan to Standard mode and save changes

general

WEB SITE MODE   FREE | SHARED | STANDARD

Figure 4.52: Change website plan to standard

3) Next, navigate to your website's Configure section
4) Click on the upload a certificate in the certificates section

certificates

You have no certificates. Upload a certificate now to get started.

upload a certificate

Figure 4.53: Upload a certificate

5) In the Upload a certificate dialog, select the certificate file (mysslcert.pfx) you created earlier using the script, or your own purchased SSL certificate. Specify the certificate password (e.g. Pass@word1) that you used for securing the .pfx file.

Upload a certificate

Upload a certificate file (.pfx) for use in your web site.

FILE

📁 myssicert.pfx

PASSWORD

••••••••••|

Figure 4.54: Upload SSL certificate

6) Click the check to upload the certificate.
7) The certificate should show up in the list as shown in Figure 4.55

certificates

SUBJECT	EXPIRATION DATE	THUMBPRINT
www.cloudapicentral.com	7/1/2022	9E0195C15CB9A763E43407C76FC7B5891377E646

upload a certificate

Figure 4.55: List of uploaded certificates

Adding SSL Bindings

SSL bindings are used to bind a certificate to a custom domain (e.g. www.cloudapicentral.com). In WAWS, you can bind your SSL certificate with your custom domain in two supported ways:

IP based SSL

IP based SSL binds a certificate with a custom domain name to the dedicated public IP address of the web server running your website. This requires you to associate a static public IP address to your domain name. This is an old method when cloud-based dynamic virtual machines were not as popular. In today's world, it is not advisable to rely on the static IP address of web servers because they are inherently stateless in the cloud. In WAWS, you can use this binding if you have a static IP address associated with your domain name.

Server Name Indication (SNI) based SSL

SNI based SSL binding allows multiple custom domains to share the same IP address, with separate SSL certificates for each custom domain. This means that if you are running multiple different websites with different domain names on the same web server, you can have a separate SSL certificate for each domain but sharing the same IP address or the underlying web server. If your users use older browsers, I recommend testing SNI based binding against these browsers because some old versions may not support this feature.

For adding SSL bindings, navigate to the SSL bindings section of the Configure tab, use the dropdowns to select the domain name, the certificate to use for binding, and the binding type as shown in Figure 4.56.

ssl bindings

| www.cloudapicentral.com | CN=Root Agency, Expires: 7/1... | SNI SSL |
| Choose a domain name ⌄ | Choose a certificate ⌄ | SNI SSL ⌄ |

Figure 4.56: Adding SSL bindings

Finally, click Save to save the changes and enable SSL.

You can then test your website by navigating to the URL using the HTTPS protocol (e.g. https://www.cloudapicentral.com). If you have used a self-signed certificate, then you will see a warning, proceed anyways to check if your site loads. Note that if you use the https protocol with the *.azurewebsites.net domain, you will not see the warning because this is a Microsoft owned domain and they already have mapped a wildcard SSL certificate to this domain. So, make sure you try with your own custom domain only. If you install an SSL certificate issued by one of the CA, you should not see any warnings (e.g. https://www.dynamicdeploy.com). The most common cause of warnings for a CA issued certificate is a failed certificate installation. Re-install the certificate before contacting support.

Other Domain and SSL Configurations

Your custom domain name and SSL configurations are not complete until you reconfigure all the links not only within your website, but also from other applications and websites that are dependent on it. For example, if you are using Windows Azure Access Control Service (ACS) for authenticating users, you need to change the Relying Party links to use the custom domain and also change the protocol to use SSL. The orchestration between your website and ACS consists of sensitive information about the user, and is based on http redirects. I highly recommend using SSL between your website and ACS. To reconfigure ACS to use your new domain name and SSL:

1) Open your website solution in Visual Studio
2) Right-Click on the project and select Identity and Access.
   Note: You can download the Identity and Access tool for Visual Studio 2012 from this location
   http://visualstudiogallery.msdn.microsoft.com/e21bf653-dfe1-4d81-b3d3-

795cb104066e

3) Change the APP ID URI and the Realm Url to use the custom domain name

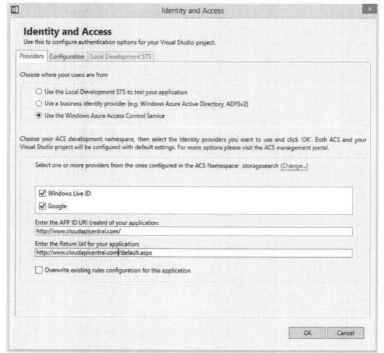

Figure 4.57: Change APP ID and Realm

4) Click on Configuration tab and check Requires HTTPS

Figure 4.58: Require HTTPS

Checking Require HTTPS will require the orchestration between your website and ACS to follow HTTPS protocol only.

5) Verify if all the parameters are saved correctly in the Relying Party configuration of your namespace in ACS portal.

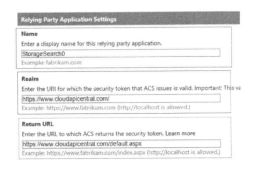

Figure 4.59: Relying Party Configuration on ACS portal

1) Next, open web.config for your website in Visual Studio and in the system.IdentityModel section verify if all the instances or [yourdomainname].azurewebsites.net (e.g. storagesearch.azurewebsites.net) are replaced by your custom domain name (e.g. www.cloudapicentral.com). Look specifically for

audienceUris and realm parameters.

2) Finally, save the website, publish it to WAWS, and test it with your custom domain and HTTPS protocol

Note: If you are using OAuth or other identity providers, you will need to make changes to your application configuration with each OAuth provider to reflect the custom domain name and HTTPS protocol.

> **Note: In order to avoid making these changes late in the project, I recommend creating the domain, SSL, and authentication infrastructure before writing the first line of code in your website. Once your domain and authentication system works flawlessly, you are free to develop your business logic.**

Forcing a website to use SSL

Most of the sites prefer operating in SSL-only mode. If a user types http://www.dynamicdeploy.com, the web server automatically redirects to https://www.dynamicdeploy.com . The advantage for this approach is that all the user communication remains encrypted and tamper-proof. The disadvantage is that if you have public facing web pages that include advertisements, some of the advertisement providers do not support HTTPS. The browser warns you on all the unsecured content on the web page and may even block these advertisements.

Running your website in SSL-only mode is a good practice provided there is no business impact to it. In order to force your ASP.NET website to run in SSL-only mode:

1) Open the website in Visual Studio
2) Open web.config and add a rewrite rule to redirect http content to https as shown in listing 4.1.

```
<system.webServer>
...
    <rewrite>
      <rules>
        <clear />
        <rule
name="RedirectToHTTPS"
```

```
stopProcessing="true">
        <match url="(.*)" />
        <conditions>
          <add input="{HTTPS}"
pattern="off" ignoreCase="true" />
        </conditions>
        <action
type="Redirect"
url="https://{HTTP_HOST}{REQUEST_URI}"
redirectType="Permanent" />
      </rule>
    </rules>
  </rewrite>
 </system.webServer>
```

Listing 4.3: Redirect to HTTPS

1) Save the website and publish to WAWS
2) Open a browser and navigate to your website using HTTP protocol
   (e.g. http://www.dynamicdeploy.com). Because of the redirect rule, you
   should be automatically redirected to HTTPS protocol (e.g.
   https://www.dynamicdeploy.com)

Configuration Settings

If you have developed an ASP.NET website/application before, you must be aware of the appSettings and connectionStrings in web.config. The appSettings element is used to store custom name-value string pairs your website can read at runtime. Similarly, the connectionString element is used to store database connection strings your website can read at runtime to connect with a database. These configuration settings are specific to ASP.NET. WAWS not only supports ASP.NET, but also PHP, Node.js, and Python.

In WAWS, from the portal, you can save name-value pairs and connection strings and read those values from your website at runtime. The values entered from the portal are readable from all the supported languages. These values are stored in the runtime database of the WAWS architecture (reference Figure 1.2). These name-value pairs remain in the database and are never stored in the text files. If there is a conflict of values between the portal settings and web.config, then the portal settings take precedence over web.config.

Setting Configuration Values

To set configuration values:
1) Navigate to the Configure section of your website in the portal.
2) You can add name-value string in the app settings section and a connection string in the connection string section. For my website, I have added one app setting (webserviceurl), and one connection string (databaseconnectionstring) as shown in Figure 4.60

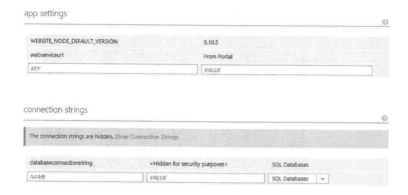

Figure 4.60: App Settings and Connection Strings

3) Save the page to persist values in the runtime database

You can now retrieve the configuration values using language specific APIs in WAWS.

Retrieving Configuration Values from ASP.NET

To retrieve the configuration values from ASP.NET:
1) Create a new empty website in Visual Studio
2) Add a new Default.aspx page to the website
3) In web.config, add the same appSetting and connectionString names as you added in the portal but enter different values, as shown in Listing 4.2.

```
<appSettings>
    <add
key="webserviceurl" value="From Local Web" />
  </appSettings>
```

```
<connectionStrings>
  <add
name="databaseconnectionstring"
connectionString="Server=(localdb)\v11.0;Integrat
ed Security=true;"/>
  </connectionStrings>
```

Listing 4.4: Local web.config

Note: You don't need to create the values in local web.config. By adding the same setting names but different values, you will be able to test whether WAWS overrides the local settings with portal settings.

---

4) In Default.aspx, add two Literal Controls to display the configuration settings.
5) Next, modify Default.aspx.cs as shown in Listing 4.3.

```
protected void Page_Load(object sender,
 EventArgs e)
{
   Literal1.Text+=
"webserviceurl=ConfigurationManager.AppSettings
 ["webserviceurl"]";

   Literal2.Text += "databaseconnectionstring="
+
ConfigurationManager.ConnectionStrings["databasec
onnectionstring"].ConnectionString.Substring(0,
15) + "...";

}
```
Listing 4.5: Read Configuration Settings Locally

Run the website locally and note down the displayed configuration values

Figure 4.61: Configuration Settings Displayed Locally

6) Publish the website to WAWS from Visual Studio

7) Test the output of the configuration settings displayed on the web page.

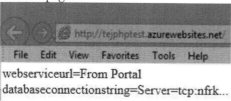

Figure 4.62: Configuration Settings From

Note that the configuration settings from the portal takes precedence over the ones in web.config. In development environment, this separation is useful because you can store development specific values in web.config and production specific values in the portal.

In order to maintain consistency across multiple languages, the portal setting values are available as system environment variables. You can retrieve the same setting values as environment variables from ASP.NET by using the System.Environment.GetEnvironmentVariable() function as shown below.

```
Environment.GetEnvironmentVariable
("APPSETTING_webserviceurl");
Environment.GetEnvironmentVariable
("SQLAZURECONNSTR_databaseconnectionstring");
```

Listing 4.6: ASP.NET Environment Variables

Observe that WAWS introduces additional conventions by prepending the configuration setting names with APPSETTING_ and SQLAZURECONNSTR_.All the appSettings must be prepended by

APPSETTING_, and the connectionStrings must be prepended appropriate database constant string. Table 4.5 lists appropriate strings to prepend specific database connection string setting names.

Table 4.5. Strings to prepend by database type[6]

Database Type	String to prepend
Windows Azure SQL Database	SQLAZURECONNSTR_
SQL Server	SQLCONNSTR_
MySQL	MYSQLCONNSTR_
Custom	CUSTOMCONNSTR_

Retrieving Configuration Values from PHP

PHP cannot access web.config values, but it can access environment variables through the getenv() function. To access configuration values from PHP, you must follow the same convention as discussed in the previous section for accessing environment variables from ASP.NET.

```php
<?php

$appSetting=getenv("APPSETTING_webserviceurl")
;
echo $appSetting;

$appSetting=getenv("SQLAZURECONNSTR_databaseconnectionstring");
echo $appSetting;
?>
```
Listing 4.7: Configuration Values from PHP

---

[6] http://blogs.msdn.com/b/windowsazure/archive/2013/07/17/windows-azure-web-sites-how-application-strings-and-connection-strings-work.aspx

Retrieving Configuration Values from Node.js

Node.js can access environment variables through the process object's env property. Listing 4.5 shows how to access the environment variables from Node.js' server.js.

```
var http = require('http');
http.createServer(function (req, res) {
    res.writeHead(200,    {    'Content-Type':
'text/html' });
    res.write('Hello, world!');

res.write('<li><label>webserviceurl:</label>'    +
process.env.APPSETTING_webserviceurl + ' </li>');

res.end('<li><label>databaseconnectionstring:</la
bel>'                                            +
process.env.SQLAZURECONNSTR_databaseconnectionstr
ing + ' </li>');

}).listen(process.env.PORT || 8080);
```

Listing 4.8: Configuration Values from Node.js

As shown in Listing 4.5, in Node.js, you can call each environment variable using the convention process.env.[ENVIRONMENT VARIABLE NAME] (e.g. process.env.APPSETTING_webserviceurl)

Summary

In this chapter, you stepped out of your developer's shoes and took a short peek into the life of an IT operator. The more you learn about the operational capabilities of WAWS, the better you will be as a developer. Traditionally, only hosting companies provided some operational capabilities to developers, but this is a paradigm shift where developers become operators of their own websites. For example, I am the sole developer and operator of the website http://www.dynamicdeploy.com . I created the idea, designed it, built it, and now I maintain it all by myself. This wouldn't have been possible just a couple of years back. Windows Azure empowered me as a developer to quickly materialize my idea to fruition. I know of several such developers who have built mobile and non-mobile web apps on WAWS, and who are the sole operators their web apps.

The objective of this chapter was to highlight some of the key operational capabilities of WAWS such as scaling, diagnostics, performance monitoring, assigning custom domains, assigning SSL certificates, and configuring your website at runtime with configuration settings. Although we covered most of the operational capabilities of WAWS, it was not an exhaustive list for a production-ready website. Different levels of testing such as functional, stress, load and regression, accompanied with global deployments and global DNS routing, are some of the capabilities I recommend including in your operations backlog from early stages of development.

Until this chapter, the focus of the book was on WAWS features for building world-class websites at a rapid pace. You learned fundamentals of WAWS architecture, tools for building, deploying, and managing websites on WAWS. But, in large scale systems, websites form only the front-end web-tier of a broader solution. For building real-world applications, you must learn solution-building skills that require knowledge of technologies beyond web-tiers. In the following chapters you will learn some of the architectural building-blocks required in running real-world solutions on WAWS. These scenarios will highlight technologies beyond Windows Azure Web Sites.

Bibliography

Microsoft Corporation. (2012). *Windows Azure Web Site Documentation.*
Retrieved from Windows Azure :
http://www.windowsazure.com/en-us/documentation/services/web-sites/?fb=en-us

Tejaswi Redkar

Chapter 5

MIGRATING
DYNAMICDEPLOY.COM

I believe, you cannot be a good developer unless you develop for yourself. I advise you to be your own customer and take accountability of the entire lifecycle of a product, even small, to realize the pains and gains associated with it. In this chapter, we will look at a real-world website that I have built in the past couple of years, and has been in production for about a year on Windows Azure. The website is named dynamicdeploy.com. It is a multi-tenant deployment-as-a-service (and a marketplace) that enables you to publish and deploy virtual machines to Windows Azure.

In a multi-tiered architecture, WAWS can host only the web-tier, whereas other Windows Azure Compute services such as Cloud Services and Virtual Machines can perform multiple roles within a solution. But, the infrastructure abstraction and ease of development makes it easier to quickly deploy your web-tier on WAWS. In this chapter, you will learn the common issues faced by developers when migrating existing websites to WAWS. The objective of the exercise is to evaluate if WAWS is a right fit for running the dynamicdeploy.com website. Although the case study is on dynamicdeploy.com, the issues discussed will apply to most of the public facing websites aspiring to migrate to WAWS.

Before diving into solutions, I would like to discuss a generic website capability model that lists the common features required by all the websites to run at production scale. This model will help you design a migration strategy for your website.

Web Site Capability Model

A website's capability model lists the core technical features required by a website to deliver value to its users. Not all capabilities are required by all the websites, but they do form a deciding factor on whether to migrate to the cloud or not. I recommend starting your migration strategy (and technical design) with this capability model to visualize core services required by your website. The website capability model is independent or any underlying web platform like WAWS. Table 5.1 represents the website capability model, and lists each capability and its description.

Table 5.1: Web Site Capability Model

Capabilities	Description
Identity Management	The authentication and authorization mechanism required by the website. This includes authentication, authorization, and identity storage.
Session Management	The mechanism used for storing and sharing session information in a web-farm.
Caching	Specifies caching requirements of a website.
Data Storage	Specifies the relational and non-relational data storage requirements of a website.
User Experience	User Experience requirements of a website.
Framework Runtime Requirements	Any specific application runtime requirements such as .NET 4.5 or PHP 5.4.
Data Security at rest	Specifies requirements for securely storing data in relational and non-relational data storage.
Data Security in transit	Specifies requirements for securely transferring data over the network.
Load-balancing	Specifies load-balancing requirements when running a website in a farm
Scale-Up	Specifies the scale-up requirements when scaling a website to meet capacity demand.
Scale-Out	Specifies the scale-out requirements when scaling a website to meet capacity demand.
Monitoring	Specifies the monitoring requirements for operating a website

Geo-deployment	Specifies the requirement for deploying a website in multiple data centers around the world.
Content Delivery Network (CDN)	Specifies the requirement for caching static content in a CDN.
Message Bus	Specifies whether a website requires to communicate with a message bus.
Integration	Specifies any integration and external API dependencies of a website.
Configuration Management	Specifies how and where the configuration of a website is managed.
Search	Specifies the search functionality requirement of a website
Analytics	Specifies if a website needs to track usage analytics.
E-commerce	Specifies the E-commerce requirements for a website.

When assessing an existing website for migrating to WAWS, Table 5.1 can be used for establishing a baseline to identify gaps and workarounds between source and destination platforms.

Migrating dynamicdeploy.com

Dynamic Deploy (http://www.dynamicdeploy.com) is an app deployment service for Windows Azure. It offers virtual machines, and cloud services for deploying to your Windows Azure subscription. It also offers additional services like StorageCopy and Private Workspaces. Because of the expansion in the feature sets, blogs, and related marketing sites, the number of supporting websites have grown, and we would like to assess if WAWS is the right fit for running dynamicdeploy.com.

Product Features

Before assessing the technical capabilities of a website, it is imperative to first understand its features. Figure 5.1 illustrates the home page of Dynamic Deploy.

Figure5.1: Dynamic Deploy Home Page

From the home page of the website, we can derive a shortlist of features as listed in Table 5.2.

Table 5.2: Dynamic Deploy Features

Feature	Description
Search	Ability to search for apps
Login	Ability for users to login using public identity providers (Microsoft Account, Google, Facebook, Yahoo)
Blog	This is a separate site not hosted with the parent website.
Publishing Your Own App	Ability to publish your own apps and virtual machines to the collection.
Deploying Apps	Ability to deploy any app to Windows Azure from the collection.
Storage Copy Service	A service for copying blobs from Amazon S3/Windows Azure Blob Storage to Windows

	Azure Blob storage.
Ecommerce	Ability to purchase Dynamic Deploy subscriptions using PayPal.
Advertising	Ability to insert Google AdSense advertisements in web pages.

Table 5.2 lists the core features of the website from a user's perspective. The next step is to take a look at the architecture of the website.

Current State Architecture

Currently, dynamicdeploy.com runs on Windows Azure Cloud Services as a multi-tiered solution. Figure 5.2 illustrates the current state architecture of dynamicdeploy.com.

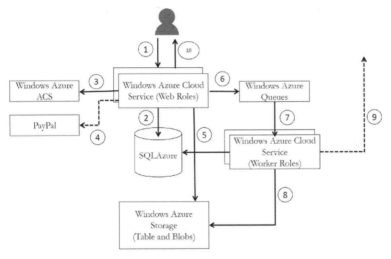

Figure 5.2: Dynamic Deploy Architecture

In Figure 5.2, there are 2 Web Roles, 2 Worker Roles and other services such as Windows Azure SQL Database, Windows Azure Storage, Windows Azure ACS, and PayPal integration. Web Role is typically used for running websites and Worker Role is used for running background services.

Typical user interaction on Dynamic Deploy website can be described in ten steps:

1) A user (or admin) navigates to http://www.dynamicdeploy.com
2) Dynamic Deploy retrieves data from the Azure SQL database or Windows Azure's Dedicated Cache running on the cloud service virtual machines.

3) User logs in to Dynamic Deploy using Windows Azure Access Control Service.
4) Optionally, user subscribes to the Dynamic Deploy Basic Subscription by making payments through PayPal.
5) Payment transaction and any user profile information is saved to Windows Azure Table Storage.
6) User initiates a deployment and the website sends a deployment message to a Windows Azure Queue.
7) One of the Worker Roles retrieves the message from the queue.
8) The Worker Role retrieves deployment profile from storage
9) Worker Role initiates a deployment of the selected app to the user's Windows Azure subscription.
10) The deployment status sent back to the user.

There are other complex interactions occurring inside the system, but in the scope of our migration discussion, these 10 steps sufficiently describes the deployment process.

From a quick observation of the architecture, we can conclude that only the Web Roles can be migrated to Windows Azure Web Sites (WAWS). The Worker Roles will continue as they are currently. Next, we will build the website capability model for the Dynamic Deploy website running in Web Roles.

Web Site Capability Model for

dynamicdeploy.com

A website capability model provides you with a clear comparison between the current and future capabilities of the website and helps you identity technical gaps that you will need to address during migration.

Table 5.2: Web Site Capability Model for Dynamic Deploy

Capability	Web Role (Current State)	WAWS (Future State)	Notes
Identity Management	ACS Azure SQL database	ACS Azure SQL database	ACS is a web-based orchestration service and works with WAWS. There might be some efforts involved if you are using certificates for

			encrypting tokens because you cannot install certificates on the virtual machines running WAWS.
Session Management	Windows Azure In-Role Cache	Windows Azure Shared Cache OR Azure SQL database	Windows Azure Shared Cache has cost associated with it.
Caching	Windows Azure In-Role Cache	In-Memory OR Windows Azure Shared Cache	In-Role Cache is not supported by WAWS, and Windows Azure Shared Cache has cost associated with it. In-Memory cache is an option but it's not distributed.
Data Storage	Windows Azure Storage (Blob and Table), Windows Azure SQL Database (Azure SQL database)	Windows Azure Storage (Blob and Table), Windows Azure SQL Database	Windows Azure Storage provides a REST interface that can be accessed from WAWS.
User Experience	ASP.NET Web Forms/HTML/AJAX	ASP.NET Web Forms/HTML/AJAX	Core ASP.NET web controls and UI works as-is in WAWS.
Framework Runtime Requirements	.NET 4.0+ ASP.NET WebApi	.NET 4.0+ ASP.NET WebApi	.NET 4.5 is supported in WAWS.
Data Security at rest	Secret Key	Secret Key	The secret key can be stored externally in Windows Azure Table storage or in the WAWS configuration.
Data Security in transit	HTTPS	HTTPS	HTTPS is fully supported in WAWS.
Load-balancing	Windows Azure Load-balancer	Windows Azure Load-balancer	Since WAWS runs on Windows Azure Cloud Services, Windows Azure load-balancer is automatically provisioned for the website.

Scale-Up	Virtual Machine Size	Standard Mode and Virtual Machine Size	Only Standard mode supports scale-up in WAWS.
Scale-Out	Add Instances	Shared or Standard Mode	Only Shared and Standard modes support scale-out in WAWS.
Monitoring & Diagnostics	Built-in Monitoring or Third-party software. Logs are stored in Windows Azure Storage	Built-in Monitoring or Third-party software (e.g. New Relic) Logs stored locally or in Windows Azure Storage	Monitoring & Diagnostics should work as-is in WAWS.
Geo-deployment	Initiate a new deployment in a new region. You can use Windows Azure Traffic Manager for geo-routing.	Initiate a new deployment in a new region. Traffic Manager is not supported in WAWS.	At the time of writing only Cloud Services (*.cloudapp.net) were supported by Traffic Manager. *.azurewebsites.net domain was not supported. This feature does not affect code migration, but may affect future expansions.
Content Delivery Network	Current website does not use CDN	Migrated website will not need CDN	WAWS can be configured to use CDN if needed in the future.
Message Bus	Windows Azure Queues	Windows Azure Queues	Windows Azure Queues provides a REST API, so it is accessible from WAWS.
Integration	No specific integration requirements	No specific integration requirements	
Configuration Management	Service Configuration	WAWS Configuration	Minor configuration management changes are expected.
Search	Uses a combination of Cache and Linq.	Can use a combination of In-Memory Cache and	Eventually, the website will use a third-party search engine such as

		Linq.	ElasticSearch or SOLR.
Analytics	Google Analytics	Google Analytics	Google Analytics JavaScript snippets work as-is in WAWS.
Ecommerce	PayPal	PayPal	Since PayPal interactions are https based, they will work in WAWS.

From the capability model, it is evident that there will be some changes required to the website for running it on WAWS. Two critical issues identified are:

1) Migrating the Session Management to Windows Azure SQL Database or Windows Azure Shared Cache

2) Migrating Caching to In-Memory cache or Windows Azure Shared Cache

Although these changes are not significant from a source code perspective, the website cannot be migrated to a production environment without making these changes. Session management and caching affect performance of a website, and therefore I recommend resolving these two issues before publishing the website to WAWS. Next, will cover these identified migration options.

Session Management

Sessions are user-specific objects that are stored on the web server when user interacts with the website. A login object is a popular example of a session. You login only once during a session, perform all the interactions with the website during that session, such as adding items to a shopping cart. You are not required to login again when you navigate from one page to another. The web server maintains your login session and identifies you in your subsequent requests. A session ends when you either close the browser, log-off from the website, or if the session times out. A web server needs to store these sessions in a temporary data store such as a database, cache, or memory throughout their lifetime. Improper session management may not only deteriorate performance, but also user experience. For managing sessions in WAWS, we have two options:

1) Windows Azure SQL Database (Azure SQL) by utilizing

ASP.NET Universal Providers

2) Utilizing Windows Azure Shared Cache

Session Management with Azure SQL Database

If your website already uses Azure SQL database, then you can share the same database for storing sessions, instead of creating a new one only for strong sessions. To manage session state in Azure SQL database, you must first install the ASP.NET Universal Providers nuget package.

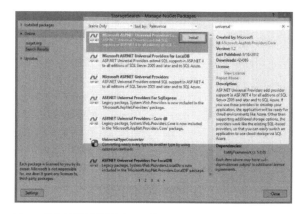

Figure 5.3: ASP.NET Universal Providers

After the Universal providers are installed, you have to set the right connection string in web.config that matches one of the supported databases such as SQL Server, SQL Server Compact or Azure SQL database. Listing 5.1 shows the session state configuration for Azure SQL database in the web.config file.

```
<configuration>
    <connectionstrings>
        <add
connectionstring="data source=myDNSName;Initial
Catalog=myDatabase;
        User ID=myUserName;Password=myPassword;
        Encrypt=true;Trusted_Connection=false;
        MultipleActiveResultSets=True"
    providerName="System.Data.SqlClient"
    name="DefaultConnection" />
        </add>
    </connectionstrings>
```

```
<system.web>
    <sessionstate
customprovider="DefaultSessionProvider"
mode="Custom">
        <providers>
          <add
type="System.Web.Providers.DefaultSessionStatePro
vider"
  name="DefaultSessionProvider"
  applicationname="/"
connectionstringname="DefaultConnection">
        </add>
  </providers>
      </sessionstate>
    </system.web>
  </configuration>
```
Listing 5.1: Azure SQL Session State Provider

In Listing 5.1, a Azure SQL database connection string is defined in the <connectionStrings /> section and the name of the connection string (e.g. DefaultConnection) is passed to the connectionstringname attribute of session state provider. After you configure the session state, you can continue using the session object in the code for storing and retrieving session objects. These session objects will be stored and retrieved from a central Azure SQL database. When you scale-out your website, the session data will be shared across all the website instances.

Session Management with Windows Azure Shared Cache

Windows Azure Cache is a distributed shared caching service that provides you with an endpoint and client-side SDK for storing objects on a server hosted by Microsoft in Windows Azure. As a developer, you can access the cache API using the caching SDK. The objects stored in this cache can be shared across multiple servers in your architecture. Because of its ability to store objects centrally on another server, Windows Azure Shared Cache can be used for storing session objects. Windows Azure Shared Cache provides an ASP.NET session provider for storing session objects without the need for modifying any source code. The Windows Azure Cache costs a minimum of $12.50/month depending on size of the cache. At the time of writing, there were three caching plans available as shown in Table 5.3.

Table 5.3: Windows Azure Shared Cache Pricing

Plan	Memory Size Range	Pricing per unit
Basic	128MB to 1GB	$12.50 per month (prorated hourly)
Standard	1GB to 10GB	$50 per month (prorated hourly)
Premium	5GB to 150GB	$200 per month (prorated hourly)

Since Windows Azure Shared Cache is not a free service, you must evaluate its usage carefully from a pricing perspective.

For latest pricing and information on Windows Azure Shared Cache, please visit the following link:

http://www.windowsazure.com/en-us/pricing/details/cache/

> **Note: At the time of writing Windows Azure Shared Cache service was in preview. Developing production websites on preview services is not recommended. Windows Azure In-Role cache is not supported in Windows Azure Web Sites**

There are four steps to incorporate Windows Azure Cache in your website:
1. Create a cache on Windows Azure portal
2. Configure the website for using Windows Azure Cache.
3. Modify the web.config file to include Windows Azure Cache as your session provider
4. Finally, start using the Session object to store and retrieve session objects.

Creating a Cache Endpoint

1. To create a new cache endpoint, login to Windows Azure portal

and click on the New > Data Services > Cache > Quick Create

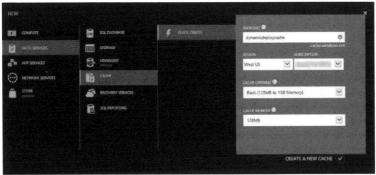

Figure 5.4: Creating a new cache

As shown in Figure 5.4, provide a unique name for your cache, the region your cache will run in, and offering. Please make sure you create the cache in the same region as your website. Click on the "Create a new cache" button to create your shared cache. The cache will be visible in the Cache section of the portal as shown in Figure 5.5.

Figure 5.5: Windows Azure Shared Cache Created

Configuring the website to use Windows Azure Shared Cache

Windows Azure Shared Cache SDK is available as a nuget package.

Note: Please ensure that you have installed the latest **Windows Azure SDK for .NET**. You can download the latest version of the **SDK** from the link below

http://www.windowsazure.com/en-us/downloads/?sdk=net

---

1. Open your website in Visual Studio, right-click on the website project in Solution Explorer, and then select Manage NuGet

Packages. (For WebMatrix, click the NuGet button on the toolbar instead)

2. Search nuget repository for "Windows Azure Caching"

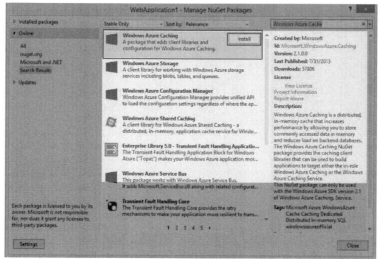

Figure 5.6: Windows Azure Caching SDK on nuget

3. Select the Windows Azure Caching package, and click the Install

4. While installing, the nuget package modifies the web.config file by inserting a dedicated section named "dataCacheClients", and commented stubs for using Windows Azure Cache as a session provider for the website.

Modifying web.config

The configuration elements created by the nuget package do not contain the endpoint information for the cache that you created earlier. You need to specify the cache endpoint details in web.config for securely communicating with the cache.

1. Open web.config of the website in Visual Studio

2. Scroll to the session state section of web.config. Comment the default session provider and uncomment the XML element representing Windows Azure Caching, as illustrated in Figure 5.7.

```
<!-- <sessionState mode="InProc" customProvider="DefaultSessionProvider">
    <providers>
        <add name="DefaultSessionProvider"
            type="System.Web.Providers.DefaultSessionStateProvider, System.Web.Providers, Version=1.0.0.0, Culture=neutral, PublicKeyToken=31bf3856ad364e35"
            connectionStringName="DefaultConnection" />
    </providers>
</sessionState> -->
<!-- Windows Azure Caching session state provider -->
<sessionState mode="Custom" customProvider="AFCacheSessionStateProvider">
    <providers>
        <add name="AFCacheSessionStateProvider"
            type="Microsoft.Web.DistributedCache.DistributedCacheSessionStateStoreProvider, Microsoft.Web.DistributedCache"
            cacheName="default"
            dataCacheClientName="default"
            applicationName="AFCacheSessionState"/>
    </providers>
</sessionState>
```

Figure 5.7: Configure Session Provider

In Figure 5.7, you configured Windows Azure Shared Cache as your default
session provider.

3.   Next, scroll to the dataCacheClients section for specifying the
     endpoint details of the cache. Uncomment the securityProperties
     element as illustrated in Figure 5.8.

```
<dataCacheClients>
    <dataCacheClient name="default">
        <!--To use the in-role flavor of Windows Azure Caching, set identifier to be the cache cluster role name -->
        <!--To use the Windows Azure Caching Service, set identifier to be the endpoint of the cache cluster -->
        <autoDiscover isEnabled="true" identifier="[Cache role name or Service Endpoint]" />

        <!--<localCache isEnabled="true" sync="TimeoutBased" objectCount="100000" ttlValue="300" />-->

        <!--Use this section to specify security settings for connecting to your cache. This section is not required i
        <securityProperties mode="Message" sslEnabled="false">
            <messageSecurity authorizationInfo="[Authentication Key]" />
        </securityProperties>
    </dataCacheClient>
</dataCacheClients></configuration>
```

Figure 5.8: Configure Cache Endpoint

The identifier attribute of autoDiscover element consists of the cache
endpoint name. The Windows Azure Caching classes communicate with the
cache endpoint using this information. Set the identifier attribute to the
endpoint of the cache. Typically, the endpoint will be of the format [unique
cache endpoint name].cache.windows.net, and can be found in the Cache
section of the Windows Azure portal.

4.   Next, from the portal, copy the cache security key by
     clicking on the Manage Keys button from the cache page.
     In web.config, set the authorizationInfo attribute of the
     messageSecurity element to the cache security key, as shown
     in Figure 5.9.

```
<dataCacheClients>
    <dataCacheClient name="default">
        <!--To use the in-role flavor of Windows Azure Caching, set identifier to be the cache cluster role name -->
        <!--To use the Windows Azure Caching Service, set identifier to be the endpoint of the cache cluster -->
        <autoDiscover isEnabled="true" identifier="dynamicdeploy.cache.windows.net" />

        <!--<localCache isEnabled="true" sync="TimeoutBased" objectCount="100000" ttlValue="300" />-->

        <!--Use this section to specify security settings for connecting to your cache. This section is not required if y
        <securityProperties mode="Message" sslEnabled="false">
            <messageSecurity authorizationInfo="XXXXXXXXXXXXXXXXXXXXXXXXXXXXXXXXXXXXXXXX" />
        </securityProperties>
    </dataCacheClient>
</dataCacheClients></configuration>
```

Figure 5.9: Cache Configuration Complete

Dynamicdeploy.com website uses In-Role cache that does not require security properties because it runs on the same virtual machine as the website. WAWS does not support In-Role cache and therefore it needs security properties of the Shared Cache, which is hosted on another server within the Windows Azure datacenter.

Using ASP.NET Session Object

There won't be any changes required to the ASP.NET Session object because only the underlying storage mechanism has changed. ASP.NET's provider model makes it possible for you to change the underlying storage mechanism without modifying your code. This technique is popularly called "Configure before Customize". I recommend following the provider model pattern in your own software development wherever you have the requirement of swapping data providers without code modifications. Listing 5.2 shows typical usage of ASP.NET Session object.

```
//Add an object to session
string sessionKey = "packageId";
string sessionValue = "XXXXXXXXXXXX";
Session.Add(sessionKey, sessionValue);
//Retrieve object from Session
string sessionValue = Session[sessionKey] as
string;
```
Listing 5.2: Using ASP.NET Session Object

When you call Session.Add() function, the ASP.NET API calls Windows Azure Caching provider as its default session provider. The provider then calls the Windows Azure Shared Caching API to store and retrieve the object.

In dynamicdeploy.com, the In-Role cache can be replaced by Windows Azure Shared Cache as a session provider. In this section, you learned to replace the default session provider with Windows Azure Shared Cache as the session provider. For caching objects independently of sessions, you need to use the Windows Azure Caching API directly without the provider model. With the new SDK, Microsoft has made the APIs between In-Role Cache and Shared Cache consistent. In the next section, you will learn to directly cache objects in Windows Azure Shared Cache from your program.

Note: For latest information on Windows Azure Shared Cache, please visit the following link

http://msdn.microsoft.com/en-us/library/windowsazure/dn386094.aspx

---

Caching with Windows Azure Shared Cache

In the previous section, you learned to configure Windows Azure Shared Cache as the default session provider. Because of the provider model pattern, you did not have to change any code for replacing session providers. Dynamicdeploy.com uses In-Role Cache for storing not only session objects, but also application objects. The website calls Windows Azure Caching API directly to save and retrieve application objects from the In-Role cache. Because the API between In-Role Cache and Shared Cache are consistent, we will require only configuration changes to replace In-Role cache with Shared Cache. For migration purposes, let's follow a 2-step process as listed below:

Step 1: Migrate Cache Configuration

Step 2: Migrate Code

Migrating Configuration

As discussed in the previous section, the Caching API has two parts to it – XML Configuration (dataCacheClients section) and the Cache API. Figure 5.10 illustrates the XML configuration of the In-Role cache in web.config.

```
<dataCacheClients>
  <dataCacheClient name="default">
    <autoDiscover isEnabled="true" identifier="ddweb" />
    <!--<localCache isEnabled="true" sync="TimeoutBased" objectCount="100000" ttlValue="300" />-->
  </dataCacheClient>
  <dataCacheClient name="ddcache" isCompressionEnabled="true">
    <autoDiscover isEnabled="true" identifier="ddweb" />
    <!--<localCache isEnabled="true" sync="TimeoutBased" objectCount="100000" ttlValue="300" />-->
  </dataCacheClient>
</dataCacheClients>
```

Figure 5.10: Cache configuration for dynamicdeploy.com

In Figure 5.10, there are two named caches – default and ddcache. The default cache is used for storing session objects and ddcache is used for storing application objects. The identifier ddweb points to the name of the Web Role. Because the configuration is for an In-Role cache, the securityProperties section is omitted, and the identifier does not require any domain name identification. For migrating this configuration to use Windows Azure Shared Cache, you will need to set the identifier attribute to the Shared Cache's endpoint name, and add securityProperties as shown in Figure 5.11.

```
<dataCacheClients>
  <dataCacheClient name="default">
    <!--To use the in-role flavor of Windows Azure Caching, set identifier to be the cache cluster role name -->
    <!--To use the Windows Azure Caching Service, set identifier to be the endpoint of the cache cluster -->
    <autoDiscover isEnabled="true" identifier="dynamicdeploy.cache.windows.net" />
    <localCache isEnabled="true" sync="TimeoutBased" objectCount="100000" ttlValue="300" />
    <!--Use this section to specify security settings for connecting to your cache. This section is not required if
    <securityProperties mode="Message" sslEnabled="false">
      <messageSecurity authorizationInfo="XXXXXXXXXXXXXXXXXXXXXXXXXXXXXXXXXXXXX" />
    </securityProperties>
  </dataCacheClient>
  <dataCacheClient name="ddcache">
    <!--To use the in-role flavor of Windows Azure Caching, set identifier to be the cache cluster role name -->
    <!--To use the Windows Azure Caching Service, set identifier to be the endpoint of the cache cluster -->
    <autoDiscover isEnabled="true" identifier="dynamicdeploy.cache.windows.net" />
    <localCache isEnabled="true" sync="TimeoutBased" objectCount="100000" ttlValue="300" />
    <!--Use this section to specify security settings for connecting to your cache. This section is not required if
    <securityProperties mode="Message" sslEnabled="false">
      <messageSecurity authorizationInfo="YYYYYYYYYYYYYYYYYYYYYYYYYYYYYYYYYYYYY" />
    </securityProperties>
  </dataCacheClient>
</dataCacheClients>
```

Figure 5.11: Shared Cache Configuration for dynamicdeploy.com

Figure 5.11 illustrates the migrated configuration that dynamicdeploy.com can use for storing application objects in Windows Azure Shared Cache.

Migrating Code

The Windows Azure Caching API follows a factory pattern. The DataCacheFactory object returns a DataCache object. The DataCache object exposes Put and Get methods to store and retrieve objects from the cache respectively. You can also initialize the DataCache object directly with its constructor. This object model is consistent between In-Role Cache and Share Cache. Detailed discussion of the Windows Azure Caching API is out of scope of this book. We will only look at the objects dynamicdeploy.com is using in its website for caching.

The two ways of initializing a DataCache object are shown in Listing 5.3.

```
// default Cache client initialized from
configuration settings.
  DataCacheFactoryConfiguration config =
  new DataCacheFactoryConfiguration("default");

  DataCacheFactory cacheFactory =
  new DataCacheFactory(config);

  DataCache defaultCache =
   cacheFactory.GetDefaultCache();
  // Store and retrieve an object from the default
//cache.
  defaultCache.Put("packageId", "XXXXXXXX");
  string packageId =
  (string) defaultCache.Get("packageId ");

  // Initialize cache client directly (without
//factory)

  DataCache ddCache = new DataCache("ddcache");
  // Put and retrieve a test object from the
default cache.

  ddCache.Put("packageConfig", "YYYYYYYYYYYY");
  string packageConfig =
  (string) ddCache.Get("packageConfig ");
```
Listing 5.3: Using DataCache object

In Listing 5.3, two named cache objects are initialized – default and ddcache. These names must match the name attributes of the dataCacheClient element in the configuration file. These two named cache objects then independently store and retrieve objects. The Put method also allows you to specify the lifetime of an object in the cache.

After migrating the configuration to support Shared Cache, the website should work without any changes to the code.

Performance Benchmarking

For public facing websites, performance is the most important quality attribute. A bad performing website will never succeed in the consumer market. The rule-of-thumb I recommend is that if the new infrastructure does not meet or exceed your website's performance benchmark, do not migrate. To achieve the desired performance, sometimes, you may need to make changes to the design, but if the trade-off is performance versus cost, I recommend siding with performance.

To capture a quick performance benchmark of dynamicdeploy.com website, I have used http://www.webpagetest.org, http://loadimpact.com, and http://www.neustar.biz. Figure 5.12 illustrates the performance results of an automated test run from NeuStar.

Figure 5.12: Neustart Load Testing Results

Load testing results from three different tools will provide you with a performance benchmark that you compare with the migrated website. If WAWS does not provide you with the same or better performance results, then you should not migrate the website to WAWS.

Estimated Operating Cost

Migration decision not only depends on the feature parity between the current and the future environment, but also the impact on operating cost in the new environment. Table 5.4 lists the pricing comparison between dynamicdeploy.com on Cloud Services and dynamicdeploy.com on WAWS.

Feature	Current Costs/month	Future Costs/month
Windows Azure Cloud Service	$231.04	$19.35 (Shared: 2 instances)

	4 Small Cores (2 Web Roles and 2 Worker Roles)	$148.80 (Standard: 2 instances) $115.32 (Worker Role: 2 instances)
Windows Azure Storage	$71.75 (1,025GB)	$71.75 (1,025GB)
Windows Azure SQL database	$9.99 (1GB)	$9.99 (1GB)
Windows Azure Caching	Not Used	$25 2 Basic Units
Bandwidth	$11.40 (100GB)	$11.40 (100GB)
Total	$324.18	With Shared Plan: $253 With Standard Plan: $382.46

Compute services represent majority of the operating costs when running the application in Windows Azure. When you migrate your website from Cloud Services to WAWS, the operating cost depends on the plan you choose in WAWS. For Standard Plan, the cost difference is not significant, but you get the benefit of running up to 500 websites in a region on a Standard instance. For Shared Plan, the cost can be significantly lower and you get the benefit of running 100 websites in the same region. If your solution consists of hundreds of websites, then migrating to WAWS may be the best choice.

Summary

In this chapter you learned to build a website capability model on an existing website that will help you decide the efforts required in migrating existing websites to WAWS. Two breaking changes were identified in the website capability model of dynamicdeploy.com – Session Management and Cache Management. Next, you learned how to migrate session management and cache from In-Role Caching to Shared Cache.

At the time of writing, dynamicdeploy.com website was fully migrated to WAWS and was in the testing phase. We chose to use Azure SQL database for session management and in-memory cache because Windows Azure Shared Cache was still in preview, and we were not ready to deploy the website in production with dependency on preview technologies. The final decision will depend on two factors – Performance impact after migration, and the cost benefit of running multiple future websites on WAWS. In the next chapter, we will migrate the popular MVC Music Store website to WAWS.

Bibliography

Microsoft Corporation. (2012). *Windows Azure Web Site Documentation*. Retrieved from Windows Azure : http://www.windowsazure.com/en-us/documentation/services/web-sites/?fb=en-us

Chapter 6

MIGRATING ASP.NET MVC MUSIC STORE

Using ASP.NET Model View Controller (MVC) framework is now considered as a norm in building ASP.NET web applications. MVC Music Store sample web application is a popular reference implementation of MVC created by Microsoft. Although the web application provides a great reference to learning ASP.NET MVC programming model, it is not designed to address real-world scalability requirements of a website. In this chapter, you will learn to publish ASP.NET MVC Music Store website on Windows Azure Web Sites (WAWS), and also extend it with real-world capabilities such as Search, Advertising, and Analytics.

Note: For this exercise, you will need to download the latest version of the MVC Music Store website from http://mvcmusicstore.codeplex.com/

Music Store Architecture

The MVC Music Store is a lightweight sample E-commerce store that demonstrates different features of ASP.NET MVC such as Razor syntax, client-side validation, ViewModels, and Entity Framework. In this chapter, we will not study the details of the web application itself, but instead focus on extending parts of the web application architecture, and publishing it in WAWS.

Note: For detailed construction of the Music Store website, please follow the link below:

http://www.asp.net/mvc/tutorials/mvc-music-store/mvc-music-store-part-1

After downloading the Music Store web application, and going through the source code and documentation, I have created a simple diagram of its architecture as illustrated in Figure 6.1.

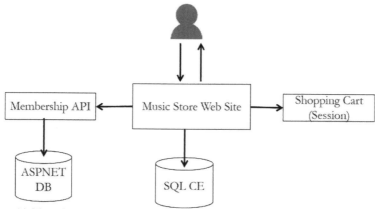

Figure 6.1: Music Store Current Architecture

In Figure 6.1, because the website is for learning purposes only, observe that it is designed to run locally on one machine. The usage of SQL Server Compact Database (SQL CE), In-Memory Sessions, and a local ASP.NET Membership database makes it a single machine website. Can this website work in a highly scalable WAWS environment? To answer this question, as learned in the previous chapter, we need to build a website capability model to visualize and estimate the efforts required to scale this website in the cloud. Table 6.1 lists the comparison between current and future capabilities of the Music Store website.

Table 6.1: Music Store Web Site Capability Model

Capability	Single Machine (Current State)	WAWS (Future State)	Notes
Identity	ASP.NET	ASP.NET	Migrating existing

Management	Membership API Local SQL Server Database stored in App_Data folder	Membership API Azure SQL database with ASP.NET Universal Providers	databases to Azure SQL database may cause issues if the databases use features that are incompatible with Azure SQL database.
Session Management	In-Memory	Windows Azure Shared Cache OR Azure SQL database	Windows Azure Shared Cache has cost associated with it.
Caching	None	Static for images	
Data Storage	SQL CE Database for application data (MvcMusicStore.sdf) Local SQL Database for Membership data (ASPNETDB.MDF)	Windows Azure SQL Database to host application and Membership and Session data	Migrating SQL CE Database to Azure SQL database may be an issue if the database requires features that are incompatible with Azure SQL database. The ASP.NET Universal Providers database schema is not compatible with the local ASP.NET Membership database schema.
User Experience	ASP.NET MVC, HTML, JavaScript	ASP.NET MVC, HTML, JavaScript	Core ASP.NET web controls and UI works as-is in WAWS.
Framework Runtime Requirements	.NET 4.0+	.NET 4.0+	.NET 4.5 is supported in WAWS.
Data Security at rest	NA	NA	Data is not secured at rest.
Data Security in transit	NA	NA	Data is not secured in transit.
Load-balancing	None	Windows Azure Load-balancer	
Scale-Up	Local Machine Size	Standard Mode and Virtual Machine Size	
Scale-Out	Cannot scale to more than one instance in	Shared or Standard Mode	Only Shared and Standard modes support

	its current state		scale-out in WAWS.
Monitoring & Diagnostics	None	Built-in Monitoring or Third-party software (e.g. New Relic) Logs stored locally or in Windows Azure Storage	
Geo-deployment	None	Initiate a new deployment in a new region. Traffic Manager is not supported in WAWS.	
Content Delivery Network	Current website does not use CDN	Migrated website will not need CDN	WAWS can be configured to use CDN if needed in the future, or use a third-party CDN.
Message Bus	None	None	
Integration	No specific integration requirements	No specific integration requirements	
Configuration Management	web.config	WAWS Configuration	
Search	Uses browse functionality that queries the database directly.	Use ElasticSearch as an external index and query service for the Music Store.,	
Analytics	None	Add custom Piwik Analytics	
Ecommerce	Custom workflow	Custom Workflow	

From the capability model, the database migration activity can be tagged as a high-risk item requiring detailed attention, estimation, and testing. We don't have experience in migrating SQL Server Compact Edition (SQL CE) database, and the ASPNET Membership database is incompatible with the ASP.NET Universal Providers. Next, Figure 6.2 illustrates the future state architecture of the Music Store website running in WAWS with ElasticSearch and Piwik Analytics.

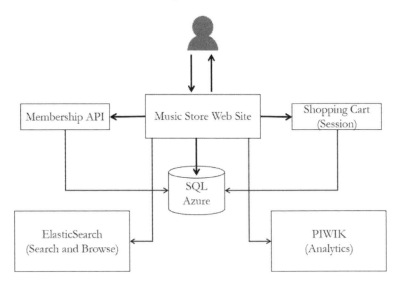

Figure 6.2: Music Store Architecture in WAWS

In Figure 6.2, the Membership and Session APIs leverage a single Azure SQL database. The ElasticSearch and Piwik are external services that do not currently run on WAWS. Therefore, we will need to run them on Windows Azure Virtual Machines. The migration is Music Store website can be split into the following six activities:

1) Migrating Databases
2) Deploying to Windows Azure Web Sites
3) Enabling Continuous Deployment
4) Adding Search with ElasticSearch
5) Adding Analytics with Piwik
6) Testing
7) Performance Testing

Migrating Databases

No matter how small your website is, your database is still the 800 pound gorilla when it comes to migrations. The application is handicapped without its databases, and based on my experience, database migration will require the most attention even in migrating smallest of the websites to the cloud. The Music Store website is no exception. The two databases that the Music Store uses are of different kinds and need different migration processes. The application database MvcMusicStore.sdf is a SQL Server Compact Edition (SQL CE) database whereas the membership database ASPNETDB.MDF is a SQL Server database. Both the databases reside in the App_Data folder of the website.

Migrating Application Database (SQLCE) to Azure SQL database

SQL Server Management Studio does not support direct migration from SQLCE to Azure SQL database. WebMatrix does support migration of SQLCE to Azure SQL database but it only offers the migration option when opened within a website. I tested the free third-party tool ExportSqlCE (http://exportsqlce.codeplex.com/) for exporting the database schema and data to an SQL file, and it worked without any issues. Listed below is a step-by-step procedure for exporting the SQLCE database to Azure SQL database.

Step 1: Download the ExportSQLCE Tool.

Download the ExportSQLCE tool from

http://exportsqlce.codeplex.com/

Note: Download the ZIP file with the name (or a recent version) exportsqlce40.3.5.2.33.zip - SQL Compact 4.0 command line utility to generate a script with schema and data

---

Step 2: Extract the tools to a known location on the file system.

Extract the tool to a known location and open command prompt to point at that location.

Step 3: Run the ExportSQLCE Tool on MvcMusicStore.sdf database.

Run the tool on MvcMusicStore.sdf, which is in the App_Data folder of the Music Store website.

```
>ExportSqlCe40.exe
"DataSource=C:\musics\App_Data\MvcMusicStore.s
df;" mvcmusic.sql
```

Figure 6.3: Running ExportSqlCE40.exe to export SQLCE database

The tool will export the data and schema of MvcMusicStore.sdf to mvcmusic.sql file.

Step 4: Create a new SQL database named mvcmusic on the local SQL Server.

Open SQL Server Management studio and create a new database named mvcmusic on the desktop SQL Server instance.

Figure 6.4: Create a new database mvcmusic

Step 5: Create database objects

Create a new query window, open the mvcmusic.sql file in it and click Execute.

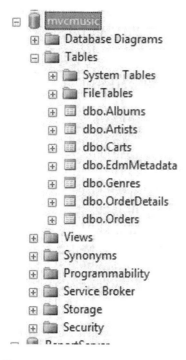

Figure 6.5: mvcmusic tables and data

After executing the commands from mvcmusic.sql, all the database objects from MvcMusicStore.sdf will be created in the mvcmusic database. In some cases, you can create the database directly in Azure SQL database, but in the case of MvcMusicStore.sdf, some of the tables don't have clustered index, which is a requirement for tables in Azure SQL database, and also a recommended best practice. If you run the mvcmusic.sql on Azure SQL database directly, you will see the following error message

Msg 40054, Level 16, State 1, Line 1

Tables without a clustered index are not supported in this version of SQL Server. Please create a clustered index and try again.

But, when you run the commands in the local SQL Server, it automatically creates clustered index for all the primary keys. You can add clustered indexes manually to the auto-generated mvcmusic.sql script, but I decided to let the local SQL Server create clustered indexes for me.

Step 6: Deploy Database to Azure SQL database

SQL Server 2012 has a built-in tool called "Deploy Database to SQL Azure". Right-click on the mvcmusic database on the local SQL Server and select Tasks > Deploy Database to SQL Azure, as illustrated in Figure 6.6

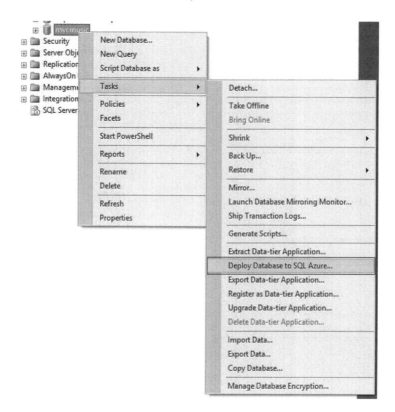

Figure 6.6: Deploy Database to Azure SQL database

On the Deployment Settings window, specify your Azure SQL database server details as illustrated in Figures 6.7, 6.8 and 6.9 below. If you have not created an Azure SQL database server before, you can login to your account in the Windows Azure portal and create a new Azure SQL database server.

Figure 6.7: Azure SQL database Deployment Settings

Note that the tool creates a temporary bacpac file and then migrates it to Azure SQL database. A bacpac file represents a Data-Tier Application which includes all the database objects required for a backup and restore procedure.

Next, click on the Connect button to specify your Azure SQL database connection details.

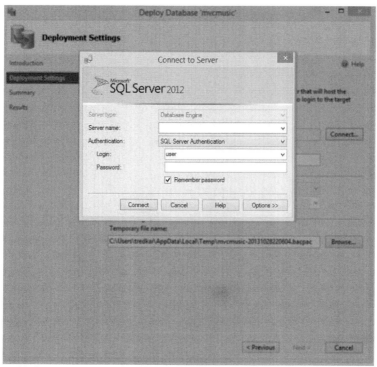

Figure 6.8: Connect to Azure SQL database server

If you have not set up firewall rules for connecting to the Azure SQL database, you will need to login to the portal and add your public IP Address to the Azure SQL database firewall access table.

After the connection is successful, you will need to choose the size and type of the Azure SQL database you want to create – Web or Business edition. For demo purposes, select 1GB size and Web Edition database.

Figure 6.9: Select Azure SQL Database Type and Size

Click Next to create the database. If the migration is successful, you will see an Operation Complete window as illustrated in Figure 6.10.

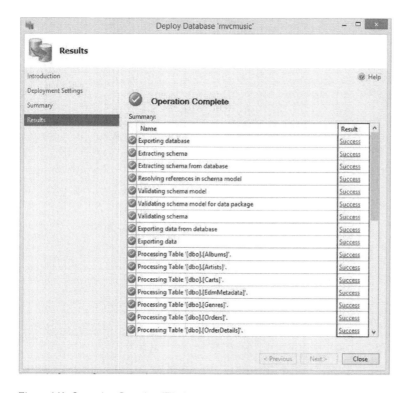

Figure 6.10: Operation Complete Window

Now that the database is created in Azure SQL, we need the connection string to add to the Music Store's web.config file.

Step 7: Copy Azure SQL Connection String

Login to the Windows Azure portal and navigate to the Azure SQL database page.

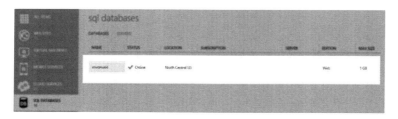

Figure 6.11: mvcmusic database in Azure SQL

From the database landing page, copy the ADO.Net connection string by clicking on View SQL Database connection strings for ADO.Net....

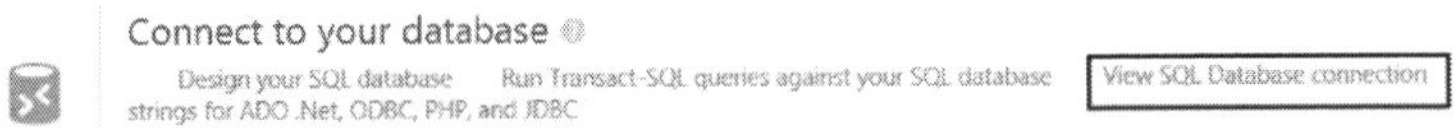

Connect to your database ◎

Design your SQL database   Run Transact-SQL queries against your SQL database   View SQL Database connection

strings for ADO .Net, ODBC, PHP, and JDBC

Figure 6.12: View SQL Database connection string

Copy the ADO.Net connection string and replace the
{your_password_here} text with your database server password.

Note: In real-world applications, I recommend
creating a dedicated user for accessing Azure SQL
database and not using the server administrator.
You can create a new login from the Azure SQL
Management portal or from SQL Server
Management studio on your desktop. Listing
below shows a sample script for creating LOGINs
and USERs for Azure SQL databases. The code
creates two users ddmyreader in the db_datareader
built-in role, and ddmywriter in the db_datawriter
built-in role.

use [master]

CREATE LOGIN ddmyreader WITH
password='Pass@word1';

CREATE LOGIN ddmywriter WITH
password='Pass@word1';

use [mvcmusic]

CREATE USER ddmywriter FROM LOGIN
ddmywriter;

EXEC sp_addrolemember 'db_datawriter',
'ddmywriter';

CREATE USER ddmyreader FROM LOGIN ddmyreader;

EXEC sp_addrolemember 'db_datareader', 'ddmyreader';

Step 8: Modify web.config

With the new mvcmusic database created in Azure SQL, you can now modify the database connection string in Music Store's web.config for pointing the website to the Azure SQL database. Figure 6.13 illustrates the new connection string.

Figure 6.13: Modified Connection String

Note that the connection string has been modified from SQL CE to SQL Server, and finally to Azure SQL. At each stage of modification, I recommend running and testing the website locally. Next, run the website locally on your desktop to retrieve data from the mvcmusic database in Azure SQL. If the connection string is accurate, the website should run without any errors.

Figure 6.14: Music Store Running Locally

Although the Music Store website is accessing the database in Azure SQL, the Membership API for managing users and roles is still accessing the ASPNETDB.MDF database in the App_Data folder. The sessions are also still managed in the machine's memory. For a real-world cloud-enabled website, you cannot use a local database and in-memory sessions. With a local database, the website is only aware of the data on its own machine, and will simple not function when running at scale on multiple instances. Therefore, we need to migrate even the ASPNETDB.MDF to Azure SQL, and enable Azure SQL to manage sessions.

Migrating Membership Database (SQL Server) to Azure SQL

When Microsoft created Azure SQL, the traditional ASP.NET tools (aspnet_regsql.exe) for creating membership and session database objects did not work on it due to the constraints imposed by Azure SQL. Some of the features used by these tools were not supported in Azure SQL. The ASP.NET team took a long time in releasing ASP.NET Universal Providers package that will install the membership and session objects in any SQL database. But, there was a catch, the new database objects created by the ASP.NET Universal Providers were (and still are) incompatible with the database objects created by the traditional tools. The ASPNETDB.MDF database in the Music Store is created using traditional tools and will not migrate easily to Azure SQL. Since this is a learning environment, I recommend deleting the ASPNETDB.MDF database and using the ASP.NET Universal Providers for membership and session management.

For migrating the membership databases, we can leverage the same mvcmusic database. Listed below is a step-by-step procedure for leveraging the Azure SQL mvcmusic database for membership and session management.

Step 1: Installing Microsoft ASP.NET Universal Providers

1) Open the Music Store website in Visual Studio.
2) Right-click on the website project and select Manage NuGet Packages....

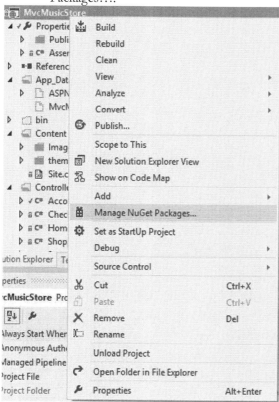

Figure 6.15: Manage NuGet Packages

3) Search and Install Microsoft ASP.NET Universal Providers Core package.

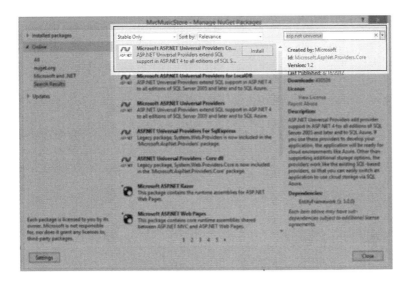

Figure 6.16: Install Microsoft ASP.NET Universal Provider Core package

Installing the universal providers will create profile, membership, role and session sections in the web.config file. Change the connectionStringName for each of these section from "DefaultConnection" to "MusicStoreEntities". In the Music Store's web.config, we don't have a database connection named DefaultConnection in the connectionstrings section. Because we plan to leverage the same mvcmusic database for application, membership, and sessions, you can point the respective configuration settings to the MusicStoreEntities database connection. Next, enable the roleManger by setting its enabled attribute to true. Figure 6.17 shows the final profile, membership, role, and session sections from the web.config file.

```
<profile defaultProvider="DefaultProfileProvider">
  <providers>
    <add type="System.Web.Providers.DefaultProfileProvider"
         name="DefaultProfileProvider"
         applicationName="/"
         connectionStringName="MusicStoreEntities" />
  </providers>
</profile>
<membership defaultProvider="DefaultMembershipProvider">
  <providers>
    <add type="System.Web.Providers.DefaultMembershipProvider"
         name="DefaultMembershipProvider"
         connectionStringName="MusicStoreEntities"
      enablePasswordRetrieval="false"
         enablePasswordReset="true"
         requiresQuestionAndAnswer="false"
         requiresUniqueEmail="false"
         maxInvalidPasswordAttempts="5"
         minRequiredPasswordLength="6"
         minRequiredNonalphanumericCharacters="0"
         passwordAttemptWindow="10"
         applicationName="/" />

  </providers>
</membership>
<roleManager defaultProvider="DefaultRoleProvider" enabled="true">
  <providers>
    <add type="System.Web.Providers.DefaultRoleProvider"
         name="DefaultRoleProvider" applicationName="/"
         connectionStringName="MusicStoreEntities" />
  </providers>
</roleManager>
<sessionState customProvider="DefaultSessionProvider" mode="Custom">
  <providers>
    <add type="System.Web.Providers.DefaultSessionStateProvider"
         name="DefaultSessionProvider"
         connectionStringName="MusicStoreEntities" />
  </providers>
</sessionState>
```

Figure 6.17: Final web.config file

Next, run the website locally and observe the membership and session tables created in the Azure SQL mvcdatabase.

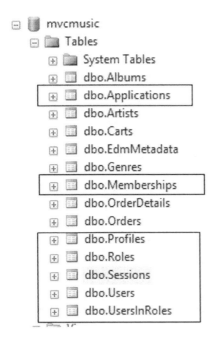

Figure 6.18: Membership and Session tables created in Azure SQL

When you run the website, the universal provider classes automatically create the membership and session tables in the specified database. Now, we have the same database that shares application, membership, and session data. We successfully moved the data-tier out of the web-tier in order to scale both the tiers independently of each other.

Step 2: Adding Administrator user to the membership database

If you remember, we deleted the ASPNETDB.MDF database that consisted of some pre-defined users such as Administrator. In the newly created database, we don't have any administrators. Without an administrator, you won't be able to manage music albums on the website. In order to create a new administrator user, we use the Membership API to create an administrator if one does not exist. We want to perform this function only once, but we should be fine performing the check every time the website restarts. In Global.asax, the Application_Start() function is called only once when the website starts. We can add the administrator account creation code in this function as shown in Listing 6.1.

```
    var memUser =
  Membership.FindUsersByName("Administrator")
  .Cast<MembershipUser>()
  .FirstOrDefault();

  if (memUser == null)

  {
  MembershipUser mu =
  Membership.CreateUser("Administrator",
"password123!",
  "admin@mvcmusicstore.com");
    if(mu != null)
    {
     Roles.AddUserToRole
     ("Administrator", "Administrator");
    }
  }else
  {
    string[]roles =
  Roles.GetRolesForUser("Administrator");
    if(roles == null || roles.Length == 0)
    {

     Roles.AddUserToRole
     ("Administrator", "Administrator");
    }
  }
```

Listing 6.1: Create a new Administrator account

In Listing 6.1, we first check if a user named "Administrator" exists in the membership database. If it does not exist, then we create a new one and then add it to the Administrator role. If an Administrator already exists, then add it to the Administrator role. Now, when the website starts, it will create a new Administrator in the newly created mvcmusic database in Azure SQL. Next, run the website to test whether you can login as an Administrator and manage the music.

Figure 6.19: Manage your music

If the website runs satisfactorily on your desktop, then you are now ready to publish it to Windows Azure Web Sites (WAWS) because you have successfully removed the dependencies that restricted it to run on a single server. In WAWS, when you scale-out the Music Store website the mvsmusic database in Azure SQL will support all the website instances in application, membership, and session data.

Deploying to Windows Azure Web Sites (WAWS)

After the website is tested successfully on your desktop with the database running in Azure SQL, it is now safe to publish the website in WAWS and test if it maintains its fidelity. Listed below is a step-by-step procedure for publishing the Music Store website to WAWS, and enabling Continuous Deployment with Visual Studio Visual Studio Online (VSOnline).

Step 1: Download Publish Profile

Login to your account in Windows Azure portal and create a new website, as illustrated in Figure 6.20.

Figure 6.20: Create a new website.

> Note: Please make sure you create the website in
> the same region as the mvcmusic Azure SQL
> database, otherwise you will incur data transfer
> and performance costs.

After the website is created, navigate to the landing page of the website and download its publish profile by clicking on "Download the publish profile" link.

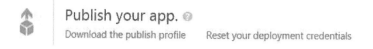

Publish your app. ⊘
Download the publish profile   Reset your deployment credentials

Figure 6.21: Download publish profile.

Step 2: Publish the website

Next, right-click on the website in Visual Studio and click Publish to open the Publish Web wizard. Click on the Import button and select the publish profile file you downloaded in the previous step.

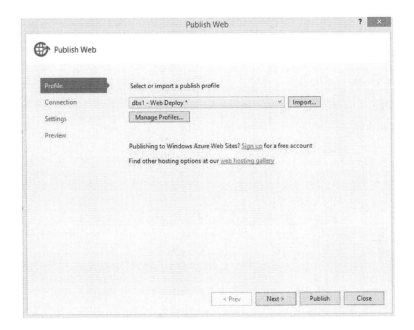

Figure 6.22: Import Publish Profile

As shown in Figure 6.22, the publish profile will show the name of your website. Click Next to validate the connection.

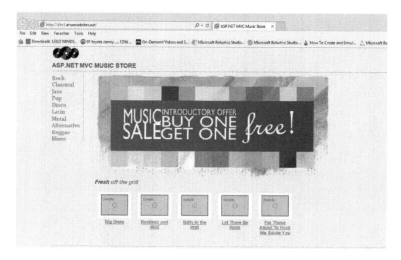

Figure 6.23: Validate Connection

Click Next to verify settings and then finally click Publish to deploy the website in WAWS. After the site is deployed successfully, Visual Studio will open a new browser window and point it to the website. If you have followed all the steps correctly, the website should run without any errors.

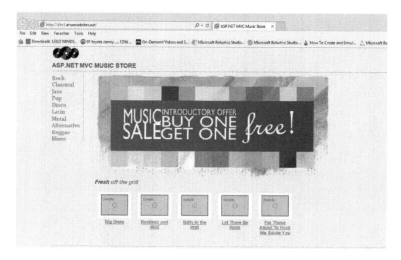

Figure 6.24: Music Store Running in WAWS

Test all the features of the website such as managing music, shopping cart, browse, checkout, etc..

Step 3: Check-In Source Code in Visual Studio Online

If you don't have a VSOnline account, open one at http://tfs.visualstudio.com. Registration is free and as an individual developer, you can create projects for free. Create a new project named MVCMusicStoreWithSearch.

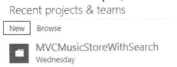

Recent projects & teams

New   Browse

MVCMusicStoreWithSearch
Wednesday

Figure 6.25: New VSOnline Project

In Visual Studio, connect to your VSOnline by clicking on Team > Connect To Team Foundation Server. Once the connection is successful, you can add the Music Store solution to the VSOnline source code repository by right-clicking on the solution and selecting Add Solution to Source Control. Select VSOnline, and then select the MVCMusicStoreWithSearch project as shown in Figure 6.26.

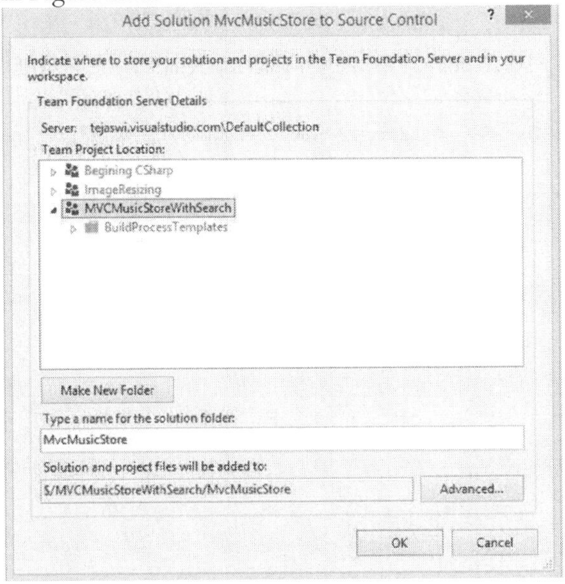

Figure 6.26: MvcMusicStore VSOnline Project

Click OK to associate the source code with the selected VSOnline project. Next right-click on the Music Store solution and click Check-In to check-in all the source code to VSOnline.

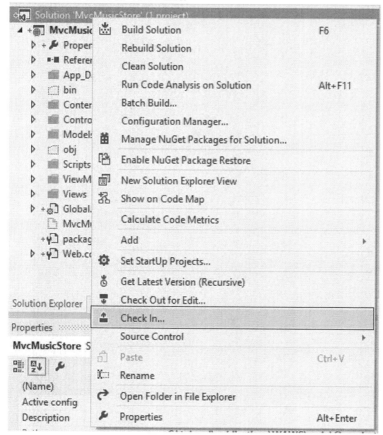

Figure 6.27: Check-In Code

On the Pending Changes window, click on Check-In. The check-in action will upload all the Music Store source code to VSOnline source code repository. The Music Store source code is now versioned by VSOnline.

Step 4: Enable Continuous Deployment

To enable continuous deployment, login to the Windows Azure portal and navigate to the website's landing page in the WAWS section.

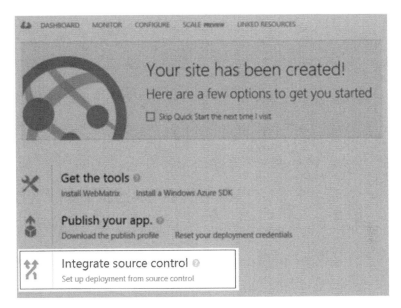

Figure 6.28: Integration source control

Click the "Integration source control" link to start the source control integration process. On the "Where is your source code?" window, select Visual Studio Online and click the next arrow button.

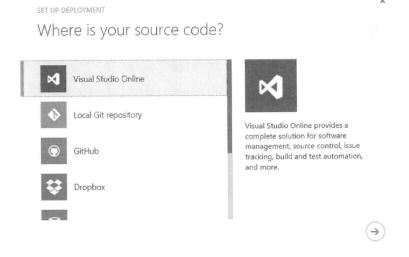

Figure 6.29: Select VSOnline

On the Connection Request window, you will be asked to authorize the connection between Windows Azure and your VSOnline account.

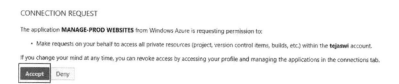

CONNECTION REQUEST

The application **MANAGE-PROD WEBSITES** from Windows Azure is requesting permission to:

• Make requests on your behalf to access all private resources (project, version control items, builds, etc.) within the **tejaswi** account.

If you change your mind at any time, you can revoke access by accessing your profile and managing the applications in the connections tab.

Accept   Deny

Figure 6.30: Approve Access

Click Accept to authorize the access. Next, on the "Choose a repository to deploy" window, select the MVCMusicStoreWithSearch project you created in VSOnline earlier.

SET UP DEPLOYMENT

Choose a repository to deploy

REPOSITORY NAME

MVCMusicStoreWithSearch

Figure 6.31: Choose MVCMusicStoreWithSearch Repository

Click the OK button to establish the link between your website in WAWS and your VSOnline project. Figure 6.32 shows the website musicstore linked to VSOnline account https://tejaswi.visualstudio.com.

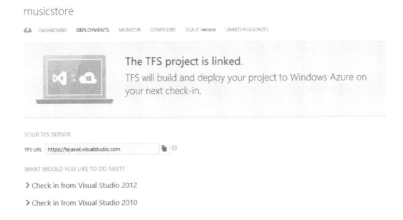

Figure 6.32: VSOnline Project Linked

Next, make some changes to the Music Store in Visual Studio and check-in the code. The deployment will automatically start in WAWS. On a successful deployment, you will see a stamp of Active Deployment in the Deployments section of your website as illustrated in Figure 6.33.

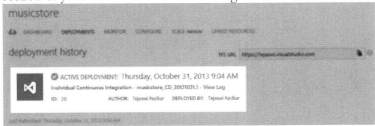

Figure 6.33: Active Deployment Stamp of Music Store

Now, whenever you check-in the Music Store code in VSOnline, a deployment will be automatically triggered in WAWS. Therefore, it is now easy to deploy changes dynamically and also pose a high risk of breaking the website if the changes are not tested.

After revisiting Figure 6.2 and the migration task list, we have successfully completed the migration of the Music Store to WAWS with a centralized application, membership, and session management database. We have also set up continuous deployment between the Music Store website and Music Store's primary source control system – VSOnline. Listed below are the completed and remaining tasks from our exercise.

1) Migrating Databases (Completed)
2) Deploying to Windows Azure Web Sites (Completed)

3) Enabling Continuous Deployment (Completed)
4) Adding Search with ElasticSearch
5) Adding Analytics with Piwik
6) Testing
7) Performance Testing

The next two chapters – Integrating with ElasticSearch and Enabling Analytics require us to use open source products and Windows Azure Virtual Machines (VMs).

Summary

In this chapter you learned important migration techniques for migrating not only ASP.NET websites to WAWS, but also other supporting components like SQLCE and SQL Server databases to Azure SQL. You also successfully setup continuous deployment with VSOnline. The exercise is not complete yet, in the interest of readability, I have broken down the migration into three chapters. In next two chapters, you will learn to quickly deploy ElasticSearch in Windows Azure VM, and also integrate search functionality in the Music Store website.

Chapter 7

INTEGRATING WITH ELASTICSEARCH

Search is a basic necessity of today's websites. If you navigate to some of your favorite websites, you will notice each website has a high-performing search feature, and probably will be its most used feature. Because of the hierarchical nature of websites, users prefer searching for information from the home page instead of navigating by clicking links. Even in large enterprise products like Microsoft SharePoint Server, search represents a core feature. In the open source domain, SOLR (from Apache Foundation) and ElasticSearch has gained enough momentum in public as well as enterprises to be considered as mainstream search engines. Both these search engines are based on Lucene indexing and search software library (also maintained by Apache Foundation). SOLR and ElasticSearch extend Lucene's core functionality by offering add-on services. Unfortunately, .NET Framework natively does not provide any search and indexing support which has been on my wish list for a long time. I think search and indexing engine should be embedded right into core .NET and ASP.NET frameworks.

In this chapter, you will learn to deploy ElasticSearch quickly and add some basic search and browse capability, powered by ElasticSearch, to the Music Store website. ElasticSearch deserves a book of its own and therefore the chapter will not cover deeper details of ElasticSearch server. I selected ElasticSearch over SOLR for this exercise because it is easier to deploy, has a scalable architecture, and runs flawlessly on Windows Azure Virtual Machines (VMs). The objective is this chapter is to build a website feature that communicates with another Windows Azure service (VMs).

Basic Search Concepts

In its simplest form, a search engine consists of three core services – A crawler, an index, and a query service. The crawler is a batch task that crawls websites at regular intervals. In very large search engines like Bing, the crawler will be continuously crawling the entire internet. The crawler captures metadata from different kinds of data sources and then forwards the data to the indexing service to index and store it. Indexing a data (also sometimes known as inverted index) is the process of storing the mapping of keywords to its location in documents. The index data structure is designed for faster retrieval of information based on keywords also known as search terms. The query service provides an API for querying data from the index. Sometimes, the query service has caching abilities to store indexed data in memory for faster retrieval. The crawler, index, and query each play a specific role in providing a complete search and retrieval capability. Figure 7.1 illustrates a high-level search engine architecture.

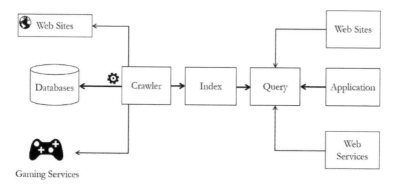

Figure 7.1: High-level search engine architecture.

In Figure 7.1, the crawler crawls different types of data sources, the index stores the data, and the query service exposes an API for searching the data in the index. Any type of web-enabled application can then call the query service to retrieve information.

Usually, the index and query services operate in tandem, whereas crawler operated independently. You don't need a crawler to build a search index. Most search engines have APIs to directly ingest data into the index. For the Music Store website, we will not be using a crawler, but instead we will be ingesting the data directly in the index using ElasticSearch's REST API. Figure 7.2 illustrates Music Store website's search architecture.

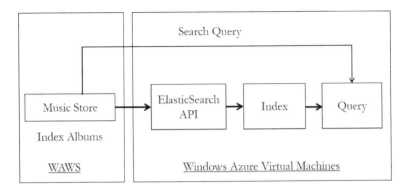

Figure 7.2: Music Store Search Architecture

As shown in Figure 7.2, the Music Store website (running in WAWS) ingests the data into the ElasticSearch server running in a Windows Azure Virtual Machine (VM). The VM hosts ElasticSearch's indexing and querying components. The Music Store then accesses ElasticSearch's query API for retrieving the search results.

This was a simplistic explanation of the search engine architecture. In reality, each component of the search engine is technologically advanced in its own sense, and cannot be detailed in this book. In the next section, let's learn more about ElasticSearch to help you understand the integration process between ElasticSearch and the Music Store website.

More about ElasticSearch

ElasticSearch is a data store, similar to a database, but the method of storing and retrieving data is completely different to a database. ElasticSearch provides you with an API to store application specific JavaScript Object Notation (JSON) objects and does not require schema definition. ElasticSearch determines the schema of the JSON object at runtime, and therefore ElasticSearch is also called a *"Schema-less search engine"*. In larger environments, you have the ability to define a schema for validation purposes.

Running ElasticSearch on Windows as well as Linux (and UNIX) operating systems requires only a few steps:

1) Install the latest Java Software Development Kit (Java SDK)
   https://java.com/en/download/index.jsp
2) Download and Unzip ElasticSearch from
   http://www.elasticsearch.org
3) Run ElasticSearch from the command prompt

```
c:\elasticsearch-0.90.5\bin>service
```

```
Usage: service.bat
install|remove|start|stop|manager [SERVICE_ID]
```

That's it, you have an ElasticSearch server running locally. You can access ElasticSearch's REST API from the browser by navigating to the following URL

http://localhost:9200/

ElasticSearch responds with a JSON file consisting of the server status as shown in Listing 7.1.

```
{
  "ok" : true,
  "status" : 200,
  "name" : "Arsenal",
  "version" : {
    "number" : "0.90.0",
    "snapshot_build" : false
  },
  "tagline" : "You Know, for Search"
}
```
Listing 7.1: JSON response from ElasticSearch

The response consists of status of the server, name of the cluster ("Arsenal"), ElasticSearch version, and a tagline that is randomly generated every time you restart ElasticSearch.

Note: You can find more detailed instructions on setting up ElasticSearch on its website

http://www.elasticsearch.org/guide/en/elasticsearch/refere
nce/current/setup-service-win.html

To scale out ElasticSearch, you have to just start another instance on the same server or network. ElasticSearch sends multicast messages to detect other instances and automatically creates a cluster. The cluster allows you to replicate your index across multiple servers, and also distribute your index across multiple files on the same server, also known as *"shards"*.

Note: Since this book is about building solutions using **WAWS**, I have covered only limited concepts about ElasticSearch. The objective of this section is to enable search capability in the Music Store website and along the way, teach you the process. In this section, I have included hyperlinks to important resources on the internet for you to learn more about ElasticSearch as a search platform.

http://www.elasticsearchtutorial.com/

http://www.elasticsearchtutorial.com/basic-elasticsearch-concepts.html

http://joelabrahamsson.com/elasticsearch-101/

http://www.elasticsearch.org

In the next section, we will use the open source NEST .NET SDK for calling ElasticSearch's REST API.

Modifying Music Store to use ElasticSearch[7]

The Music Store website does not support search functionality in its original design. But, in today's real world websites, search is a basic necessity. As the volume of music grows on the website, it will be difficult for the users to search for music they want to purchase. Search makes it easier for users to quickly search and that reduces the purchasing time of the user. From a

---

[7] Joel Abrahamsson has written a nice blog article on extending Music Store with ElasticSearch
http://joelabrahamsson.com/extending-aspnet-mvc-music-store-with-elasticsearch/

business perspective, as quickly a user can find his favorite music on the website, the faster the purchase transaction is going to be. In our design, we will ingest the music albums from the Music Store database into ElasticSearch directly from the website administrator's user interface.

Listed below is a four-step procedure for enabling search functionality in the Music Store website:

Step 1: Deploying ElasticSearch from dynamicdeploy.com
Step 2: Install NEST ElasticSearch Client
Step 3: Updating Music Store Source Code
Step 4: Testing Search and Browse with ElasticSearch

Step 1: Deploying ElasticSearch from dynamicdeploy.com[8]

The website dynamicdeploy.com offers point-click deployment of ElasticSearch virtual machine on Windows Azure for free. It also supports a cluster deployment for subscribed users, but for this exercise, we will use the free virtual machine.

1) Navigate to http://www.dynamicdeploy.com and register as a user (free)
2) Search for ElasticSearch and click on details to go to ElasticSearch details page. You can also navigate directly to the ElasticSearch details page by navigating to the following link
   https://www.dynamicdeploy.com/packagedetails.aspx?pkgid=89
3) On the package details page, click on the Deploy button

---

[8] Dynamicdeploy.com has a blog published on deploying ElasticSearch on Windows Azure

http://www.opensourceazure.com/blog/2013/05/29/point-click-deploy-elasticsearch-on-azure/#sthash.qQO4w8mB.dpbs

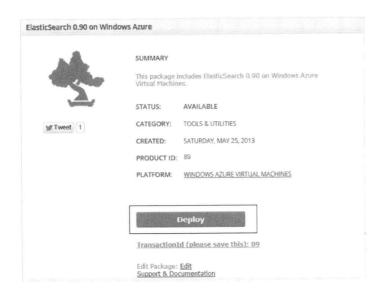

Figure 7.3: Click Deploy button

4) On the "Select a Supported Datacenter" page, select a supported datacenter and click Next.

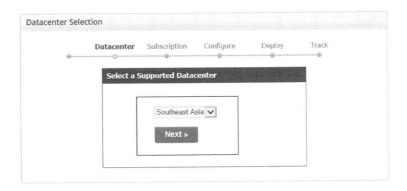

Figure 7.4: Supported Datacenter

5) Next, on the Subscription Information page, upload the .publishsettings file of your subscription.

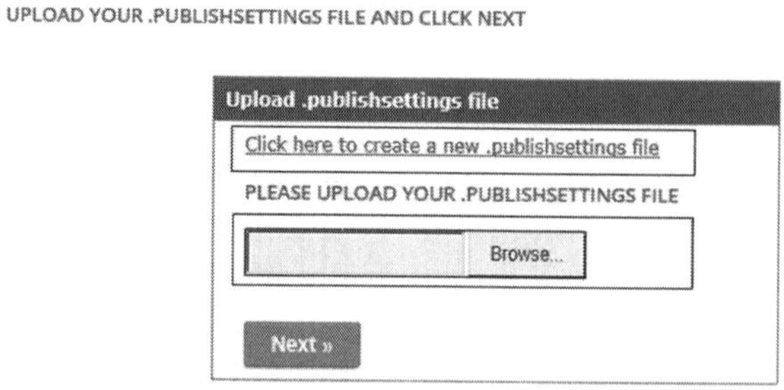

UPLOAD YOUR .PUBLISHSETTINGS FILE AND CLICK NEXT

Figure 7.5: Upload .publishsettings file

Note: You can also download a .publishsettings file by navigating to the following the link below

https://windows.azure.com/download/publishprofile.aspx

---

6) After you upload the .publishsettings file, dynamicdeploy.com will query your subscription and provide you with a list of cloud services and storage accounts within the selected datacenter. You can also create new cloud services and storage accounts.

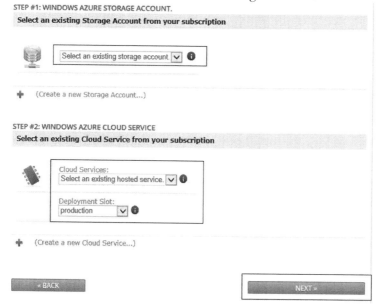

Figure 7.6: Select Cloud Services

Click Next to navigate to the provisioning process screen.

7) From the provisioning process screen, note down the following items:

i)   Administrator's user name

ii)   Administrator's password

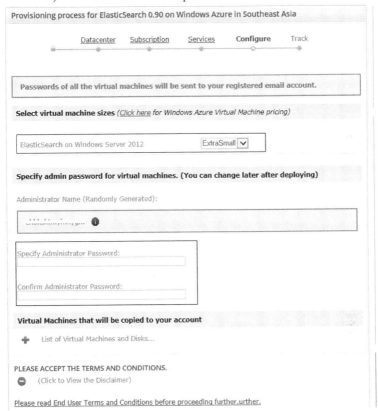

Figure 7.7: Provisioning process screen for ElasticSearch

iii)   Click Accept to start the deployment. After deployment is complete, you will see a screen with the cloud service running, VM running, and deployment time updated; as shown in Figure 7.8.

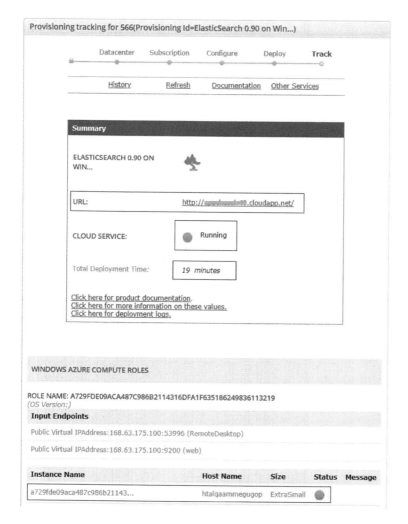

Figure 7.8: ElasticSearch deployed in Windows Azure

In Figure 7.8, the URL field points to the URL of the Windows Azure Cloud Service that is hosting your virtual machine. Till the deployment time appears, the deployment is not complete. The WINDOWS AZURE COMPUTE ROLES section provides you with the list of roles, instance names, hostnames, VM size, and the VM status of the deployment.

8) You can now test the ElasticSearch deployment by typing the URL of the ElasticSearch REST API endpoint in your browser.

   http://[your could service name].cloudapp.net:9200

   e.g. http://elasticsearch.cloudapp.net:9200

   If the deployment is successful, you will receive a JSON file similar to Listing 7.1.

Note: dynamicdeploy.com has a blog article published on deploying ElasticSearch cluster on Windows Azure Virtual Machines here

http://www.opensourceazure.com/blog/2013/10/01/point-click-2-node-elasticsearch-cluster-on-windows-azure-in-minutes/#sthash.9zU5rNF4.dpbs

Step 2: Install NEST ElasticSearch Client

NEST client provides a strongly-typed .NET API for accessing ElasticSearch's REST API.

Note: Source code for NEST is available at https://github.com/Mpdreamz/NEST and the website itself runs on WAWS at http://nest.azurewebsites.net/.

Open the Music Store website in Visual Studio and install NEST – ElasticSearch Client nuget package as illustrated in Figure 7.9.

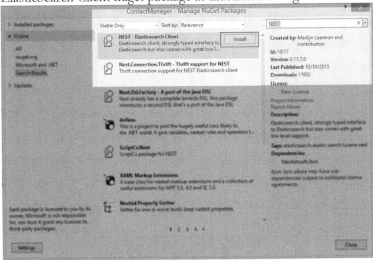

Figure 7.9: Install NEST Client

Installing NEST client will create an assembly reference named "Nest" in the Music Store project. The package also installs JSON.NET nuget package in the project.

Note: Other ElasticSearch clients you can try to experiment with are:

ElasticSearch.Net
https://github.com/medcl/ElasticSearch.Net

PlainElastic.Net
https://github.com/Yegoroff/PlainElastic.Net

Any client you program with, you will still be accessing the same ElasticSearch REST API. Therefore, I recommend testing performance and usability of the APIs before selecting the right one for your project.

Step 3: Updating Music Store Source Code

In this step will follow 3 sub-steps:

a) **Modifying web.config**

Adding the ElasticSearch server's connection Uri and index name to the web.config will make it flexible for you to change the connection at runtime. Index name is the name of the storage index that will consist of the data you store in ElasticSearch. An index name is analogous to a database name where one database server can host multiple databases. Similarly, one ElasticSearch server can host multiple indexes. We will be using only one index for storing Music Store's data.

Open Music Store's web.config and add the following keys (Listing 7.2) and values to the appSettings section.

```
<add
key="elasticsearchUri" value=
"http://[your_cloudservice].cloudapp.net:9200"
/>
  <add
```

```
key="elasticsearchindexname"
value="mvcmusicstore" />
```

Listing 7.2: Modify web.config

You will need to change the [your_cloudservice] text to point to the cloud service where your ElasticSearch deployment exists. The mvcmusicstore is the name of the index and must be unique within the ElasticSearch deployment. So, it can remain the same - mvcmusicstore.

b) Ingesting Albums in ElasticSearch Index

In the Music Store website, the StoreManagerController class consists of all the administrative actions, and therefore would be a perfect place for inserting indexing capabilities. Typically, you would index an album when it is created, but we are adding search functionality on an existing website therefore we need to index all the existing albums. There is already an Index() action in the StoreManagerController class that represents ASP.NET MVC's Index action and has no relationship with the search index whatsoever. We will call our MVC action ReIndex() that will call the NEST API to index the music albums. As a Music Store administrator, you should be able to index the albums by typing the URL http://[music_store_url]:9200/StoreManager/ReIndex in your browser.

Listing 7.3 shows the code snippets for the ReIndex action added to the StoreManagerController class.

```
//Add the assembly reference to NEST
using Nest;

//...

//Define a ReIndex Action
public ActionResult ReIndex()
{
  //Retrieve the elasticsearch Uri from
  //configuration
    string elasticSearchUri =
ConfigurationManager.AppSettings
["elasticsearchUri"];
  //Create a connection settings object with the
```

```
//Uri
  var setting =
new ConnectionSettings(new
  Uri(elasticSearchUri));
  //Create a new ElasticClient object with the
  //connection settings
    var client = new ElasticClient(setting);

  //Retrieve theindex name from configuration
    string elasticsearchindexname =
ConfigurationManager.AppSettings
["elasticsearchindexname"];

  //For each album call the Index() function
    foreach (var album in db.Albums)
    {
        client.Index(album,
elasticsearchindexname, "albums", album.AlbumId);
    }

  //Redirect back to the Index() action
    return RedirectToAction("Index");
}
```
Listing 7.3: Action for Indexing albums

In Listing 7.3, similar to a database connection, you create an ElasticClient connection and then for each album, call the ElasticClient's Index() function with the album information as parameters. The Album class (in the Models folder) consists of a reference to the Genre class, whereas the Genre class includes a list of Albums. This causes circular references in the index and may create an ingestion or indexing problem. For avoiding circular references in the index, modify the Genre class by adding JsonIgnore attribute the Albums property. With this change, the Albums in the index will point to the Genre property, but the Genre objects will not store any Albums. Listing 7.4 shows the changes made to the Genre class as required.

```
using Newtonsoft.Json;
//...

//This attribute prevents circular references
```

```
// between Genre and Albums when serializing.
[JsonIgnore]
public List<Album> Albums { get; set; }
```

Listing 7.4: Modified Genre class to avoid circular references

The JsonIgnore property excludes the property and its value from serializing to a JSON object.

If the continuous deployment was setup successfully for the Music Store, the moment you check-in these code changes, an automatic deployment will be triggered. If not, you can publish it manually as a Windows Azure Web Site. After the home page loads, you can index the albums by typing the following URL.

http://[your_music_store_website]/StoreManager/ReIndex

e.g. http://musicstore.azurewebsites.net/StoreManager/ReIndex

Note that you will be asked to login as an administrator to execute this action. In a real-world application, you will typically index an album when it is created, updated or deleted. Some large applications may run batch job for indexing changes on a regular basis instead of burdening the website with indexing.

After the indexing is complete, you will be redirected to the StoreManager page. To check the contents of the actual index in ElasticSearch, you can navigate to the elastic search head URL

http://[elasticsearch_cloudservice_url]:9200/_plugin/head/

The ElasticSearch Head (http://mobz.github.io/elasticsearch-head/) is a separate plugin that dynamicdeploy.com installs automatically during deployment. The plugin provides you with an administrator's view of the ElasticSearch server and index. When the ElasticSearch head page loads, click on the Browser tab to view the contents of the index. You should see a list of albums as illustrated in Figure 7.10.

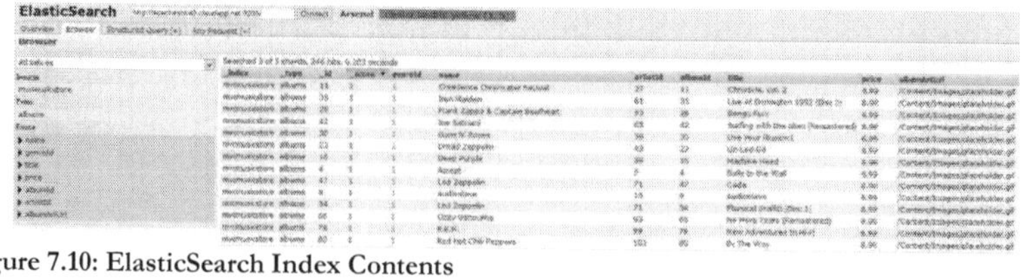

Figure 7.10: ElasticSearch Index Contents

Figure 7.10 illustrates that the data now resides in the index and is available for searching. You can test your search in the "Structured Query" or "Any Request" tabs of the ElasticSearch plugin head web page.

c) Modifying the Browse functionality to return results from ElasticSearch

In Music Store, the Browse action can be found in the StoreController, and it used for browsing albums by their genre. Listing 7.5 shows the default implementation of the browse functionality.

```
public ActionResult Browse(string genre)
{
// Retrieve Genre and its Associated Albums
//from database
  var genreModel =
storeDB.Genres.Include("Albums")
            .Single(g => g.Name == genre);

    return View(genreModel);
}
```
Listing 7.5: Default Browse Functionality

The default implementation uses a Linq query on the storeDB Entity object. The query retrieves all the albums belonging to the specified genre. Listing 7.6 shows the same query on the ElasticSearch server using NEST client.

```
using Nest;
...

  private static ElasticClient ElasticClient
  {
    get
    {
        string elasticSearchUri =
```

WINDOWS AZURE WEB SITES

```
ConfigurationManager.AppSettings
["elasticsearchUri"];

        var setting =
new ConnectionSettings
(new Uri(elasticSearchUri));

        string elasticsearchindexname =
ConfigurationManager.AppSettings
["elasticsearchindexname"];

setting.SetDefaultIndex(elasticsearchindexname);
        return new ElasticClient(setting);
    }
}

public ActionResult Browse(string genre)
{

    var result =
  ElasticClient.Search<Album>(body =>
    body.Query(query =>
    query.ConstantScore(
    csq => csq.Filter(filter =>
    filter.Term(x =>
    x.Genre.Name, genre.ToLower())))))
    .Take(1000));

    var genreModel = new Genre()
    {
        Name = genre,
        Albums = result.Documents.ToList()
    };

    return View(genreModel);

}
```

Listing 7.6: Query Albums by Genre from ElasticSearch

In Listing 7.6, the first step is creating an ElasticClient property for initializing connection to the ElasticSearch server. In the Browse function, you create a filter on albums that matches the specified genre term. The filter is then wrapped in a query with a constant score to avoid any search relevance scoring. Search relevance adds performance burden to the query, and therefore we won't use it here. To test the browse functionality, click on one of the genres on the side menu of the Music Store website. The MVC website invokes the StoreController's Browse action, retrieves the results from ElasticSearch and presents them through the View object. Note that we have made changes only to the controller class; the model and view classes of the website are unchanged. This shows the flexibility of the ASP.NET MVC architecture where you can modify one-tier of the application without affecting the other.

d) Adding Free Text Search

Free text search allows you to search for albums using a search string. To add free text search to Music Store, create a new function Search() in StoreController.cs, as shown in Listing 7.7.

```
//GET: /Store/Search
public ActionResult Search(string q)
{
    var result =
  ElasticClient.Search<Album>(body =>
    body.Query(query =>
    query.QueryString(qs => qs.Query(q))));

    var genre = new Genre()
    {
        Name = "Search results for " + q,
        Albums = result.Documents.ToList()
    };

    return View("Browse", genre);

}
```
Figure 7.7: Search function in Music Store

In Listing 7.7, we call the NEST API's Search() function and pass it a QueryString query to the request body. The results are passed to a Genre object that is passed to the Browse view for rendering. Since we don't have a dedicated view for Search functionality, we will reuse the Browse view for rendering search results. To test free text search, type the following URLs in your browser window.

http://[your_music_store_website]/store/search?q=Incognito

e.g.

http://musicstore.azurewebsites.net/store/search?q=Miles Davis
http://musicstore.azurewebsites.net/store/search?q=Incognito

Step 4: Testing Search and Browse with ElasticSearch

After completing Step 3, check-in the code and with continuous deployment in place, the Music Store website will be automatically published to WAWS. Figure 7.11 illustrates the search results for the term "jazz".

Figure 7.11: Search term jazz

For testing the Browse functionality, you need to click on the genre menu as illustrated in Figure 7.12.

Figure 7.12: Browse genre metal

After revisiting Figure 6.2 (from Chapter 6) and the migration task list, we have successfully completed the migration to WAWS, set up continuous deployment, and added a search engine to the website. Listed below are the completed and remaining tasks from our exercise.

1) Migrating Databases (Completed)
2) Deploying to Windows Azure Web Sites (Completed)
3) Enabling Continuous Deployment (Completed)
4) Adding Search with ElasticSearch (Completed)

5) Adding Analytics with Piwik
6) Testing
7) Performance Testing

In the next chapter, you will learn to enable analytics on the Music Store website for capturing usage information, and deriving trends to help you further improve your website's user experience.

Summary

In this chapter, a typical .NET developer's ego was challenged. We deployed a Java-based ElasticSearch on Windows Azure VM and successfully integrated it with the Music Store website. One important point to note of is that in this architecture, the endpoints of ElasticSearch VMs are exposed to the internet. In real-world, you would add IP filtering or an additional layer of secure communications between the Music Store website and the ElasticSearch VM. Through a series of steps, you learned the invaluable skill of integrating search engines into ASP.NET websites. In the next chapter, in a similar manner, you will learn to deploy and integrate Piwik analytics application in the Music Store website.

Chapter 8

ADDING CUSTOM ANALYTICS

Piwik (http://piwik.org/) is a leading open source web analytics platform. It helps you analyze the usage history and trends from your website. It is built in PHP and is available to run on multiple platforms. In this chapter, you will learn to quickly deploy Piwik using dynamicdeploy.com, and add Piwik analytics code to the Music Store website for tracking purposes.

Note: Since this book is about building solutions using WAWS, I have covered only limited concepts about Piwik. The objective of this section is to enable analytics capability in a website. Listed below are some of the hyperlinks to important resources on the internet for learning more about Piwik as a web analytics platform.

http://piwik.org/

http://www.dynamicdeploy.com/packagedetails.aspx?pkgid=99

http://piwik.org/features/

Using dynamicdeploy.com to deploy Piwik

A single instance Piwik VM is available on dynamicdeploy.com for free. Listed below is a step-by-step procedure for deploying Piwik to a Windows

Azure Virtual Machine (VM).

Step 1: Locate Piwik on dynamicdeploy.com

Navigate to http://www.dynamicdeploy.com and search for Piwik. On the results page, click the details button.

Figure 8.1: Search for Piwik on dynamicdeploy.com

Step 2: Note the Default Login Information

On the Piwik details page, note the Default parameter values and register for a dynamicdeploy.com account as shown in Figure 8.2.

Figure 8.2: Sign in to dynamicdeploy.com

After signing in, you will be automatically navigated to the same package details page, but this time with the "Deploy" button visible.

Step 3: Click on the Deploy button, as shown in the Figure 8.3.

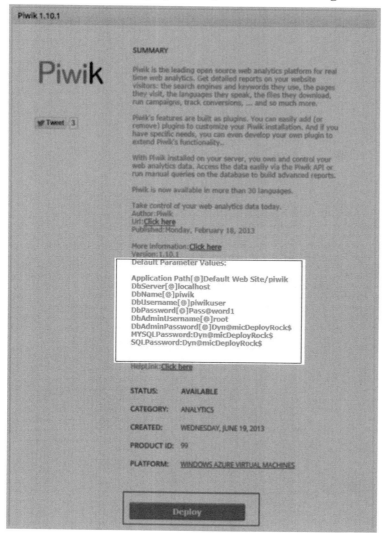

Figure 8.3: Click Deploy

This will start the provisioning process.

Step 4: Select Datacenter

Dynamicdeploy.com uses datacenter affinity to reduce the deployment time as well as avoiding the data-transfer costs during copying VMs between datacenters. It takes at least 60-75 minutes to copy a VM from one datacenter to another; but with datacenter affinity, you can copy it in much shorter time than that.

On the "Datacenter Selection" page, select an available datacenter, but also make sure it is in the same datacenter where your Music Store website and ElasticSearch VMs are running.

Figure 8.4: Select a datacenter

Step 5: Select a subscription

If you have already deployed a VM from dynamicdeploy.com, you will see an existing subscription. If not, you will need to upload a publish settings file for your subscription. Optionally, you can download a new publish settings file by clicking the "Click here to create a new .publishsettings file" link.

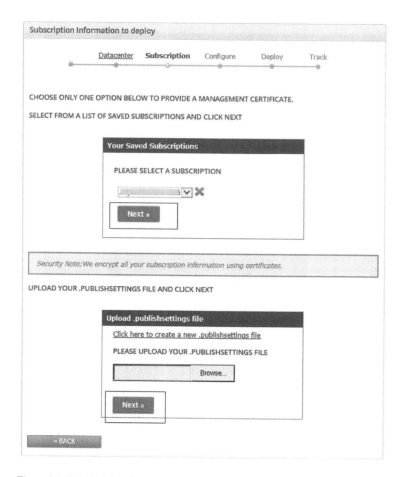

Figure 8.5: Provide Subscription Information

Click Next to navigate to configuration page.

Step 6: Provide Storage and Compute Details

On the services screen, based on the datacenter you selected, you will see a list of storage accounts and cloud services to select for the deployment. After selecting a storage account and an empty cloud service, click Next, as shown in Figure 8.6.

Figure 8.6: Select a storage account and cloud service

Step 7: Final Configuration

On the configuration page, select the VM size, and administrator password for logging into the VM, as shown in Figure 8.7. Please note down the randomly generated administrator name for the VM (you can change that later when you login).

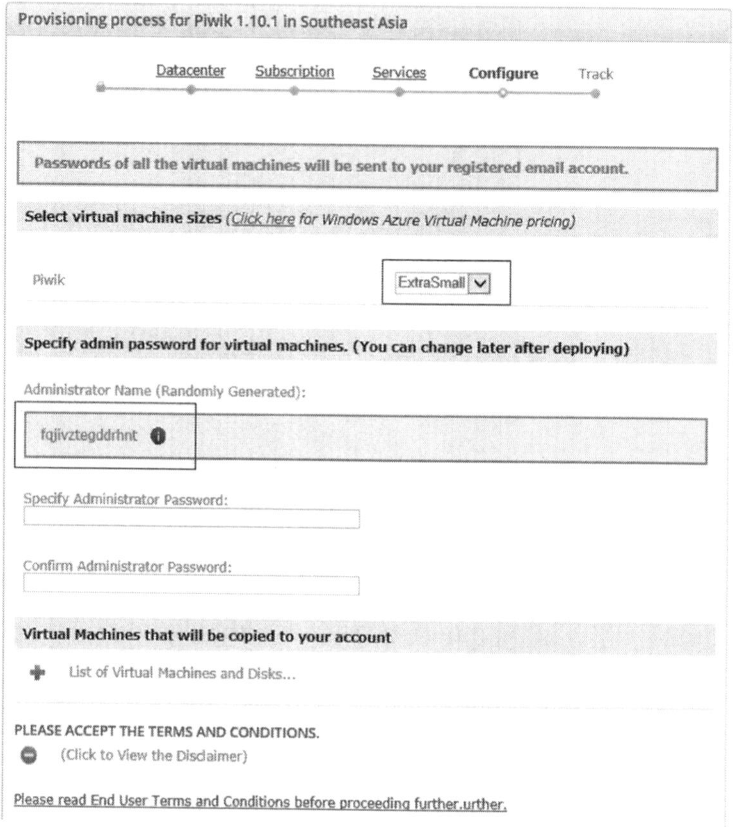

Figure 8.7: Configure VM

Please read the Terms & Conditions and Click Accept. This will start deployment of the Piwik VM in your subscription. After the deployment is complete, you will see the status and the time it took for deploying the VM, as shown in Figure 8.8.

Summary

PIWIK 1.10.1   Piwik

URL: http://ddtejaswi.cloudapp.net/

CLOUD SERVICE: ● Running

Total Deployment Time: | 22 minutes |

Click here for product documentation.
Click here for more information on these values.
Click here for deployment logs.

Figure 8.8: Deployment Complete screen.

Step 8: Start Piwik Setup

After the deployment is successful, Piwk will be running on the VM, and you will need to setup and configure it such that it starts capturing your website's usage data.

To access Piwik's configuration page, navigate to http://[piwk_cloud_service].cloudapp.net/piwik .
You will see a welcome screen as shown in Figure 8.9.

Figure 8.9: Piwik Welcome Screen

Click Next to navigate to the System Check screen. If the system check succeeds, as shown in Figure 8.10, click Next.

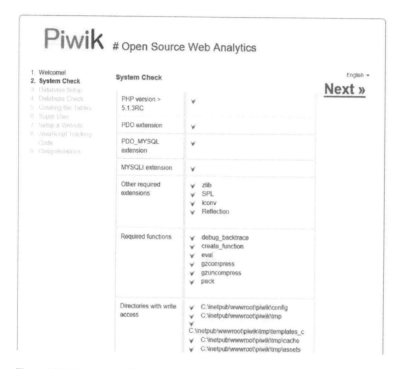

Figure 8.10: Piwik System Check

The system check looks for components that were installed and can predict if the Piwik software will run successfully. Note that the underlying operating system of the VM is Windows Server.

Step 9: Database Setup

On the database setup page, specify the database details Piwik will use. In the deployment, the database is on the same VM as Piwik, therefore keep the defaults and specify the password **Dyn@micDeployRock$**. This is the default password that was setup during deployment. For this exercise, we will keep it to default, but please change it if you want to deploy it in production environments.

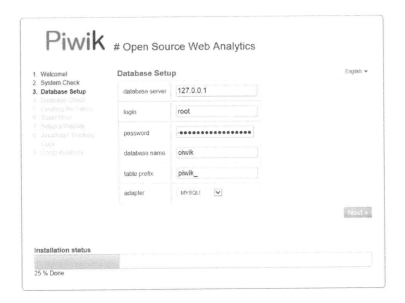

Figure 8.11: Piwik Database Setup

Click Next to create the database and Piwik tables. Figure 8.12 illustrates successful creation of the database and the Piwik tables.

Figure 8.12: Piwik Database Created

Click Next to navigate to the super user setup for your Piwik website.

Step 10: Super user setup

On the super user setup screen, enter a login, password, and email of the Piwik site administrator. As an administrator, you will be able to manage users, websites, and reporting capabilities of Piwik.

Figure 8.13: Setup Super User

Click Next to setup a target website. Target website is the website you want to capture usage data from, such as the Music Store website.

Step 11: Setup a website

On the "Setup a website" page, specify a website name (can be anything for your knowledge), a website URL (e.g. http://musicstore.azurewebsites.net), the time zone, and E-commerce capabilities of the target website.

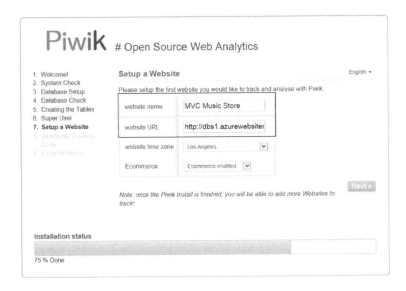

Figure 8.14: Setup a Target Web Site.

After the default setup process is complete, you can even add more websites for Piwik to track. By adding multiple sites, you can use the same Piwik VM for analyzing a number of websites. Click Next to get the client-side JavaScript code to embed in your website.

Step 12: Setup JavaScript Tracking Code

From the "Tracking code for MVC Music Store" page, copy the JavaScript code snippet and paste it before the </body> tag in ~/Shared/ _Layout.cshtml file of the Music Store website. Figure 8.15 illustrates the JavaScript tracking code page.

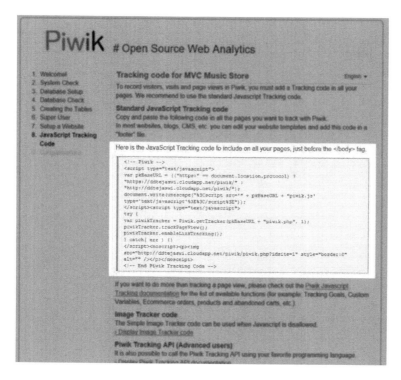

Figure 8.15: JavaScript Tracking Code

The _Layout.cshtml file defines the master layout for all the Music Store web pages, therefore, adding the tracking code to this file will help you track usage data on all the pages that are based on _Layout.cshmtl. Listing 8.1 shows the JavaScript code copied to the _Layout.cshtml file.

```
...
<!-- Piwik -->
<script type="text/javascript">
    var pkBaseURL =
(("https:" == document.location.protocol) ?
"https://ddtejaswi.cloudapp.net/piwik/" :
 "http://ddtejaswi.cloudapp.net/piwik/");

    document.write(unescape("%3Cscript src='" +
pkBaseURL + "piwik.js'
 type='text/javascript'%3E%3C/script%3E"));
</script>
<script type="text/javascript">
```

```
    try {

        var piwikTracker =
Piwik.getTracker(pkBaseURL + "piwik.php", 1);
        piwikTracker.trackPageView();
        piwikTracker.enableLinkTracking();
        } catch (err) { }
    </script>
<noscript>
<p><img
src="http://ddtejaswi.cloudapp.net/piwik/piwik.ph
p?idsite=1" style="border:0" alt="" /></p>
    </noscript>
        <!-- End Piwik Tracking Code -->
</body>
</html>
```

Listing 8.1: JavaScript Tracking Code in _Layout.cshtml.

The tracking code downloads a JavaScript in every web page that loads in the browser, and then transfers the usage information to the Piwik web service. This procedure can slow down the performance of the web page, therefore in a real-world production website, you must save the JavaScript on a CDN and scale-out the Piwik VM.

Click Next to complete the installation, as shown in Figure 8.16.

Figure 8.16: Successful Piwik Installation

Click on the "Continue to Piwik" link to navigate to the administrator login page.

Step 13: Login as administrator (super user)

Login to your Piwik website using the super user privileges you created in Step 10 of this exercise.

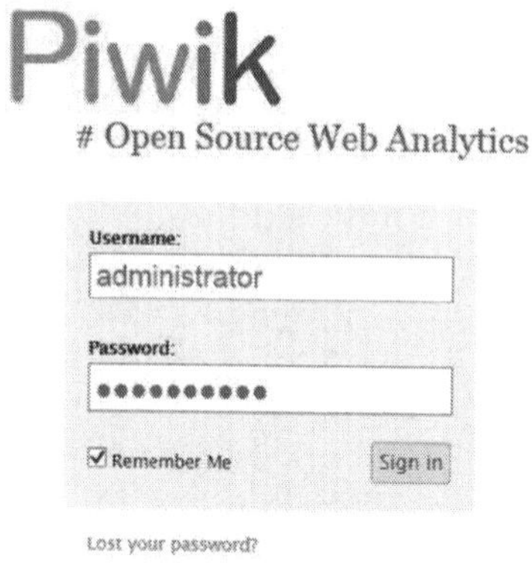

Open Source Web Analytics

Username:
administrator

Password:
●●●●●●●●●●

☑ Remember Me   Sign in

Lost your password?

Figure 8.17: Administrator login

After you login, you will be navigated to the Piwik Dashboard page showing usage tracking information for your Music Store website, as illustrated in Figure 8.18.

Figure 8.18: Usage Tracking

In order to capture more tracking information, you can run a web page test with http://www.webpagetest.org . This will provide some usage and performance data for your Music Store website.

Figure 8.19 illustrates the usage captured on the Piwik website after running a few webpagetest.org tests on the Music Store website.

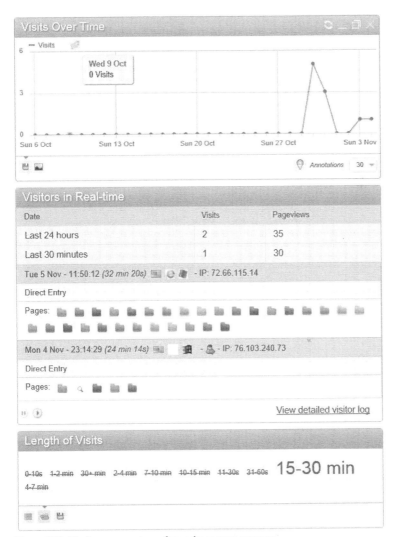

Figure 8.19: Piwik usage capture after webpagetest.org tests.

From Figure 8.19, we can confirm that the analytics capability of the Music Store website is fully functional. So, from a basic infrastructure testing perspective, we have our architecture functional on WAWS.

After revisiting Figure 6.2 (Chapter 6) and the migration task list, we have successfully migrated the website and databases to WAWS, set up continuous deployment, added a search engine, and adding analytics to the website. Listed below are the completed and remaining tasks from our exercise.

1) Migrating Databases (Completed)
2) Deploying to Windows Azure Web Sites (Completed)
3) Enabling Continuous Deployment (Completed)
4) Adding Search with ElasticSearch (Completed)
5) Adding Analytics with Piwik (Completed)
6) Testing (Completed)
7) Performance Testing

In the next section, we will take a look at the captured performance report from webpagetest.org to identify performance improvement opportunities.

Performance Testing

In the previous section, we ran a few tests on our Music Store website from webpagetest.org online testing tool. The grading system implemented by webpagetest.org provides valuable insights into improving performance of your website.

Figure 8.20 illustrates the web page performance test results from a webpagetest.org run on the Music Store website running in WAWS (free plan), with search and analytics enabled.

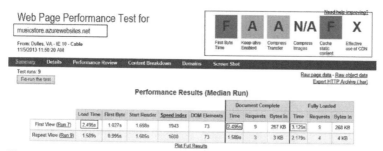

Figure 8.20: Web Page Performance Test

From Figure 8.20, it is clear that there is a lot of room for improving performance of the Music Store website. The top-right corner shows the grades on each basic performance metric. We need to improve on the following metrics: First Byte Time, Cache static content, and Effective use of CDN metrics.

First Byte Time

First Byte Time (FBT) is the time your browser spent waiting on the web server to send back the first byte of data (or page). The recommended FTB for static websites is 100ms and for dynamic websites is between 300ms-500ms. If you click on the "F" grade for FBT in Figure 8.20, you will see the actual and target FBT value for the Music Store website. For the test I ran, I received the following results:

1027ms First Byte Time

300ms Target First Byte Time (recommended target is 300ms-500ms)

FBT is influenced by several factors such as DNS lookup, web server caching, database lookup, website loading/unloading, etc. Because we are running on a WAWS free plan, we don't have control over automatic loading and unloading of the website from the WAWS infrastructure. To improve FTB, we can implement one or all of the following recommendations:

1) Continuously hit the website through a monitoring service like Pingdom.com. This will prevent the website from unloading due to limited usage.

2) Leverage Windows Azure Shared Cache or In-Memory cache in Music Store for caching dynamic content.

3) Upgrade to Shared or Standard Plan for larger VM with more memory and powerful CPU.

4) Use CDN for static content.

Cache Static Content

As listed in the Top 10 performance gain tips in Chapter 4, you can enable static content in IIS by adding the following code snippet to Music Store's web.config in the <system.webServer> section.

```
<staticContent>
    <clientCache
cacheControlMode="UseMaxAge"
cacheControlMaxAge="20.00:00:00" />
    </staticContent>
```
Listing 8.2: Enable Client Caching

In Listing 8.2, the static content is cached for 20 days by adding **Cache-Control: max-age=20** header value to the HTTP response.

Effective Use of CDN

At the time of writing, the Windows Azure CDN service was not available to new customers because the Windows Azure team was revamping the service completely. As a result, you will need to use a third-party CDN such as

Akamai for caching static content from your website.

Summary

In this chapter you learned to deploy and integrate Piwik into your website. Usage analytics provides you with the ability to continuously improve your content and also track the demographics of users on your website. Such analytics is invaluable not only to website operators but also to business owners of the website who can intelligently place content throughout the website to attract more users, and improving the interaction of existing users.

This chapter brings an end to the in-depth architecture and guidance journey we started in Chapter 6. I hope the knowledge you acquired through this reading and exercises will help you build large-scale websites on Windows Azure. In the next (and last) chapter, I am introducing a new concept called "The Lightening Round". The lightening round will provide you with a list of scenarios and best resources available to successfully execute these scenarios. As a reader, you can pick one scenario, and then navigate to the resources for that scenario for further reading.

Chapter 9
WEB SITES LIGHTENING ROUND

In this chapter, I will share some of the best practices I have learned over the several years in building large-scale web solutions on Windows Azure. I have tried to stay within the Windows Azure Web Sites (WAWS) context, but any deviations are only due to focus on solution-design best practices for WAWS. Windows Azure Web Sites is an ever-improving service that will be updated several times a year with new features. In this lightening round chapter, I have tried my best to provide you with the best of the practices and relevant resources on real-world solution scenarios. These scenarios and resources will take you beyond this book and challenge your imaginations in building websites on Windows Azure.

The scenarios in this book are grouped into four topics:
1) Hybrid Connectivity -- Connecting WAWS to your datacenter
2) Authentication Models -- Different ways of authenticating website users
3) Data Storage
4) SignalR and Web Sockets

Each of these categories will include at least one scenario and reference to resources for implementing it. Note that ultimately, these categories will fulfill one of the Web Site Capability you learned in Chapter 5.

Hybrid Connectivity

Hybrid connectivity is concerned with connecting your cloud applications with applications residing in your own datacenter, typically behind a firewall. For connecting these two applications, you need to configure connectivity either at the network-level or at the application-level. At the time of writing, Windows Azure Web Sites (WAWS) did not support network-level connectivity such as a virtual network[9]. But, WAWS does support application-level connectivity using Service Bus[10]. In this section, we will take a quick peek at architectures that enable hybrid connectivity.

Scenario: You want to connect your Windows Azure website to a web service or an application in your datacenter behind a firewall.
Examples:

1) You want your website to retrieve customer data from a Line of Business (LOB) system such as a purchase order or a Customer Relationship Management (CRM) application residing in your datacenter behind a firewall

2) You want to retrieve data from a data repository such as a database or a search engine that cannot be migrated to the cloud due to compliance and regulatory reasons

Solution Architecture

The solution architecture includes Service Bus Relay messaging technology for communicating between WAWS and a web service running in your datacenter. Figure 9.1 illustrates one hybrid connectivity scenario for connecting a website running in WAWS with a LOB web service in your datacenter.

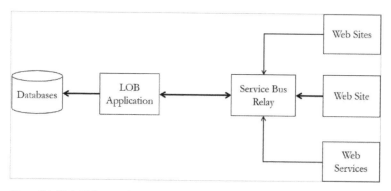

Figure 9.1: Hybrid Connectivity

In Figure 9.1, the websites running in WAWS makes a one-way outbound connection to a Service Bus Relay namespace in Windows Azure. In your data-center, the LOB application (or a proxy) creates an outbound bi-

---

[9] Virtual Network (http://www.windowsazure.com/en-us/documentation/services/virtual-network/)

[10] Service Bus (http://www.windowsazure.com/en-us/documentation/services/service-bus/)

directional socket connection to the same Service Bus Relay namespace in Windows Azure. Now, the Service Bus infrastructure is aware of the two connection-points on the same namespace. When the website calls a method on the LOB web service, the Service Bus networking infrastructure routes the message to the LOB application connection on the same namespace. Because of the bi-directional connection, the message is delivered to the LOB application behind firewall.

Implementation Resources

To design a Service Bus relay connectivity application, you need to follow a step-by-step procedure in creating the Service Bus namespace in Windows Azure, and then designing the Windows Communications Foundation (WCF) interfaces for the LOB application for websites and web services running in WAWS to call. Currently, WCF façade is the only supported interface for exposing LOB applications over Service Bus relay.

1) .NET On-Premises/Cloud Hybrid Application Using Service Bus Relay
   This reference article from Microsoft is a step-by-step procedure in building a simple hybrid connectivity between applications.
   http://www.windowsazure.com/en-us/develop/net/tutorials/hybrid-solution/

2) How to Use the Service Bus Relay Service
   This is another basic tutorial on getting started with Service Bus
   http://www.windowsazure.com/en-us/develop/net/how-to-guides/service-bus-relay/

3) How to integrate a Windows Azure Web Site with a LOB app via a Service Bus Relay Service
   This is an advanced article on integrating WAWS with an LOB app using Service Bus Relay and the author also adds Windows Azure Notification Hubs for sending back notifications to mobile devices when the product catalog changes. I recommend reading this article after finishing 1) & 2)
   http://blogs.msdn.com/b/paolos/archive/2013/10/24/how-to-integrate-a-windows-azure-web-site-with-a-lob-app-via-a-service-bus-relay-service.aspx

Tools

Other than the Windows Azure portal, Microsoft does not offer any supported Service Bus tools. Some developers have contributed the following tools that are used by the development community when working with Service Bus.

Service Bus Explorer

This is client tool for monitoring and managing Service Bus namespaces. You can download the code from the following location.

http://code.msdn.microsoft.com/windowsazure/Service-Bus-Explorer-f2abca5a

Port Bridge

Port Bridge is a proxy server that abstracts TCP connection bindings between the client and the server in a Service Bus interaction. Means, with Port Bridge, you no longer have to build WCF interfaces for the service, but instead add a Port Bridge indirection layer between the client and the service. Port Bridge will then forward web service calls to the appropriate on-premises LOB application or service. Port Bridge was originally built by Clemens Vasters and it is not updated or supported by Microsoft. You can learn more information about Port Bridge at the following locations.

Port Bridge Concepts

http://blogs.msdn.com/b/clemensv/archive/2009/11/18/port-bridge.aspx

Integrating On-Premises Web Services with Windows Azure Service Bus and Port Bridge

http://msdn.microsoft.com/en-us/library/windowsazure/hh697517.aspx

Authentication Models

In the past few years, authentication models for websites have changed drastically due to surge in consumer and enterprise cloud identities. When you build a website today, you may need to design it for enterprise identities as well. Office 365 is a popular enterprise domain that runs in the cloud and hosts enterprise identities. In this section, you will learn to authenticate your website users with an Office 365 domain.

Authentication with Office 365 Domain

You want to enable single sign-on between your website and Office 365 domain. Developing single sign-on is a two-step process:
1) Registering for Office 365 Domain
2) Configuring your ASP.NET website to federate authentication with the Office 365 Domain

Registering for Office 365 Domain

You can open an Office 365 account or a preview account by navigating here
http://www.microsoft.com/office/cxm/en-us/home-premium/

After you acquire an Office 365 account and a domain, you can login to your account and navigate to the domains section to copy the domain name.

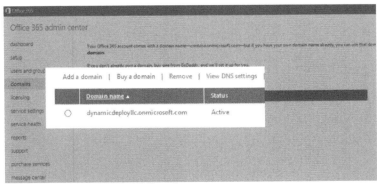

Figure 9.2: Acquiring Office 365 Domain

Copy the domain name as you will need it later to configure your website.

Configuring your ASP.NET website to federate authentication with the Office 365 Domain

Step 1: Create a new ASP.NET website in Visual Studio 2013

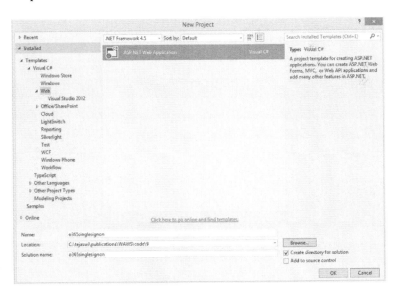

Figure 9.3: Create a new ASP.NET Project in Visual Studio 2013

Click OK and then on the Select a template screen click on Change Authentication. On the Change Authentication window, select Cloud – Single Organization and then copy the domain name in the Domain text box as illustrated in Figure 9.4.

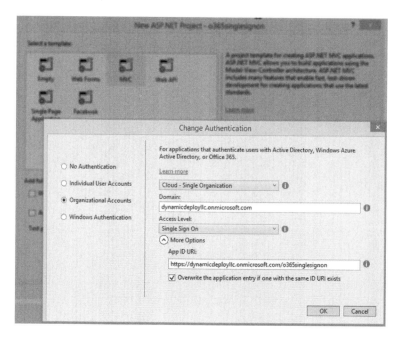

Figure 9.4: Change Authentication

After you click OK, you will be required to sign into the domain before Visual Studio creates identity-related entries in the web.config.

Note: If you are using Visual Studio 2012, you will need to download ASP.NET Tools for Windows Azure Active Directory (WAAD) from this location

http://dl01.blob.core.windows.net/waad/AspNetToolsForW AAD_VS2012.msi

---

Run the website on the local machine to test the federated authentication with Office 365.

Step 2: Create a Windows Azure Web Site

Next, create a Windows Azure Web Site (e.g. o365singlesignon.azurewebsites.net) as shown in Figure 9.5.

Figure 9.5: Windows Azure Web Site

After the website is created, download publish profile for the website and save it in a secure location on your hard drive.

Figure 9.6: Download Publish Profile

Before you publish you website to WAWS, there are a few activities you need to perform.

1) Migrate the default SQL Server database from the website's App_Data folder to Azure SQL. Without this migration, your website will not work.

2) Modify the replyUrl , and any other reference to localhost from the <system.identityModel.services> section in web.config to point to the URL of the WAWS you created.

```
<federationConfiguration>
      <cookieHandler requireSsl="true" />
      <wsFederation
        passiveRedirectEnabled="true"
        issuer=
  "https://login.windows.net/dynamicdeployllc.on
microsoft.com/wsfed"

realm="https://dynamicdeployllc.onmicrosoft.com/o
365singlesignon"

requireHttps="true" reply="[Your Reply URL]" />
      </federationConfiguration>
```

Listing 9.1: Modify Federation Configuration from web.config

Finally, during publishing, Visual Studio will ask you to enter your Office 365 domain credentials again in the File Publish Options screen as shown in Figure 9.7.

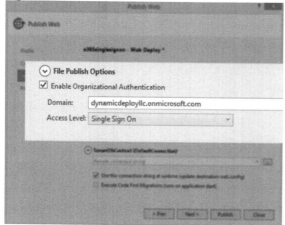

Figure 9.7: Specify Domain in File Publish Options

If the configuration and deployment is successful, you will be redirected to the Office 365 login screen when you browse to the website's URL. On successful login, you will see your domain credentials on the website's home page as illustrated in Figure 9.8.

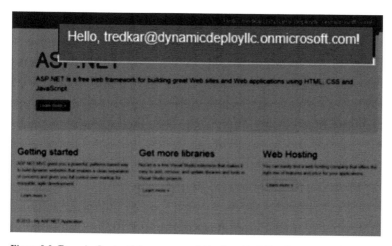

Figure 9.8: Domain Credentials on successful login with Office 365.

The domain configuration for federating with Office 365 is not a complicated task. The configuration of the source code (web.config) and migration of the database needs to be successful before running the federated website live on WAWS. The follow-up tasks like authorizing users upon authentication requires careful attention because the security boundaries in the cloud are not as stringent as in your own datacenter.

Using OAuth 2.0 Providers in websites

Scenario: You want to authenticate the website users against publicly available OAuth 2.0 (OAuth) identity providers such as Twitter, Facebook, Microsoft, Yahoo, and Google.

OAuth is based on the concept that an application (or a website) can request access to your identity and profile stored by another application (or identity provider) such as Twitter, Facebook, Microsoft, etc. The user holds the rights to grant or revoke the application access. Figure 9.9 illustrates the OAuth 2.0 authentication/authorization orchestration between the user, a website (e.g. Music Store), and the identity or profile provider (e.g. Facebook).

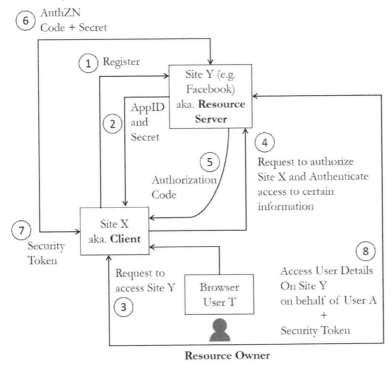

Figure 9.9: OAuth 2.0 Orchestration

Figure 9.9 illustrates the following interaction between the user "T" (aka. Resource Owner), your website "X" (aka. Client) and the service "Y" (aka. Resource Server) that stores your profile (identity).

1) You register your website X with service Y, usually through their developer web interface.
2) The service Y provides you with an AppId and Secret Key.
3) During browsing, the Resource Owner (T) requests the website X to call service Y such as Facebook for authenticating and providing access to T's profile information (e.g. email).
4) Service Y presents an authorization screen to User T to confirm and approve the access request. This is the same screen you saw when authorizing access to GitHub and Visual Studio Online from WAWS, earlier in the book.
5) After User T approves or allows the transaction, Site Y redirects the request back to Site X with an Authorization Code.
6) Site X then passes the Authorization Code and the Secret Key (from 2) to service Y
7) Service Y responds with a Security Token.
8) Site X then packages this Security Token and makes request to service Y on behalf of the User T. This way Site X can retrieve the profile properties approved by the user.

Note that OAuth 2.0 orchestration mainly focuses on empowering the user to make the decision on allowing access to his/her profile information stored with the Resource Server. OAuth 2.0 does not define any encryption requirements for passing data between Resource Owner, Client and Resource Server. It is usually assumed that the orchestration happens over an HTTPS protocol.

Implementation Resources

Visual Studio 2013 and Asp.NET MVC 5 is packed with default support for accessing OAuth 2.0 providers. When you create a new ASP.NET MVC project in Visual Studio 2013, click on the Change Authentication button and select Individual User Accounts as shown in Figure 9.10

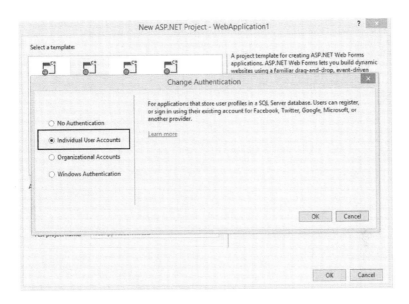

Figure 9.10: Select Individual User Accounts

Next, for enabling OAuth 2.0 support, you must uncomment the OAuth 2.0 provider code and then add AppId and Secret Key for you application. You will receive an AppId and a Secret Key for reaching out to the table reads developer's site for each of the provider consists of AppId and Secret Key. Listing 9.2 shows for passing the App credentials to the Resource Server.

```
// Uncomment the following lines to enable
logging in with third-party login providers
//app.UseMicrosoftAccountAuthentication(
//    clientId: "",
//    clientSecret: "");

//app.UseTwitterAuthentication(
//    consumerKey: "",
//    consumerSecret: "");

//app.UseFacebookAuthentication(
//    appId: "",
//    appSecret: "");
```

```
//app.UseGoogleAuthentication();
```
Listing: 9.2: Uncommented code for enabling OAuth 2.0 identity providers.

The code for Listing 9.2 is auto-generated by Visual Studio in the /App_Start/Startup.Auth.cs file. Note that each of the authentication, except Google requires you to provide and Id and Key, which corresponds to Step 1 in Figure 9.10. Listed below are the URLs of each provider's developer portal for registering your app.

1) **Microsoft Account**
   https://account.live.com/developers/applications/index
   Registration Instructions
   http://www.windowsazure.com/en-us/develop/mobile/how-to-guides/register-for-microsoft-authentication/

2) **Facebook**
   https://developers.facebook.com/
   Registration Instructions
   http://www.windowsazure.com/en-us/develop/mobile/how-to-guides/register-for-facebook-authentication/

3) **Google**
   https://accounts.google.com/SignUp
   Registration Instructions
   http://www.windowsazure.com/en-us/develop/mobile/how-to-guides/register-for-google-authentication/

4) **Twitter**
   https://dev.twitter.com/apps
   Registration Instructions
   http://www.windowsazure.com/en-us/develop/mobile/how-to-guides/register-for-twitter-authentication/

After you acquire AppId and the Secret Key, you can then uncomment the required providers in Listing 9.2, for running a quick authentication test between the website and the selected providers.

In a real-world applications, you will need more profile information about the user for maintaining in the website's ASP.NET Membership database. The IdentityModel.cs file in the /Models directory of the website will let you add addition profile information about the user. The following resources will help you with step-by-step procedures in enabling OAuth 2.0 on your website.

1) Deploy a Secure ASP.NET MVC 5 app with Membership, OAuth,

and SQL Database to a Windows Azure Web Site
http://www.windowsazure.com/en-us/develop/net/tutorials/web-site-with-sql-database/

2) Create an ASP.NET MVC 5 App with Facebook and Google OAuth2 and OpenID Sign-on
http://www.asp.net/mvc/tutorials/mvc-5/create-an-aspnet-mvc-5-app-with-facebook-and-google-oauth2-and-openid-sign-on

Further Reading

OAuth 2.0 Simplified by Aaron Parecki
http://aaronparecki.com/articles/2012/07/29/1/oauth2-simplified

Using OAuth Providers with MVC 4
http://www.asp.net/mvc/tutorials/security/using-oauth-providers-with-mvc

Customizing the login UI when using OAuth/OpenID
http://blogs.msdn.com/b/webdev/archive/2012/08/24/customizing-the-login-ui-when-using-oauth-openid.aspx

Integrate OpenAuth/OpenID with your existing ASP.NET application using Universal Providers
http://blogs.msdn.com/b/webdev/archive/2012/09/12/integrate-openauth-openid-with-your-existing-asp-net-application-using-universal-providers.aspx

Extra Information from OAuth/OpenId Provider
http://blogs.msdn.com/b/webdev/archive/2012/08/22/extra-information-from-oauth-openid-provider.aspx
Create an ASP.NET MVC 5 App with Facebook and Google OAuth2 and OpenID Sign-on (C#)
http://www.asp.net/mvc/tutorials/mvc-5/create-an-aspnet-mvc-5-app-with-facebook-and-google-oauth2-and-openid-sign-on

Deploy a Secure ASP.NET MVC 5 app with Membership, OAuth, and SQL Database to a Windows Azure Web Site
http://www.windowsazure.com/en-us/develop/net/tutorials/web-site-with-sql-database/

http://blogs.msdn.com/b/webdev/archive/2013/03/12/deploy-a-secure-asp-net-mvc-application-with-oauth-membership-and-sql-database.aspx

Security

In the Web Site Capability Model (defined in Chapter 5), I have split security into two categories – Data Security in transit and Data Security at rest. In this section, we will looks at SSL, the most common in-transit data security requirement. Data security at rest typically requires encryption methods that are application specific and thus out-of -scope for this book.

Data Security in Transit

Data Security in transit is concerned with security data that is transferred over the network, either intranet or internet. The most popular protocol for securing data in transit is HTTPS. HTTPS creates an encrypted channel between the client (e.g. browser) and the server to protect the data-transfer from spoofing or tampering in transit. In the cloud, data security in transit needs careful attention because you don't have control over the cloud provider's network for you to deploy network-security tools of your own. Listed below are some of the common scenarios and patterns that I have recommended for securing your website data in transit over and above setting up HTTPS.

Scenario: Forcing WebApi Clients to use SSL

If you have a WebApi combined in a public facing website in which you want to force only the WebApi to use SSL, then you need to write a custom action attribute requiring the WebApi clients to use HTTPS for communicating with the web services. Implementing this scenario is a two-step procedure:

1) **Creating the custom HTTPS action Attribute as shown in Listing 9.3**

```
using System;
using System.Linq;
using System.Net.Http;
using System.Web.Http.Filters;
using System.Web.Http.Controllers;

namespace Com.DynamicDeploy.Web.Security
{
//Inherit from the ActionFilter Attribute
 public class CustomHttpsAttribute :
```

```
ActionFilterAttribute
{
//Overide the OnActionExecuting method.
  public override void
  OnActionExecuting(HttpActionContext
actionContext)
    {

  //Verify whether the Url scheme is HTTPS

    if
(!String.Equals(actionContext.Request.RequestUri.
  Scheme,
  "https",
  StringComparison.OrdinalIgnoreCase))
    {

  //Send the BadRequest HTTP Status Code to the
  // browser

  actionContext.Response =
  new HttpResponseMessage
  (System.Net.HttpStatusCode.BadRequest)
    {
  //Send a response message

      Content = new StringContent
  ("Only HTTPS is supported for this method.")
      };
      return;
    }
   }
  }
 }
```

Listing 9.3: Custom HTTPS Attribute

In Listing 9.3, we simply check whether the URL scheme used for accessing the API is HTTPS or not. If not we send back a BadRequest status code to the client.

2) Registering the custom attribute

The attribute code created in Listing 9.3 needs to be registered with the ASP.NET MVC routing configuration in Global.asax.cs as shown below

```
GlobalConfiguration.Configuration.Filters.Add(
new CustomHttpsAttribute());
```

Finally, you can test the custom attribute from the browser by invoking the web service using HTTPS and HTTP.

You can use IIS URL Rewriting for redirecting all the HTTP traffic to HTTPS, as shown in Listing 9.4.

```
<system.webServer>
    <rule name="Force HTTPS" enabled="true">
        <match url="(.*)" ignoreCase="false" />
        <conditions>
            <add input="{HTTPS}" pattern="off"
/>
        </conditions>

        <action type="Redirect"
url="https://{HTTP_HOST}/{R:1}"
appendQueryString="true" redirectType="Permanent"
/>
    </rule>
</system.webServer>
```

Listing 9.4: Force HTTPS at the Web Server level

Scenario: IP Filtering in Windows Azure Web Sites

In Windows Azure Web Sites, developers can configure the Dynamic IP Restrictions (DIPR) feature from IIS 8 for their websites.

Note: For more information on DIPR, please visit the following link

---

http://www.iis.net/learn/get-started/whats-new-in-iis-8/iis-80-dynamic-ip-address-restrictions

The DIPR feature provides two features:
- Blocking of IP addresses based on number of concurrent client requests
- Blocking of IP addresses based on number of requests over a period of time from a client

Listing 9.5 shows the configuration for blocking IP Addresses that try to connect to the web server with more than 25 concurrent connections, or that have made more than 1000 total requests within a 10 seconds time window. This concept is useful in protecting your website from Denial of Service (DOS) attacks.

```
<dynamicIpSecurity>

<denyByRequestRate enabled="true"
maxRequests="1000"
requestIntervalInMilliseconds="10000"/>

<denyByConcurrentRequests enabled="true"
maxConcurrentRequests="25" />

</dynamicIpSecurity>
```

Listing 9.5: DIPR in IIS

Note: At the time of writing, the IIS <ipSecurity> feature was not enabled in WAWS.

Further Reading

For IIS IP Address Security restrictions, please read the following article
http://www.iis.net/configreference/system.webserver/security/ipsecurity

IIS Request Filtering
http://www.petefreitag.com/item/741.cfm

Configuring Dynamic IP Address Restrictions in Windows Azure Web Sites
http://blogs.msdn.com/b/windowsazure/archive/2013/08/27/confirming-dynamic-ip-address-restrictions-in-windows-azure-web-sites.aspx

IP Filtering in Windows Azure VMs
http://michaelwasham.com/2013/06/03/windows-azure-powershell-june-2013-update-for-iaas-and-paas/

IP Filtering in Windows Azure Web Sites
http://ntotten.com/2013/09/12/client-ip-address-filtering-with-windows-azure-web-sites/

Storage Object Distribution Pattern

If I have to rank the top 3 design features an architect must focus on when designing a cloud application, they would be:
1) Data Storage
2) Security & Identity
3) Performance

Typically, software developers are used to programming with two basic assumptions:
a) Their website will have access to the local file system
b) They can scale-up and scale-out the database by adding more hardware.

In the cloud, you don't have any control over the hardware and have to operate within the constraints of the cloud provider's environment. For example, when you run compute (or VMs) instances in Windows Azure, you are constrained by the following at the minimum:
1) The disk space available to you is limited by the size of the VM instance
2) The network and disk IO is constrained by the size of the VM
3) Azure SQL database size is limited to 150GB
4) Azure SQL infrastructure is shared and your performance may be affected by some else's poorly designed database running on the same server as yours
5) In WAWS, you don't have a local file system to store application data

For building real-world applications, these constraints are significant, but flexibility offered by Windows Azure sometimes outweighs these constraints. For example, you automatically get a highly available Azure SQL database and Windows Azure Storage. Windows Azure provides you with virtually unlimited storage capacity for storing data in Blobs and Tables.

As an architect, you are constantly challenged to think beyond traditional methodologies and patterns to take advantage of services offered by cloud platforms such as Windows Azure. In WAWS, as mentioned earlier, there is no access to local file system and the network IO performance also depends on size of the VM your website is running. As a result, to get the most out of your compute instances, you have to run the website in the costliest available plan (i.e. Standard Plan with Large VM). As a traditional architect, you would quickly think of increasing VM size for performance gains, but in today's world of a billion-plus mobile devices, your scale is challenged even with largest of the VMs available in the cloud.

For building high-performing websites, I am introducing a pattern called Storage Object Distribution pattern that would provide you with scale and efficiency in delivering objects to a large volume of devices. The Storage Object Distribution pattern allows you to leverage the scale and bandwidth of storage services, yet access application objects like if you were calling a REST API to retrieve the object. The pattern allows you to distribute application objects to a storage service such as Windows Azure Blob storage, and enables convention-based URL routing on each object. The client application accesses the object using the HTTP URI similar to a REST URI. For example, a client will access a customer object with the URI http://www.dynamicdeploy.com/customers/[customer id]. The customer object, instead of retrieving from a web service, will be retrieved from the blob storage.

Scenario: You want to build a highly-scalable website (gaming, advertising, or social) to support millions of mobile devices.
Figure 9.11 illustrates the approach that a traditional architect will take for building such a large volume website on Windows Azure Web Sites.

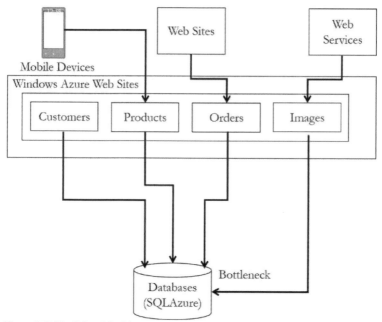

Figure 9.11: Traditional Architecture

In Figure 9.11, WAWS hosts all the web services and websites for supporting the high-volume website. Considering the volume, you will need to run it in the Standard Plan with Large instances. Even if your compute is able to manage the load, your database will be the bottleneck in handling these request. To reduce the load on the database, you will implement a caching layer for caching some of the data in Windows Azure Shared Cache. As a result, you will face a compute-cost bottleneck. A compute-cost bottleneck is where your compute costs rises proportionately with the user volume.

If you ask me about the most important takeaway from this book, I would answer, without hesitation, the Storage Object Distribution (SOD) pattern. SOD pattern leverages cloud storage blob capabilities (or Windows Azure Blob Storage) for delivering high-volume responses to mobile devices. Windows Azure Blob storage is a static repository, but it also doesn't have any constraints based on the plan you use. What that means is that if you are achieving 10000 transactions/seconds for your objects stored in Windows Azure Storage, unlike compute service (e.g. WAWS), you will not be throttled based on your plan. Though throttling is still in place, but it applies to all the storage accounts, not dependent on the plan you use. From a cost perspective, Windows Azure Storage is significantly cheaper than compute.

SOD Pattern Architecture

SOD pattern periodically distributes live dynamic objects to cloud blob storage, such as Windows Azure Blob Storage, for client applications to consume directly based on pre-configured URI schemes.

A dynamic object is the one that changes not more than 24 times a day and the client application does not require the latest object every time it accesses the web service. A real-time object is the one that may change any-time, whereas, a static object is the one that remains unchanged for more than 8 hours. SOD works well for static and dynamic objects. For real-time objects, it is better to use compute services directly. Figure 9.12 illustrates the architecture of SOD pattern.

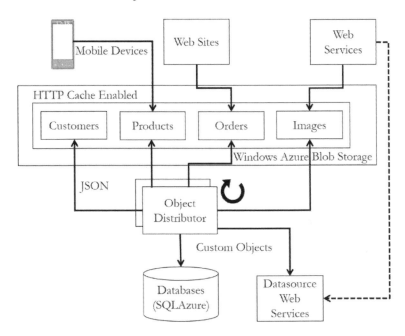

Figure 9.12: SOD Architecture

In SOD architecture in Figure 9.12, the Object Distributor is a scalable batch process that reads custom objects (i.e. C# or Entity Framework) from varied data sources such as database(s) or web services, and then distributes them into the appropriate Windows Azure Blob containers. Each container consists of objects belonging to its type. For example, the Customers container will hold all the individual customer objects as well as objects representing pre-defined queries such as, Customers by Location, or Products by Category. When you store these objects in the Blob storage, you can set several HTTP header properties such as Cache-Control and Content Type, that will help you scale up to the volume you desire. From the mobile browsers or other client devices, you can access the JSON objects directly without going through the compute VM. For example, for retrieving the list

of all products, you can access it using the following URL
http://appsforazurestorage.blob.core.windows.net/products/products-all.json

The Object Distributor retrieves native objects from data sources (databases or web services), serializes them as JSON or XML objects, and then copies them to the Blob containers. The Object Distributor can itself run as a Cloud Service or a Windows Service in a Virtual Machine. If your architecture demands, you may even run it on-premises as a Windows Service. The clients requiring fresher data can bypass the Blob storage and call the data source web services directly (see dotted line Figure 9.12). If the object in the client-cache becomes stale, the HTTP Cache-Control options max-age and must-revalidate will make sure a fresh object is retrieved when the max-age expires.

In a scaled-out environment, the Object Distributor can create a lease-lock and verify the Last Modified Time property on a blob to avoid multiple instances of Object Distributor updating the same blob within the update cycle.

Listing 9.6 shows the code-snippets for quickly building an Object Distributor that retrieves objects from a WebApi and then copies them to a Blob container.

```
public static string DistributeObject(
string containerName,
string blobName,
string restUrl,
string cacheControl = "public, max-age=3600, must-revalidate",
string contentType="application/json")
  {
    try
    {
      using (WebClient w = new WebClient())
      {

        if (StorageHelperNew.DoesBlobExist
(containerName, blobName))
          {

  ICloudBlob blob =
   StorageHelperNew.GetBlob(containerName, blobName, fetchAttributes:true);
  /*
```

```
    if the different between now and blob's last
modified is greater than 45 mins, then only modify
    */
            if ((DateTime.UtcNow -
    blob.Properties.LastModified)
    < TimeSpan.FromMinutes(45))
        {
                return "";

        }


    }
    //Download the JSON blob from Web Api and upload
//it to Blob Storage
    string ret = StorageHelperNew.PutBlob
    (containerName, blobName,
     w.DownloadData(restUrl), true);

    //Set the Cache Control and the Content Type of
the blob

    StorageHelperNew.SetCacheControlContentType(
    containerName,blobName,cacheControl,
contentType);

    //return the Blob Uri
          return ret;
        }

    }
      catch (Exception ex)
    {

    //Log errors
     }

     return "";
    }
```

```
//Extension to the Blob Class
public static class BlobExtensions
{
//A convenience method to set the Cache-Control
//header.
    public static void SetCacheControl
(this ICloudBlob blob, string value)
    {
        blob.Properties.CacheControl = value;
        blob.SetProperties();
    }


    public static void SetContentType
(this ICloudBlob blob, string value)
    {
        blob.Properties.ContentType = value;
        blob.SetProperties();
    }

//Set both the properties from a single method
    public static void
    SetCacheControlContentType
(this  ICloudBlob  blob,  string  cacheControl,
string contentType)
    {
        blob.Properties.ContentType =
contentType;
        blob.Properties.CacheControl =
cacheControl;
        blob.SetProperties();
    }
}
```
Listing 9.6: Distribute Object Method

In Listing 9.6 note the Cache Control and Content Type HTTP header parameters set as Blob properties. The Cache Control header instructs the client browser to cache the blob for 1 hour and must revalidate the blob again after it expires. The public parameter instructs the browser to cache authenticated responses. When the browser retrieves the file for the first time, the caching instructions are embedded in the header as illustrated in Figure 9.13.

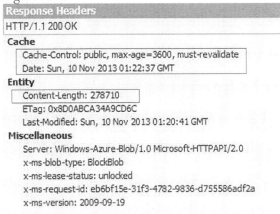

Figure 9.13: Cache Control on First Time Blob Load

Second time the client loads the blob within 1 hour, the response looks like Figure 9.14.

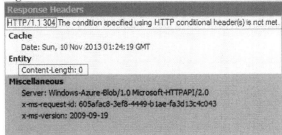

Figure 9.14: Cached response

In Figure 9.14, the HTTP 304 (Not Modified) status code and the Content-Length=0 confirms that the blob is loaded from the client's cache and not from the Windows Azure blob storage. Thus, with SOD, you can leverage the client's caching abilities and reduce the load on the valuable and costly compute server resources. If the object is loaded from the client's cache, you will not be paying any bandwidth (egress) costs for loading the object, which is not true for server-side caching. Even if you don't cache the response, it might still be worth loading the objects from the Blob storage instead of web service to take advantage of the higher I/O and scale of the Windows Azure Storage service.

SOD pattern, though not directly related to Windows Azure Web Sites (WAWS), is an invaluable design pattern to complement WAWS. For the right scenario, the scale and performance you can achieve with SOD will seldom be met by the compute services.

Further Reading

Save Money by Setting Cache-Control on Windows Azure Blobs
http://alexandrebrisebois.wordpress.com/2013/08/11/save-money-by-setting-cache-control-on-windows-azure-blobs/

IIS7 + Azure Blob Storage Cache-Control
http://www.bondigeek.com/blog/2011/08/16/iis7-azure-blob-storage-cache-control/

ASP.NET Web API and Azure Blob Storage
http://blogs.msdn.com/b/yaohuang1/archive/2012/07/02/asp-net-web-api-and-azure-blob-storage.aspx
http://code.msdn.microsoft.com/Uploading-large-files-386ec0af

A guide to asynchronous file uploads in ASP.NET Web API RTM
http://www.strathweb.com/2012/08/a-guide-to-asynchronous-file-uploads-in-asp-net-web-api-rtm/

Dealing with large files in ASP.NET Web API
http://www.strathweb.com/2012/09/dealing-with-large-files-in-asp-net-web-api/

Asynchronously streaming video with ASP.NET Web API
http://www.strathweb.com/2013/01/asynchronously-streaming-video-with-asp-net-web-api/

Async Streaming in ASP.NET Web API
http://blogs.msdn.com/b/henrikn/archive/2012/02/24/async-actions-in-asp-net-web-api.aspx

Resources on SignalR

SignalR helps you add real-time interaction to your websites. It pushes contents to the connected clients (e.g. browser) as the content becomes available. With SignalR, the clients don't need to poll the web server to retrieve data. Gaming, Stock updates, etc. are some of the common examples where SignalR can add significant value in user experiences.

SignalR leverages the WebSocket transport protocol wherever available, and falls back to older transports when the browsers or web servers don't support WebSocket. Windows Azure Web Sites recently announced support for Web Socket. Listed below are resources that you can leverage for building SignalR enabled websites on WAWS. For your SignalR website running on WAWS to use WebSocket as the underlying protocol, you must enable it in the Configure section of the website in Windows Azure portal.

WEB SOCKETS	ON	OFF

Figure 9.15: Enable Web Sockets on WAWS.

If you don't enable Web Sockets protocol, SignalR will fall back to traditional communications. In the Further reading section, I have listed resources for you to quickly bring yourself up to speed on SignalR. All other aspects of the WAWS infrastructure remains the same when running a SignalR website.

WebSocket

IIS 8.0 supports WebSocket protocol out-of-the-box. By default, ASP.NET SignalR uses WebSocket for communication, but falls back to other available mechanisms in its absence.

For more information on WebSockets, please visit http://www.websocket.org/aboutwebsocket.html

For more information on WebSockets support in IIS, please visit

Further Reading

Official SignalR Web site
http://www.asp.net/signalr
Windows Azure Websites, Web API and SignalR
http://blogs.blackmarble.co.uk/blogs/sspencer/post/2013/01/09/Windows-Azure-Websites-Web-API-and-SignalR.aspx
Publish the SignalR Getting Started Sample as a Windows Azure Web Site
http://blogs.msdn.com/b/timlee/archive/2013/02/27/deploy-the-signalr-getting-started-sample-as-a-windows-azure-web-site.aspx
Developing Single Page, Real Time Websites on Windows Azure
http://developusing.net/2012/06/08/DevelopingSinglePageRealTimeWebsitesOnWindowsAzure.aspx
SignalR chat on Azure
http://briankeating.net/post/2012/09/13/SignalR-chat-on-Azure.aspx
CloudSurvey Demo Web Application
https://github.com/WindowsAzure-Samples/CloudSurvey

SignalR Developer Code Samples on MSDN
http://code.msdn.microsoft.com/site/search?query=signalr&f%5B0%5D.Value=signalr&f
%5B0%5D.Type=SearchText&ac=2

Summary

The lightening round was designed to enlighten the solution architect in you and letting you take a step back from WAWS and think of a holistic picture. WAWS on its own may not add significant value in building real-world solutions, but when integrated with other Windows Azure services, it becomes a powerful web-tier of your solution. WAWS is designed to be the fire-and-forget component in your architecture. You build the website, integrate with source control, automate the test, and then forget about it. Microsoft will manage the lifecycle of the infrastructure as per your configuration. In this chapter, you learned three key concepts – Hybrid Connectivity, OAuth Authentication, Storage Object Distribution Pattern, and SignalR. I usually tell my customers, "If you nail down Authentication and Storage, the cloud is yours." What I mean by that is that design your authentication and data storage architecture upfront, and then move on to the other components of the system.

Chapter 10

BUILDING NODE.JS APPS

This book would have been incomplete without Node.js (aka NodeJS). Microsoft supports Node.js in Windows Azure Web Sites, and also provides development tools and native SDK for programming with Windows Azure APIs. Node.js is a JavaScript runtime engine for building client and server applications. Node.js includes an asynchronous I/O framework that helps it handle thousands of concurrent connections on a single process with minimal CPU or memory overhead. The core Node.js engine is built in C++ on top of Google's V8 JavaScript engine designed for the Chrome browser. In this section, I will give you a brief overview of Node.js followed by an exercise to try it out for yourself on Windows Azure Web Sites (WAWS). Through these exercises, you will be able to build REST web services, access MongoDB, and build web user experience in Node.js.

Components of Node.js

Node.js consists of the following two components:

Core/Kernel

The kernel of Node.js is written in C++ on top of Google's V8 JavaScript engine. The core itself is single-threaded and is capable of load-balancing between CPUs.

Modules

Modules are similar to nuget packages. Node.js Package Manager (npm) is the tool for managing Node.js packages. Modules spawn new process or threads depending on the I/O intensity of the task. Examples of some popular modules are – http, MongoDB, Express (web template framework), etc.

For a list of popular modules, please visit https://nodejsmodules.org/

Web Request Processing Model

To best understand the Node.js processing model, let's look at its visual representation (Figure 10.1) of the HTTP Request/Response processing pipeline.

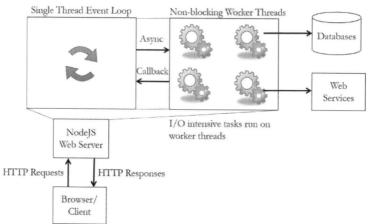

Figure 10.1: Node.js Processing model

In Figure 10.1, the Node.js engine starts a single main thread for handling concurrent client connections. Now because there is a single thread already initialized, there is no initialization overhead required for processing the rise in requests. If the HTTP Request incudes a long-running or I/O intensive task, such as database access or web service call, it is executed asynchronously in non-blocking worker threads. Once the long-running task are complete, the worker threads return the results as callback to the main thread. The main thread then returns the results back to the client. For understanding this model further, let's build a small HTTP server in Node.js.

Building an HTTP Server in Node.js

Listed below is a step-by-step procedure for running a Node.js HTTP server on Windows.

Step 1: Downloading and Installing Node.js

Node.js runs on Windows and can be downloaded and installed from the following location:

http://nodejs.org/#download

The installer installs Node.js runtime and "npm" – The Node.js package manager.

Step 2: Creating an HTTP Server

To create an HTTP Server in Node.js, open your favorite text editor and type the following code.

```
var http = require("http");

http.createServer(function(request, response) {
  response.writeHead(200, {"Content-Type":
"text/plain"});
  response.write("Hello WAWS! Book");
  response.end();
}).listen(8080);
```
Listing 10.1: Node.js Web Server

Listing 10.1 creates a web server and listens on TCP port 8080. Save the code as webserver.js.

Step 3: Running the HTTP Server

To run the HTTP server, open command prompt and navigate to the folder where you saved the webserver.js file and type the following:

```
>"C:\Program Files\nodejs\node.exe"
webserver.js
```

This will start the web server, and you can test it by navigating to http://localhost:8080.

Figure 10.2: Node.js Web Server running on your local machine

It was simple, wasn't it? Initially, as a .NET developer, I had doubts about productivity in building Node.js apps, but only after writing this chapter, I have gotten comfortable with it. In the next section, you will learn to deploy Node.js in WAWS.

Running Node.js on Windows Azure Web Sites

In this section, you will learn to build a simple Node.js website, based on an existing template called Express, and run in Windows Azure. We will use

Web Matrix 3 as our primary development tool for the remainder of this chapter. WebMatrix provides powerful capabilities and extensions for building Node.js applications.

Step 1: Creating a Windows Azure website

Create a new Windows Azure website from the Windows Azure portal as illustrated in Figure 10.3.

Figure 10.3: Create a website

Step 2: Creating an Express Template website in WebMatrix

1) Open Web Matrix 3
2) Click on New > Template Gallery, and under the Node.js category, select the Express Site template. Express is a lightweight Node.js web application framework that provides basic HTTP capabilities and makes it easier to create websites and REST APIs (which we will create in the next exercise).

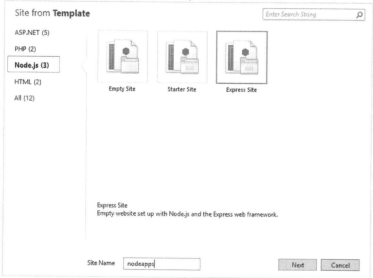

Figure 10.4: Select Express Site Template

Specify a site name and click Next to install IISNode and Express site template.

Figure 10.5: IISNode and Express Site Installation

Note: WebMatrix installs IISNode for IIS Express. IISNode allows you to host Node.js application on IIS. You can get more details about IISNode at the following GitHub repository
https://github.com/tjanczuk/iisnode.

Figure 10.6 illustrates the file structure created by the express template and the source code for server.js.

Tejaswi Redkar

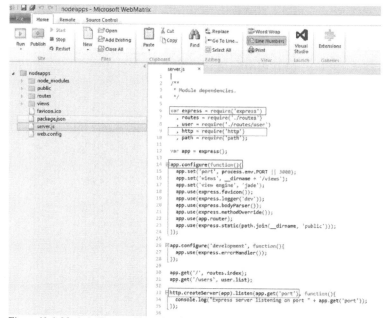

Figure 10.6: Node.js Express Template Site Structure.

Step 3: Running the website locally

Click the Run button on WebMatrix to test the website on your local machine.

Figure 10.7: Express site running

Because the Express template also installed a Jade template engine, the index.html contents are rendered from /views/index.jade and /routes/index.js. These routes are setup on lines 16, 17, and 30 in server.js as shown in Figure 10.6 above. For more information on Jade template engine, please visit http://jade-lang.com/.

Step 4: Publishing the website to WAWS

Click on the Publish button to start the website publishing process. Import the publish profile for your website into WebMatrix and follow the publishing wizard.

292

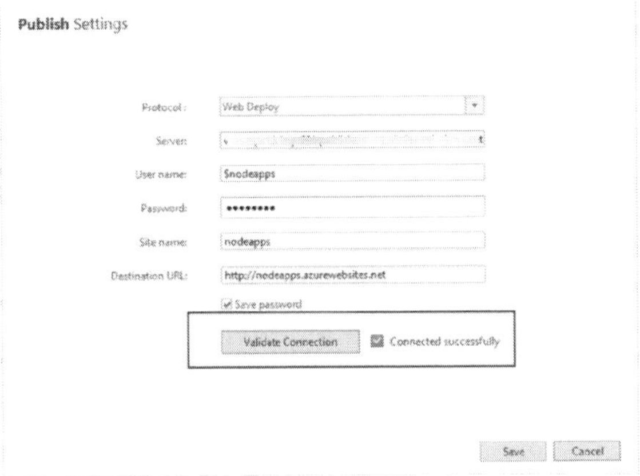

Publish Settings

Protocol :	Web Deploy
Server:	
User name:	$nodeapps
Password:	••••••••
Site name:	nodeapps
Destination URL:	http://nodeapps.azurewebsites.net

☑ Save password

Validate Connection ☑ Connected successfully

Save   Cancel

Figure 10.8: Publish Settings

After the publishing process completes, WebMatrix will load your website in Internet Explorer as shown in Figure 10.9.

http://nodeapps.azurewebsites.net/

File   Edit   View   Favorites   Tools   Help

Express

Welcome to Express

Figure 10.9: Express site running in Windows Azure.

This exercise was basic but showed you quick steps for deploying a Node.js website in WAWS. In the next section, we will enhance the previous example to build a REST web service in Node.js that retrieves data from a MongoDB database.

Creating a REST Web Service using Node.js, Express, and MongoDB

Node.js and MongoDB complement each other because Node.js is a JavaScript engine and MongoDB is a No-SQL database for storing JSON documents. JSON objects are JavaScript objects and thus are native to Node.js. In this section, let's build a REST web service that retrieves JSON objects from MongoDB database running in Windows Azure.

Architecture

Before starting the exercise, let's first understand the overall architecture of the solution. Figure 10.10 illustrates the architecture of the solution we will be building in this exercise.

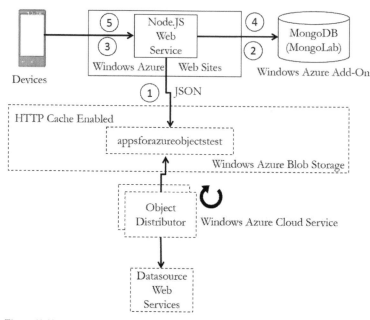

Figure 10.10: Node.js Web Service Architecture.

In Figure 10.10, as discussed in the previous chapter, a Storage Object Distributor distributes JSON objects hourly in Windows Azure Blob storage. One of the object is a list of all the apps available in dynamicdeploy.com. The JSON object is available at

http://storage.appsforazure.com/appsforazueobjectstest/servicepackages.json

I thought, this data would serve as good sample data for loading in MongoDB, and then retrieve that data from the Node.js REST web service. So, the JSON object will be used only as a sample data in this exercise. When a user calls the Node.js web service, it checks if the data exists in MongoDB, and if empty, loads the JSON object from Windows Azure Blob storage into MongoDB. The data from MongoDB is then served by the REST web services to a website or a device. The REST web services will expose the following URIs:

GET: /pkgs (Retrieves all the apps from MongoDB database)
GET: /pkgs/:id (Retrieves app by id)
GET: /pkgs/remote (Retrieves the JSON object directly from Blob storage)
POST: /pkgs (Adds a new app to MongoDB)

PUT: /pkgs/:id (Updates an app in MongoDB)
In the exercise, we will route these URIs to appropriate JavaScript functions in Node.js.

Step 1: Installing MongoDB in Windows Azure

MongoDB is available in Windows Azure Store as an add-on and you can install a sandbox version for free. Login to your Windows Azure portal and install MongoDB (MongoLab) from the New > Store > Add On menu.

Figure 10.11: MongoDB Add-On

On the Personalize Add-On screen, select the Sandbox version, and please make sure that you install the MongoDB instance in the same region as your website.

Figure 10.12: Configure MongoDB Add-On

Step 2: Copying Connection String

After the installation is complete, navigate to the add-on page.

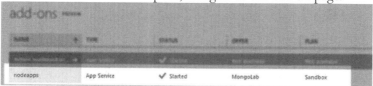

Figure 10.13: Add-Ons page

Click on Connection Info and copy the connection string for the installed database.

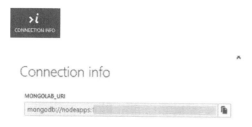

Figure 10.14: Copy Connection Info

Step 3: Installing WebMatrix Extensions

Open the mynodeapps website (or the website you created in the previous exercise) in WebMatrix and click on the Extensions menu. From the list of extensions, search and install NPM Gallery as shown in Figure 10.15.

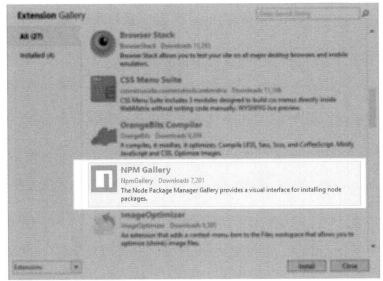

Figure 10.15: Install NPM Gallery

The NPM gallery allows you to install npm packages right from WebMatrix. I am personally not a proponent of command prompt because I believe that it is more error prone than UI driven configurations. Therefore, wherever possible, I have tried to use a UI drive option over a command-driven. Open NPM Gallery and install mongodb, which is the native driver for connecting node.js to MongoDB.

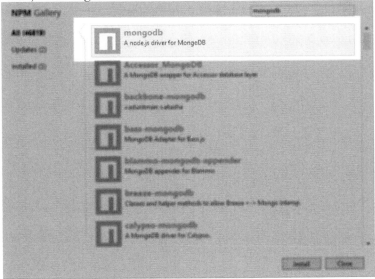

Figure 10.16: Install mongodb driver

We will need the mongodb driver to save and retrieve data from MongoDB from Node.js. To connect to MongoDB from Node.js, there are several drivers available such as native MongoDB driver, Mongoose and Mongolia. A comparison of these drivers is beyond the scope of this book. In this exercise, I have selected native Node.js driver. Next, also install nconf module to help us read configuration files from Node.js.

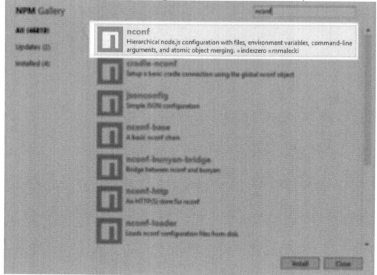

Figure 10.17: Install nconf

After the mongodb and nconf modules are installed, you have completed all the pre-requisites for setting up a Node.js and MongoDB development environment. In the next step, we will start programming the web service.

Step 4: Creating and Testing Skeleton Web Services

To create REST web services, we must first define dependencies and routes in server.js as shown in Listing 10.2.

```
var express = require('express')
, routes = require('./routes')
, user = require('./routes/user')
, http = require('http')
, path = require('path'),
pkgs=require('./routes/pkgs');
```
Listing 10.2: server.js routes

Depending on the installation, you may need to only include ./routes/pkgs dependency. Next, we must define the REST functions in the /routes/pkgs.js file because in Listing 10.2, we are delegating the function handling to the pkgs module. In the routes folder create a file named pkgs.js as shown in Listing 10.3.

```
exports.findAll = function(req, res) {
    res.send([{name:'app1'},      {name:'app2'},
{name:'app3'}]);
};
exports.findRemote = function(req, res) {
    res.send([{name:'app1'},      {name:'app2'},
{name:'app3'}]);
};
 exports.findById = function(req, res) {
    res.send({id:req.params.id,           name:
"DisplayName", description: "description"});
};
exports.addPkg = function (req, res) {
    res.send("Success");
};
exports.updatePkg = function (req, res) {
    res.send("Success");
};
```
Listing 10.3: REST Methods

Note that we have only created function skeletons returning static data.
In server.js, define the route methods that correspond to the module methods you created in Listing 10.3. Listing 10.4 shows the mapping between the route and its corresponding function in pkgs.js.

```
app.get('/pkgs', pkgs.findAll);
app.get('/pkgs/remote', pkgs.findRemote);
app.get('/pkgs/:id', pkgs.findById);
app.post('/pkgs', pkgs.addPkg);
app.put('/pkgs/:id', pkgs.updatePkg);
```
Listing 10.4: Defining REST URI method routes

With these signatures and definitions in place, you can test if the routes are working properly by running the website locally as well as in WAWS. The URLs to test are, http://[web site url]/pkgs, http://[web site url]/pkgs/remote, and http://[web site url]/pkgs/1. If these URL return the expected values then the routes are working fine and we should proceed with MongoDB integration.

Step 5: Adding MongoDB data interactions

Now we need to start implementing data access functionality in our REST API functions. The three steps that I followed while implementing the functions were:

1) Creating a config.json file and store MongoDB connection string
2) Defining global variables such as MongoDB client and retrieving connection string from config.json
3) Populate MongoDB with sample data
   In this step the function makes an HTTP GET call to
   http://storage.appsforazure.com/appsforazureobjectstest/servicepackages.json
   and stores the retrieved data into the MongoDB instance.
4) Implement the data access functions for retrieving and storing data in MongoDB

Listing 10.5 shows the code for pkgs.js file with all the functions implemented.

```
//Initialize dependencies
http = require('http');
var nconf = require('nconf');
var mongo = require('mongodb');
var MongoClient = mongo.MongoClient
, format = require('util').format;

var Server = mongo.Server,
    Db = mongo.Db,
    BSON = mongo.BSONPure;
//Define the configuration file
nconf.env().file({ file: 'config.json' });

//Read the connection string
var connectionString =
  nconf.get("MONGOLAB_URI");

//Initialize MongoDB connection
MongoClient.connect(connectionString,
function (err, db) {
    if (err) throw err;

    if (!err) {

        db.collection('pkgs', { strict: true },
```

```
function (err, collection) {
          if (err) {
//Populate the db by calling the function
              populateDB(db);
          }
      });
    }

})

//find an app by id
exports.findById = function (req, res) {
      var id = req.params.id;
      MongoClient.connect(connectionString,
  function (err, db) {
          if (err) throw err;

          if (!err) {

              db.collection('pkgs',
  function (err, collection) {
  //Find the object by id
                  collection.findOne({ '_id':
  new BSON.ObjectID(id) }, function (err, item)
{

                      res.send(item);
              });
          });
        }
      })
    };

//Get all apps
exports.findAll = function(req, res) {

      MongoClient.connect(connectionString,
function(err, db) {
```

```
    if(err) throw err;

     if(!err) {
        db.collection('pkgs',
function(err, collection) {
//find all
collection.find().toArray(function(err,  items)
{
            res.send(items);
        });
      });
      }

    })



  };

  exports.addPkg = function (req, res) {
      var pkg = req.body;

      MongoClient.connect(connectionString,
function (err, db) {
          if (err) throw err;

          if (!err) {
              db.collection('pkgs',
function (err, collection) {
                  collection.insert(pkg,
  { safe: true }, function (err, result) {
                      if (err) {
  res.send({ 'error': 'An error has occurred' });
                      } else {

  res.send(result[0]);
                      }
                  });
```

```
        });
    }
  })
};

exports.findRemote = function (req, res) {
    var body = "";
    var url =
"http://storage.appsforazure.com/appsforazureo
bjectstest/servicepackages.json";

//call HTTP GET
    http.get(url, function (res2) {

//Retrieve data into body
        res2.on('data', function (chunk) {
//Since this is an async function we need to
//add
            body += chunk;

    });

//When response ends
        res2.on("end", function
//Set the header to application/json
//you may also set caching header here
    res.setHeader("Content-Type",
"application/json");
            res.send(body);
    })

        res2.on("error", function (error) {
            res.send(error);
    })


    });
}
```

```
exports.updatePkg = function (req, res) {
    var id = req.params.id;
    var pkg = req.body;

    MongoClient.connect(connectionString,
function (err, db) {
        if (err) throw err;

        if (!err) {
            db.collection('pkgs',
function (err, collection) {
    collection.update({ '_id': new
    BSON.ObjectID(id) }, pkg, { safe: true },
function (err, result) {
                if (err) {

res.send({ 'error': 'An error has occurred' });
                } else {
    res.send(pkg);
                }
            });
        });
    }

    })
};

// Populate database with sample data -- Only
//used once: the first time the application is
//started.
var populateDB = function (db) {
    var body = "";
    var url =

"http://storage.appsforazure.com/appsforazureobje
ctstest/servicepackages.json";
    http.get(url, function (res2) {
```

```
res2.on('data', function (chunk) {
    body += chunk;

});

res2.on("end", function () {
//Need    to    parse    because    stringifying    was
//converting JSON into strings.
    var pkgs = JSON.parse(body)
    db.collection('pkgs',    function    (err,
collection) {
        collection.insert(pkgs,    {    safe:
true }, function (err, result) { });




});




});

res2.on("error", function (error) {
        //you can log here further
    })



});
```

Listing 10.4: Source Code for pkgs.js

You can save and run the website locally first and then publish it to Windows Azure Web Sites to test each REST function. Along with the web service, I have also implemented a website that shows the contents of the data from MongoDB. As a basic template to start with, I selected Christophe Coenraets' nodeceller sample application from
http://coenraets.org/blog/2012/10/nodecellar-sample-application-with-backbone-js-twitter-bootstrap-node-js-express-and-mongodb/

Note: The complete source code for the REST

web service and the website is available at
https://github.com/dynamicdeploy/appsforazure

To test whether the sample data was loaded, you can visit the MongoLab's management console as illustrated in Figure 10.18.

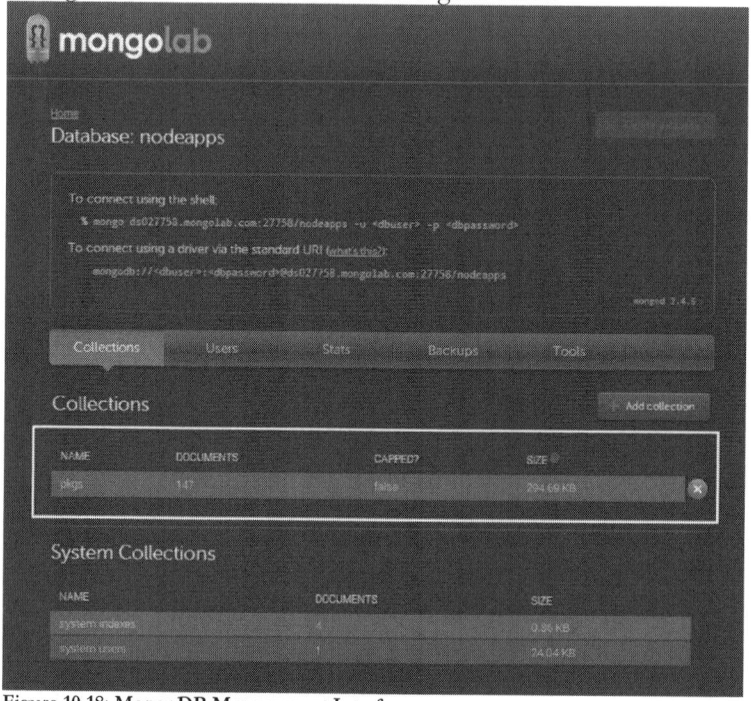

Figure 10.18: MongoDB Management Interface

Observe in figure 10.18 that the pkgs collection is created with 147 documents. The live website (called apps for azure) for this entire application can be found at http://mynodeapps.azurewebsites.net
To retrieve all apps: http://mynodeapps.azurewebsites.net/pkgs
To retrieve remote JSON = http://mynodeapps.azurewebsites.net/pkgs/remote
To retrieve by Id =
http://mynodeapps.azurewebsites.net/pkgs/ 5282bdba7689651c0b00001c

Figure 10.19 and Figure 10.20 illustrate the final look of the website that calls REST services for displaying MongoDB data.

Figure 10.19: Node.js Apps for Azure Home Page

Figure 10.20: Node.js Apps for Azure Browse Page

After you are comfortable with Node.js, you can fork the code for the above website from GitHub, and build your own web services and websites.

Step 6: Continuous Integration with GitHub

And finally, I will end this chapter and the book with my favorite feature in WAWS – Continuous Deployment. Continuous deployment makes it easier for small development teams to quickly implement agile test and development cycles.

To implement continuous deployment for the Node.js website:

1) Create a public GitHub repository (note: do not initialize it). I have named my repository appsforazure, but you can name it anything you want.

2) Open the website in WebMatrix 3 and select Git Init from the Source Control tab.

Figure 10.21: Git Init from Web Matrix

The initialization process will install Git Tools for WebMatrix. Follow the installation procedure.

3) Commit the source code to the local Git repository

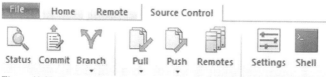

Figure 10.22: Commit Locally

4) Click on Remotes button and add your GitHub repository to the Remotes repository.

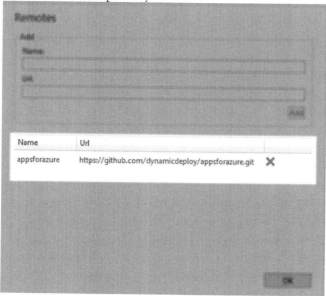

Figure 10.23: Add Remote Repository

5) Next, login to the Windows Azure portal and setup GitHub the source control system for continuous deployment of this website.

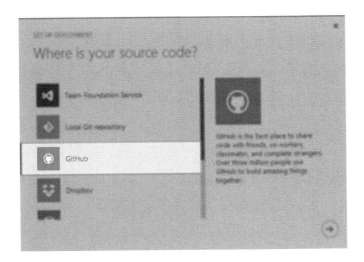

Figure 10.24: Select GitHub

When prompted for the source control repository, select the repository you created for storing this website.

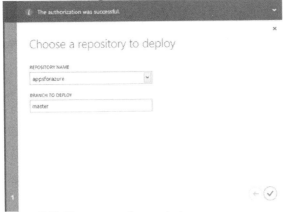

Figure 10.25: Choose a repository to deploy

6) Go back to WebMatrix and click on the Push button to upload the committed changes to the GitHub repository.

Figure 10.26: Push source code to GitHub

After the source code is committed to GitHub, the continuous deployment hooks will be fired initiating a deployment to WAWS. Within minutes, your website will be running live.

Figure 10.27: Web Site in deploying mode

Any subsequent check-ins of the source code in the configured GitHub branch will start the auto-deployment process.

Summary

This chapter helped you understand the basics of Node.js as a web development platform. I have seen a significant number of real-time and gaming websites running on Node.js. But, I have still not formed an opinion on whether it is ready for building large-scale mission critical applications. When building applications on Node.js, you do have to research open source components that will increase your productivity. The ideal test would be to fit Node.js website in the Web Site Capability Model. Each of the capabilities will test the completeness of the platform. Nevertheless, I enjoyed learning a new programming platform, and hope you did too.

Since this is the concluding chapter, I will wish you all the best in your Windows Azure Web Site development endeavor and for any questions, you know my number -- @tejaswiredkar.

Bibliography

Coenraets, C. (n.d.). *Creating a REST API using Node.js, Express, and MongoDB*. Retrieved from http://coenraets.org/blog/2012/10/creating-a-rest-api-using-node-js-express-and-mongodb/

Coenraets, C. (n.d.). *NodeCellar: Sample Application with Backbone.js, Twitter Bootstrap, Node.js, Express, and MongoDB*. Retrieved from http://coenraets.org/blog/2012/10/nodecellar-sample-application-with-backbone-js-twitter-bootstrap-node-js-express-and-mongodb/

Microsoft Corporation. (2012). *Windows Azure Web Site Documentation*. Retrieved from Windows Azure : http://www.windowsazure.com/en-us/documentation/services/web-sites/?fb=en-us

Further Reading

Creating a REST API using Node.js, Express, and MongoDB
http://coenraets.org/blog/2012/10/creating-a-rest-api-using-node-js-express-and-mongodb/

Getting Started with MongoDB and Node.JS
http://www.slideshare.net/ggoodale/getting-started-with-mongodb-and-nodejs?from_search=8

Node.js explained with examples
http://de.slideshare.net/gabriele.lana/nodejs-explained-with-examples

Windows Azure NodeJS Developer Site
https://www.windowsazure.com/en-us/develop/nodejs/
http://nodeblog.azurewebsites.net/running-mongodb-on-azure-and-connect-from-a-nodejs-web-app

Node.js Tutorials
http://nodetuts.com/

INDEX

COPY BLOBS IN BULK

http://www.dynamicdeploy.com/storcopy.aspx

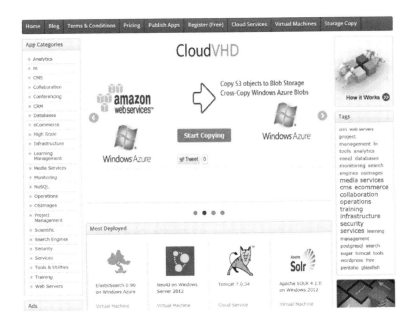

Follow: @opensourceazure

DYNAMIC DEPLOY

Tejaswi Redkar

DEPLOY APPS TO
WINDOWS AZURE

http://www.dynamicdeploy.com

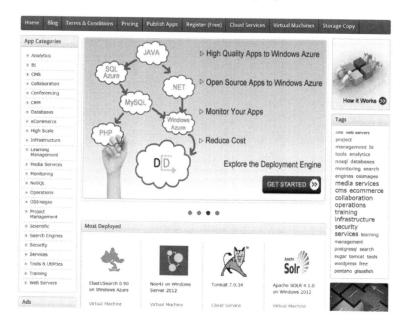

Follow: @opensourceazure

DYNAMIC DEPLOY

Thank You,
Tejaswi

Made in the USA
San Bernardino, CA
13 January 2014